TAKEAWAY

Hardeep Singh Kohli

was born in Glasgow in 1969. A BAFTA-winning broadcaster, he was the writer of the Channel 4 hit *Meet the Magoons*, a presenter of Radio 4's *Saturday Live*, *Midweek* and *The Food Programme*, as well as a contributor to numerous radio programmes such as Radio 4's *Front Row* and Radio 3's *Nightwaves*, and a movie reviewer on BBC Radio 5 Live. His weekly column, 'Hardeep is your love?', appears in *Scotland on Sunday*. Hardeep is often found clad in turban and kilt as a panellist and presenter of *Newsnight Review*, and has appeared on *Question Time*. He is currently presenting the BBC hit programme *The One Show*. He was also a runner-up on *Celebrity Masterchef*. This is his first book.

INDIAN
TAKEAWAY

A VERY BRITISH STORY

Hardeep Singh Kohli

First published in Great Britain in 2008 by
Canongate Books Ltd, 14 High Street,
Edinburgh EH1 1TE

This paperback edition published in 2009 by Canongate Books

2

Copyright © Shyness Productions Ltd, 2008

The moral right of the author has been asserted

British Library Cataloguing-in-Publication Data
A catalogue record for this book is available on
request from the British Library

ISBN 978 1 84767 143 1

Typeset by Sharon McTeir, Creative Publishing Services

Printed and bound in Great Britain by Clays Ltd, St Ives plc

www.meetatthegate.com

For the big fella

In loving memory of Clara,
who is now serving soup to angels.

CONTENTS

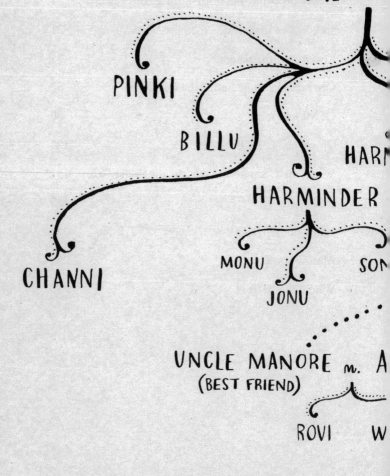

HARBANS SINGH KOHLI m.

PINKI

BILLU

HAR

HARMINDER

MONU   SON

JONU

CHANNI

UNCLE MANORE m. A
(BEST FRIEND)

ROVI   W

a family

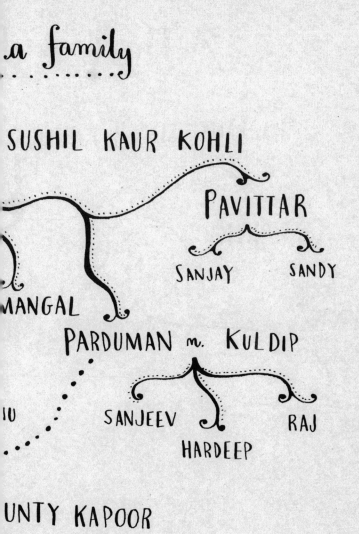

SUSHIL KAUR KOHLI

PAVITTAR

SANJAY   SANDY

MANGAL

PARDUMAN m. KULDIP

IU   SANJEEV   RAJ

HARDEEP

UNTY KAPOOR

OVI

WHERE DO YOU COME FROM ... ORIGINALLY?

H ome.
The most innocuous and yet the most complex of words. Both comforting and confusing.

I grew up on an estate in the north of Glasgow, a place called Bishopbriggs. It was a slightly over-planned sixties-built concept estate; basically a load of Wimpey houses on a few fancy little streets with slightly avant-garde names like Endrick Bank, Lyne Croft and Bowmont Hill.

It was down Bowmont Hill that my idyllic childhood collided with Glaswegian reality. It was the height of the summer holidays and all the kids on the estate ended up playing together in the street. The craze that summer was for home-made ice lollies. It seemed every freezer in every house contained moulds filled with any variety of frozen concoction. The kids would pile back to each other's houses to try the latest home-made blend. I recall being rather taken with a milk and Coke version. Then, one day, we ended up heading into the garden of some random child. There must have been eleven or twelve of us. We were met at the garden gate by his mum who allowed every child in, every child with the exception of me. She looked at me rather pointedly.

'Youse can all come in . . . but not him . . .'

It was clear that I was not welcome. I stood on the pavement, numb, watching the backs of my friends as they disappeared into the garden and left me on my own.

I had no idea why I had been singled out, and ran home crying. But my mum knew exactly why I had been ostracised.

'Don't worry,' she told me. 'This is life; what can you do? It is not our job to rock the boat.'

It was clear that she felt that we were visitors in another man's country. Well, maybe she felt like a visitor, but I was born in this country. I felt compelled to rock as many boats as they would let me board. I had no knowledge of anywhere else, of anytime else. Glasgow in 1974 was the beginning, middle and end of my reality.

I can't say I have ever forgotten that feeling of standing alone on Bowmont Hill. Those are the sorts of experiences that never soften with time; they stay with you; you replay them in your head so that the next time it happens, you will be better prepared. Unfortunately, there was no shortage of next times.

As I got older I would be asked time and again where home was and they would laugh when I suggested Glasgow. 'Where do you come from?' they would ask, adding: 'Originally,' if I was glib enough to suggest the Great Western Road. Implicit in all of their interrogations was the accusation that I did not belong, that I was other, that my home was not here. To them I could never be Scottish.

Yet neither did I feel particularly Indian. Of course, I was born to Indian parents and grew up in an Indian house. But that Indian house was always somewhere in Glasgow. It was all very confusing.

As a young child my sense of self was a cultural car crash, a collision between the values of my parents and the ridicule of the playground. In those days it was commonplace for my brothers and me to be referred to as 'chocolate drops', which I preferred to the more casually vicious 'darkie'. (Perhaps this is why I have never been a great fan of chocolate drops.) The perception of India was that all Indians were smelly, smelling, presumably, of curry. The fact that Britain later adopted Indian food as its own was an irony lost on Charlie McTeer, the celebrated school thug, as he spent the entire day with a clothes peg on his nose, complaining of the aroma that apparently emanated from my body. I have to confess to having been unaware of any smell, other than my mum's spittle from where she had invariably cleaned some breakfast off my face.

Yet, this idea of India was radically different from the place I watched on TV or saw splashed across the newspapers. The Indians I saw on TV were either starving or poor or both; cyclone-hit Bangladeshis, emaciated and barely alive. Surely this was not where I fitted in?

As I grew older, perceptions of India changed. I became aware of the more spiritual side of India through the Beatles and their beads and cheesecloth, and their discovery of their guru, the Maharishi Mahesh Yogi. I remember being faintly embarrassed by the idea of this bearded Svengali owning a legion of Rolls Royces in a country which was in the throes of famine and pestilence. The India of the early 1980s was a world away from the economic superpower it is today. I didn't understand how, to the young, free-minded, drug-addled youth, India was a place worth visiting. India was the home of mysticism, the epicentre of spirituality, the birthplace of religious civilisation. But I found it impossible to access any of the cool associated with that world. Lank-haired hippies would trail their way across three continents to find themselves in the warm waters of the Arabian Sea in Goa. I never quite grasped how this worked, or what they did once they found themselves. What did anyone hope to find in India that wasn't already present in their Scottish life? I had spent most of my childhood being ridiculed for being Indian and yet here were these white folk off to the selfsame country to find enlightenment.

And then there was the *Kama Sutra*. Why did the *Kama Sutra* have to be Indian? The idea of an ancient book all about sex – with drawings – could not have been further from my experience of India. In my house I never saw my parents kiss, and still never have. My mum gets a hug once a year on her birthday and a sideways hug at that, lest there be any intimacy. I would be appalled if my mother or father ever used the word 'love' in relation to each other. I know they love each other; they have been together for over forty years and have slowly, through the attrition of time, moulded each other into shapes that fit together; much like pebbles on the seashore.

But then again, my India was just a version of India as defined through a childhood in Glasgow. Sunday was our day to be Indian. After a week of mundane Scottish life, my mother would wrangle her three sons into smart clothes and assault us with a damp facecloth before tramping us off with our dad to experience the delights of the *gurdwara*, the Sikh temple. I never understood why we had to be smartly dressed to visit the temple. If, as my mother so very often told me, God (who was omnipotent and omniscient and all other words beginning with *omni-*) judged who we were rather than how we appeared, then why did we need to ensure that our trousers were freshly pressed and our shirts free of ketchup? This philosophical musing of an eight-year-old was often met with the counter-argument of a skelp across the back of the thighs.

Temple was great. The religious component of praying and being holy was simply one of a myriad of activities that took place in what was no more than a rundown, near-derelict house on Nithsdale Drive in the Southside of Glasgow. As kids we mostly ran around at breakneck speed in our ironed trousers and ketchup-free shirts, trying our best to crumple our trousers and mark our shirts with ketchup. *Gurdwara* was where the entire community gathered; it was our parents' single chance to re-engage with Sikhism and Sikh people. It must have been a blessed relief for them to feel relaxed amongst their 'ain folk', for at least one day of the week. When I think about the hard time I used to get as a small brown boy in Glasgow, I forget that my parents had to deal with yet more abuse in a more sinister, less forgiving adult world.

There were two good things about *gurdwara*, apart from the fact that about a hundred kids were at liberty to play and laugh and generally have a great time. At the end of the religious service, after the hordes had prayed collectively, the holy men would wander amongst the congregation who were sat cross-legged on the floor, handing out *prasad*. *Prasad* is a truly amazing thing. If you ever needed convincing that the universe has some form of higher power at its helm, then *prasad* would be the single substance to convert you. It's a semolina- and sugar-based concoction bound together with ghee. It is bereft of any nutritional value, but it is hot and sweet and lovely. And it's holy. What more could you want?

After *prasad* the congregation would filter downstairs to enjoy *langar*. I believe the Sikh religion to be the grooviest, most forward thinking of all world religions. Obviously, I have a vested interest, but given the fact that as an organised belief system Sikhism is little over 300 years old, one begins to understand the antecedents of its grooviness. It is a young, vibrant religion that is not bogged down with ancient scripture and dogma. Sikhs were able to experience the other great religions of the subcontinent and construct a new belief system that accentuated positives whilst attempting to eradicate the negatives. And no more is this innovation exemplified than with the beautifully egalitarian concept of *langar*. Every temple is compelled to offer any comer a free hot meal. In India this happens on a daily basis, but when I was growing up in Glasgow, Sunday was the day of the largest communion. You can be the wealthiest man in Punjab or the lowliest cowherd, but together you sit and share the same modest yet delicious meal, cooked in the temple by devotees. This is *langar*. It's a practical manifestation of the theological notion that all are equal in the eyes of God. A tenet at the very heart of Sikhism. And it happens with food. I was meant to be born a Sikh: generosity and food, my two favourite things.

Our bellies full of *langar*, we would drive a few miles from the temple into the centre of Glasgow, to the Odeon on Renfield Street. In the seventies and early eighties, cinemas were closed on Sundays, a fact utilised by the Indian community the length and breadth of Britain. For six days of the week, cinemas were bastions of British and American film, but on Sunday the sweeping strings and sensuous sari blouses of Bollywood took over. And it felt like every brown person in Glasgow was there. From three o'clock in the afternoon we had a double bill of beautiful women dancing for handsome moustachioed men; of gun fights and fist fights; of love and betrayal. These films were in Hindi, a language lost on us boys; we barely spoke any Punjabi. But the images were bold and strong and most importantly Indian. And guess what? There was also food involved. Hot mince and pea samosas were handed round and occasionally the cinema would fill with the sound of old men blowing cooling air into their hot triangular snacks. Pakoras would be illicitly eaten with spicy chutney. There would be the inevitable spillage and some fruity Punjabi cursing, involving an adult blaming the nearest innocent kid for their own inability to pour cardamom tea from a thermos whilst balancing an onion bhaji on their knee. It was only some years later that I discovered that the eating of food within the cinema was banned.

Not content with a morning of running around the temple, we spent most of the afternoon and early evening running around the cinema; there's something quite exhilarating about sprinting in the dark while a woman in a skimpy sari is caught in a monsoon shower. The single unifying factor between the Bollywood blockbusters and Glasgow was that it seemed to rain incessantly in both places; but for very different reasons.

My sense of being Indian was further embellished by my gran, the late Sushil Kaur. She came over from India some years after my grandfather passed away, staying with her first born, my dad. I had a special relationship with Gran; I was her favourite. I'd like to think that, of all her grandsons, she selected me because I have the most vibrant personality, that I am the most entertaining and loving of her tribe, the child in whose eyes she saw herself. I'd like to think that. The reality was, however, that I had the warmest body and she felt the cold of Glasgow. There is no medical or anatomical explanation for my higher than average body warmth. It was something I was born with, like my oversized posterior.

Many people have sentimental memories of their gran; baking cakes together, going for fish and chips, or being allowed to stay up that extra bit later. My gran was different. Very different. She was a matriarch, a survivor, a strong woman who had held a family together for years. She loved her family, and she looked after us. My gran played a very big part in my growing up. With two working parents, she was the one who was always there. She taught me Punjabi since she spoke very little English, and in return I taught her English to enable her to teach me more Punjabi. It was beautifully symbiotic. But we all believed that as an uneducated woman from the heart of the Punjab it might be one struggle too many for her to learn the complex and challenging language of English. That was until we overheard her gossiping with Grace Buchanan from next door. She was very good at that; if gossiping had been an Olympic sport she might well have been approached to captain the Indian team. That was my gran.

She would tell us stories of India, of politics and of family. We cooked together, she taught me to sew, and every morning she would wake up and make us all a cup of tea. She would do this thing of adding half a teaspoon of sugar to the pot to encourage it to brew. I abhorred tea with sugar and would always moan the way only a grandson can moan at a grandmother when drinking her tea but, from her lack of response she was clearly used to dealing with complaints. I can still see her now, squatting over a tea tray in our house in Bishopbriggs, stirring the slightly sweetened, discernibly stronger tea.

This was my sense of Indianness: at home with Mum and Dad, temple and Bollywood movies, aunts and uncles, and Gran and her stories. I'm not sure that my day-to-day experience of being Indian in Glasgow was any more accurate than the image I was offered from the wider culture around me; I had yet to actually visit the sprawling subcontinent. The India I was imbibing at the tender age of nine was an India fed to me by parents still stuck in 1960's India. All of which was topped up with dislocated images on the silver screen, weekly visits to the Sikh temple, my grandmother and her slightly sweetened tea.

When I eventually got to India in January 1978 for my uncle's wedding, the country I saw was contained within my grandfather's house, my uncle's farm, the streets of the city my father grew up in. It was rural Punjab: ox-drawn carts, old-fashioned trains, squat toilets, rundown towns. I saw very little of the real India, south to north, east to west. And in the years that followed I could never travel all the way to India and not visit my family; that was unconscionable and also restricting. Therefore, I'd never had the chance to explore this place I felt such a deep affinity with whilst simultaneously experiencing a sense of estrangement.

Now, my outward appearance may be Indian but my mind, my heart and my stomach are very much from Glasgow. English is my first language, by quite some way. I can get by with the Punjabi my grandmother taught me but my Hindi is more from movies than from commerce or poetry. Yet, as a turbaned Sikh, Indians expect me to be a fluent Hindi and/or Punjabi speaker. It seems wherever I go in the world the expectation of who I might be is never in sync with who I actually am.

Perhaps this is what I was searching for in India – the secret formula to reconcile the expectations of those around me with the reality. Or maybe it was something much more profound: maybe I had to manage my own confusion, my own expectation. To make some sense of the life I had led thus far, I needed to know why my father had left India, uprooted and had a family in Britain.

There is no better time to ask my dad searching questions about life, the universe and everything than when he has a freshly made mug of tea in his hand and a plate of biscuits on standby. He is captive. (The fact that I had to wait till my mid-thirties to ask such questions is another matter.)

'Why did you leave India, Dad?' I asked, more in hope than expectation.

'To better myself. For a better life for you,' he replied.

'But you didn't even know you were going to have a family when you left.'

'We didn't ask so many questions in those days, son.' He sipped his tea. 'Life was much easier then. Why are you asking all these questions?'

'It's difficult to explain, Dad. I feel like something is missing in my life. A reason for being.' I looked at him.

'If you think something is missing, then you should try and find it.' He finished his tea and looked straight at me. 'Son . . . '

I leaned in. I could sense from the pregnancy of the pause that he was about to offer some insight, some revelation.

'Did you sign those documents?'

I should explain that my dad runs a property business and is forever sending me documents to sign. Property businesses are built not of bricks and mortar but on documents, battalions, legions, armies of papers, all officially sanctioned and in my dad's case, invariably requiring my signature. I never seem to manage to sign them correctly or at the right time. As I searched high and low for this latest clutch, I realised that they weren't the only thing missing. I was thirty-seven years old, the same age my father was when I was born, and I had no idea who I was. My father left the country of his birth and travelled halfway around the planet to set up a new life. What had I done with *my* life? Maybe the hippies were onto something. Perhaps it was time to start looking for myself, to start making sense of my upbringing, to make sense of me.

'Dad, I've got a plan. I'm going to India.'

'Good.' He was always happy when I travelled. 'Work or pleasure?'

'I'm going to travel to India to find myself.' I felt triumphant. It was clear what I had to do.

'Find yourself?' he asked. 'Where did you lose yourself?' He laughed, heartily and happily.

It was time to go home.

Wherever home might be.

What You Need To Know About My Dad:

I knew that my father would want me to make the journey. He had always been obsessed with travel, his feet never stopped itching. This desire to travel was perhaps foreshadowed in his first job. When he was twenty-four he left Ferozepure, the town of his birth in Punjab, to become a customs officer in Delhi. It was 1959, ten years before I was born. He had trained for a short while in Amritsar, the spiritual capital of the Sikh religion. For a young, single man the bright lights of the big city couldn't have been more different from the almost medieval squalor of Ferozepure. In Delhi he spent five years living the quintessential bachelor life with his best friend, a man we have come to know as Kapoor Uncle. But Delhi was not the real destination; it was but a stop on the way. America beckoned my father. Her silky whispers travelled halfway across the world to entice him. His plan was to come to London, make some money, research opportunities in America and then take himself over there, to a brave new world.

One absolutely charming thing about my father is that if you ask him where he intended to settle in the States, he has absolutely no idea. His thesis was simple: he was going there to make money; it was thought at that time (and borne out) that there was more money to be made in America than anywhere else, that dreams came true, and my father had dreams. He was so brave to travel halfway across the world not knowing where he'd end up and with no one there to help him.

My father met my mother shortly before they got married. When I say 'shortly' I mean about twenty minutes or so before the ceremony itself. That was the beauty of the arranged marriage. My mother was part of the East African diaspora. My grandfather had worked on the railways in India and had been taken over to Nairobi by the British to build more railways. That's what the British gave their colonies: railways and paperwork. My mum, her two sisters and her brother were brought up as Kenyan Indians. My maternal grandmother died when she was very young; my mother was raised by her elder sister, Malkit, my Massi.

My father is six foot two, my mother is five foot two: that is the least of their differences. They are testament to the success of the arranged marriage system. On paper they have very little in common, no shared interests – she was working-class immigrant Indian, my father was lower middle class from the heart of the Punjab – yet somehow, forty or so years later, they are still very much together. My dad never laughs as much as when my mum is telling a story. His eyes fill with tears and he coughs and splutters with joy.

Soon after their marriage, midway through the swinging sixties, my parents made their way to London, where my mum had family. We lived with my Malkit Massi. I say we, although neither my elder brother Raj, myself nor Sanjeev were around. My mother fell pregnant with Raj in 1965, which is what stopped my father's plans for his stateside domination. Raj was born shortly after England lifted the World Cup and I followed three years later. The following year Sanjeev popped out and my mother found herself in a house full of men.

This is where the story becomes interesting. I believe that if we had stayed in London and become another of those Hounslow Indian families, we would have all led fairly unremarkable lives. But my father had discovered Scotland after a stint training to be a teacher in Dundee, which gave him a plan B for when he'd had enough of my mum's family, which he most certainly had by 1972. We piled into our spearmint green Vauxhall Viva and drove the eight hours to Glasgow. I remember with vivid clarity driving down the Great Western Road for the very first time. It was predictably wet but the night was twinkling.

That was my father's story. So it was no surprise that he liked the idea of his son travelling around India. I wanted to travel the country on my own and discover it for myself, starting at the southernmost tip and travelling north via some prominent and pertinent places. I would cook in each city, town or village and discover a little of India and hopefully a lot of myself. I would complete my journey in Ferozepure at my grandfather's house, the place of my father's birth.

My father seemed equally excited about my journey. Having travelled extensively round India, he spoke unpunctuated about all the possible places I could go, all the sights I might see, all the people I might meet. He regaled me with stories of Ladakh, villages on the Pakistan border he once visited as a child, a house he had seen in a magazine once, set on a clifftop near Bombay.

'Dad, calm down,' I said. 'It's still very much in the early stages.'

'You have to go to Kashmir. You have to.' He was insistent. 'I have a friend in Simla, he will be more than happy to look after you. And Manore Uncle will sort your flights and trains.' He was planning my entire trip in his head.

'You seem happy that I'm going,' I said.

'Why not?'

He *was* happy.

Very happy. As if he was going himself.

And maybe he was.

What You Need To Know About My Mum:

My mother is an amazing cook. I have rarely tasted Punjabi food better than that lovingly prepared by my mum. So good is my mother's food that I have stopped cooking Indian food myself, knowing that I will never come close to her standard. My lamb curry will never have that melt-in-the-mouth consistency, the sauce will never be as well spiced and rich, my potatoes never as floury and soft. My daal will be bereft of that buttery richness, that earthy appeal that warms you from inside. My parathas will never be as flaky and delicious and comforting.

Not only did she cook, clean and prepare four men (my father and her three sons) for the world, she also worked. And how she worked. Our wee newspaper shop on Sinclair Drive in the Southside of Glasgow was like a jail for my mother. While she counted down the days of her sentence, my brothers and I learnt Latin and literature, maths and music, all paid for by the money she garnered from her seven-day-a-week, twelve-hour-a-day existence. Luckily her resolve was harder than the concrete floor she had to stand on. Later in life she had both her knees replaced, no doubt a consequence of that concrete floor and the unforgiving workload. And while she worked, uncomplaining year after year, giving us everything an education can provide for the children of immigrants, she was systematically taking years off her life. Ironically we, her progeny, the very objects of her sacrifice, became strangers to her, educated away from the loving mother that gave life to us.

There is a place in Southall, in the Sikh ghetto west of London, where the food, whilst not quite achieving the heady standards of my mum's, comes pretty close. In fact it's the only Indian restaurant I will ever take my parents to in Britain. The food is delicious and it's like eating at home. Sagoo and Thakar, renamed now as the New Asian Tandoori Centre, is my home from home.

I have often been known to pile my family into the car and drive forty-five minutes to devour their food. They seldom complained, knowing what was coming. (Whenever I go there I am reminded of my parents.) One such day when I was planning my trip to India I realised that so much of contemporary Britain is based around Indian food. There I was in Sagoo and Thakar, a place originally designed to feed immigrants from the Punjab who had come to drive the buses, sweep the streets and staff Heathrow airport, and the joint was full of every sort of person: black, white and everything in between joining the massed ranks of Indians. The common theme seemed to be that we were all British. Food unites. That much is clear. And as I sat there, a devoured plate of lamb curry in front of me and the remnants of a paratha, I started to think that maybe I should return to India what India has so successfully given Britain: food. If I was to find myself in India, I must take some of myself with me. And what better to take than my love of food and cooking? I resolved to take British food to India.

I have always thought that my ability to cook allows me to share a little of my soul with my guests. My parents always instilled in me the generosity of entertaining. No one was ever turned away from our house unfed or unwatered. The breaking of bread breaks down barriers. Food soothes and assuages. Romance is continued over breakfast. Friendships are made over lunch, enmities resolved over dinner. That is the power of food.

In my repertoire I have a number of powerful classic British dishes. This is food to fall in love over, food to fight over, food that I hope will make me friends across a subcontinent. My shepherd's pie is well practised and relatively unique in that I use nuggets of lamb rather than mince. It's an innovation I am quietly proud of. I have perfected the art of roasting lamb, beef, pork and chicken. Obviously, I will have to be canny about where I cook pork in India, and given the Hindu majority, I will rule out any beef-based dishes entirely. I have been known to work my culinary magic on fish and shellfish and I am no stranger to vegetable accompaniments, if a little bemused by fully vegetarian meals.

Then I mentioned my idea to my dad . . . Now, my dad really likes my cooking. He calls me Masterchef and whenever I'm at home in Glasgow he turns up with some exotic shellfish or a special cut of meat or baby quail and expects me to do something amazing with it.

'Look at this cheeky onion. Can you do anything with it?' he asked once, brandishing a banana shallot in one hand. From the other hand he produced a clutch of razor clams. 'And what about these buggers? They're not very clever. You know what to do with them . . . And I need you to sign some documents.'

I love his belief in me. However, he was less than impressed by my new plan.

'So, Dad, I'm going to cook British food in India when I am travelling.'

Silence on the Glasgow end of the phone.

'Dad?'

'What?'

'I said that when I am in India I am going to cook British food.'

Pause. 'Why?'

'I just thought that it would be a good idea . . . you know . . . to take back to India what India has given Britain . . . '

He pauses. Again. 'Son, if British food was all that good then there would be no Indian restaurants in Britain.'

My father's logic seemed watertight . . .

'Would there?' he persisted.

'And did you sign those documents?'

SIKH AND YE SHALL FIND

Decision made, and with my father's help, I needed to sketch a rough journey around the vast subcontinent; between the big fella and me I was hopeful that somewhere I would find some answers. An old hippy in a cake shop off the Byres Road in Glasgow once told me that you needed seven lives of seven decades to truly experience the spiritualism and profundity of India. (He did say this while trying to haggle down the price of an almond croissant, however . . .) I didn't have seven lives; I didn't have seven decades; I didn't even have seven months. But I would make a start . . .

'Kovalam. Start in Kovalam. It is the most beautiful place on the planet, son. Paradise. True paradise . . . '

My dad would always talk about the beauty of southern India, a beauty I'm not sure he ever experienced firsthand while he lived in India despite his travels. He would explain the differences between us northern Indians and the southern Indians, the *real* Indians.

'They are smaller, darker and more . . . well, more Indian looking. They are Dravidians. They are the true Indians.'

This, to a slightly overweight Sikh boy growing up in Glasgow in the seventies was more than a little perplexing.

'What are we then, Dad, if we're not Indian?' I was compelled to ask.

He waited a moment, his face as stern and handsome as ever. 'We, son, are the descendents of the Aryan people. Our ancestors trekked from Middle Europe across the Russian Steppes through Persia and ultimately into northern India.'

This was amazing. We were white people. We weren't really Indian after all. I couldn't wait to get back to the playground and explain this; perhaps then they would stop calling me names.

'Our ancestors ultimately settled in and around modern-day Punjab. And if you have ever been to the Punjab you would soon realise that it's a great place to stop.'

Dad had laughed that rarest of laughs. He clearly loved the Punjab.

'That's how the Aryan race ended up in the Punjab.'

And I distinctly remember telling kids in the playground that I was part of the Aryan race. It was the late seventies and the National Front was on the march. Little did I realise that a brown-skinned fat kid from Glasgow telling everyone that he was somehow linked to the rise of Hitler and Nazi Germany had consequences. That is where my confusion over my identity must have begun . . .

'Kovalam, son,' repeated my dad, fast-forwarding me thirty years back into the present. 'Start in Kovalam. They weren't stupid those Portuguese.'

I had never suggested that they were . . . The Portuguese had colonised tracts of southern India, taking chillies and vinegar to the Indians.

' . . . and sign those documents. But start in Kovalam . . . '

Kovalam is about as far away from my 'home' in India as I can possibly get. The Punjab is the most northerly point in India and if Kovalam were any further south it would be in the sea. Apart from the fact that the weather is discernibly warmer and consequently the scenery is different, I wasn't altogether sure what to expect, but it seemed logical to start in a place unlike the India I knew and recognised. (When I was a very young kid I thought India was full of Punjabis.)

'You really ought to go to Pondicherry, son. The French influence on India is crucially important to the geo-politics of the age.' I had never heard my dad use the word 'geo-politics'.

'It's too close to Trivandrum, not different enough,' I argued.

'Then?'

'Madras,' I suggested. Chennai as it is now called. The big fella needed convincing.

Madras is India's fourth largest city and is the capital city of the state of Tamil Nadu, a state rich with ancient history and culture. This seems to jar more than a little with the connotations of the word 'Madras' in Britain. As far as most of our population is concerned, Madras is a curry that is hotter than a creamy Korma, but less virulent than a Vindaloo. It's quite amazing how millennia of history can be summed up on a spiceometer. For me, Madras would be the sole representative for the east coast of India.

'After Madras?' He was keen for me to venture further north up that coast. He and I had always planned a trip to Assam and Darjeeling. He loves his tea, and I could think of few things more rewarding than having a cup or two with him in the heart of tea-growing India. But I wasn't going to Assam or Darjeeling on this trip; nor was I going with him.

'Too far north-east, Dad', I explained. 'I need to come inland'.

'Bangalore?' he asked.

'Eventually,' I replied.

From Madras and its mild curries I would venture west to Mysore. My father-in-law went to medical college in Mysore, and it is famed for its Sandalwood soap, a fragrance that instantly transports me to India. A few months before I'd met an American Filipino hippy type who had started a yoga school in Mysore. We had exchanged email addresses and it seemed daft not to explore the place whilst combining it with a gentle stretch.

'Then Bangalore?'

'Yes,' I replied. Dad was happy; he liked Bangalore.

Bangalore is the epitome of everything modern India wishes to be, a microcosm of the unfolding second millennium. Bangalore is famous for many things: it is the centre of India's technology revolution and it is also Geoffrey Boycott's favourite Indian city. For me it will always be the city of my wife's family, a place of great parties, weddings and much fun. A city run by urban sophisticates.

'You have to go to Goa, son.'

At this point I was beginning to wonder who was making this journey. But I did have to go to Goa.

'For many Westerners it was their primary source of knowledge of the Indian subcontinent.' My dad was on fire with insight.

Goa. It would be churlish not to go and find myself in the same place so many others attempted self-discovery. And it would be nice to spend a little time on a beach in India; although the idea of brown-skinned people on a beach still strikes me as wholly incongruous.

'And after Goa?'

'Bombay, Dad.' Dad liked Bombay, too, and I think it is my favourite city in the world.

Is there a more vibrant and exciting place on the planet? I doubt it. As well as being home to the world's largest film industry, Bombay is the most cosmopolitan of all Indian cities, drawing every sort of Indian into its ample and warm bosom. I love Bombay.

'You have to spend some time with Manore Uncle in Delhi. Rovi will look after you. Send him an email. Wait, I'll call him now on the other line . . . '

My dad was bad enough with one phone; the free market and subsequent deregulation of the telecommunications business meant that he now had a mobile and two landlines in the house; he was able to sort my entire itinerary out single-handedly. Manore Uncle is my dad's best friend and they are like family to us. In many ways they are closer than family. Rovi is Manore Uncle's second son and an all-round angel. They make Delhi feel like home to us. We would always fly into Delhi, staying for a day or two before going to the Punjab. I have strong childhood memories of the city and it has become a de facto annexe of the Punjab, so full is it of my north Indian brethren.

'There's a place called McLeod Gunj where they have some Scottish missionaries . . . '

The big fella is off on one. He spent some time in Leh on a walking pilgrimage. He loves walking. Walking and tea; he's some man. The pilgrimage involved a high-altitude walk across a tiny path in the foothills of the Himalayas. He was keen for me to visit there. I, too, was keen to be in Kashmir but I explained to him that I couldn't risk travelling to remote places and getting stranded. We are talking about the Himalayas here. Snowfall, mudslides and general meteorological mayhem. It was simply too risky. Instead I would head for Srinagar in the Kashmir Valley.

'Good,' he said approvingly.

The Kashmir Valley: one of the most beautiful places on earth and a place my father spoke about often when we were kids. I spent a summer there once when my aunt and her husband, a colonel in the army, were stationed there. My aunt is a great cook and her date and walnut cake is still spoken about in hushed tones.

'Then home?' asked my dad.

'Then home,' I concurred.

Not London but Ferozepure: my home in India, a place I was not born in, a place I had never lived in. But home, nonetheless.

I was beginning to wonder what home actually meant to me; what Britain meant to me; what India meant to me. I was doing a lot of wondering. I hadn't even left Blighty and my mind was whirring with the potential of this journey.

In some ways I could have turned round and gone back to Cricklewood and my life would have already been affected deeply merely by considering these questions of home, identity, of who I was and where I was going in life. The fact that I was actually going to step on a plane and make this journey . . . .well, the mind boggled with opportunity. I know my dad felt the same way, too. I have never felt closer to him than when we were discussing planning this trip. His excitement and enthusiasm were infectious. I knew that he wished he could come with me, but he couldn't. This was a journey I had to make alone. But he would never be too far from my thoughts.

Less than a month later I was standing in Heathrow airport. I've always loved Heathrow airport. Everyone in the world seems to have passed through this place at one time or another. And there I was, trolley bag in one hand, bacon roll in the other, wondering why I was undertaking this journey. What was I expecting to achieve from this quest? How exactly was I going to find myself?

The bacon roll consumed, my heart slightly aflutter, the departure board suggested that I make my way to Gate 32 and prepare to board my flight. I had one thing left to do before leaving for India. I dialled my dad's number.

'Dad?'

'Son? All set?' he asked.

'Ready to go . . .' I hesitated. 'Just wanted to say thanks . . .'

There was a moment. I could hear his mind turning. I could sense him searching the words, the phrases, the emotions. I knew he had something to say to me at this point, at which his dreams and hopes and fears became my hopes and dreams and fears.

'Son . . .'

'Yes, Dad?'

'Did you sign those documents?'

'Yes, Dad. Signed and in the post.'

'Good,' he said. 'Call me when you get there.'

I headed for Gate 32.

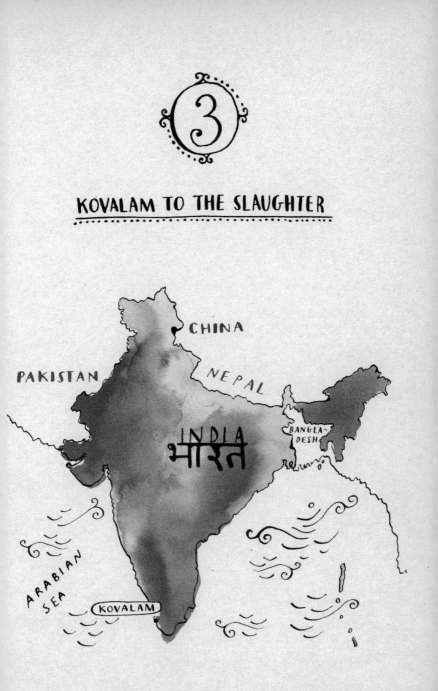

3

KOVALAM TO THE SLAUGHTER

CHINA

PAKISTAN

NEPAL

INDIA
भारत

BANGLA-
DESH

ARABIAN
SEA

KOVALAM

In a little over eight hours I will be touching down on Indian soil; Bombay, gateway to India. But what makes this trip so very different to the numerous other trips I have taken to the subcontinent is that this is my first as a tourist. This thought unsettles me. It's mealtime on the plane. Quite which meal it's time for I'm not wholeheartedly sure, but trollies are furiously dispensing food all around me, the dimmed lights catching the crumpled foil that bestows little surprise on the eater. I happily take my eight-inch by four-inch meal, peel away the astonishingly hot foil to reveal roast chicken with potatoes and vegetables. Ironic or what? Here I am flying over to India to explore the country and myself and to cook British food, and I am about to tuck into a roast dinner. What am I thinking? Am I thinking at all? Why would Indians be the least bit interested in shepherd's pie, toad in the hole, cock-a-leekie soup? And why would they be the least bit interested in me cooking it for them? Troubled though I am, never before has anxiety come in the way of this man and his belly. I devour my roast dinner wishing only for one thing: bread sauce.

Ten hours later and I find myself in another airport, shuffling in search of my connecting flight to Cochin. The plush grandeur of the new domestic departure terminal at Bombay airport is an oasis of calming marble, steel and glass, a world away from the mayhem that exists but yards from the terminal entrance. The air-conditioned serenity, the gently ordered protocol of check-in couldn't be more blatantly anti-Indian in its sensibility. Where are the betel nut-chewing fat men, their shirts stiff with days of perspiration as they attempt to wedge themselves between you and the ticketing counter? Where is the dried daal seller, chanting the words he has chanted a thousand times a day, rendering their meaning meaningless? Where is the teeming mass of humanity, struggling to fit its own circumstances?

The tannoy announcements beckon and lull and herd us travellers into some brave, new world of becalmed tranquillity. Our queues are orderly, our voices unraised as we wait patiently in our marble edifice to undergo security checks.

Although India has had a woman Prime Minister and beloved manifestations of the female form come in many of their polytheistic deities, one soon realises the sweet quaintness of Indian pre-feminist culture as one negotiates security. Women are siphoned off into a separate queue, off to a dedicated channel where they pass through the beeping security doorway into a small curtained area where the outline of their bodies is discreetly described by the handheld detecting machine. (Quite what it detects but harmless items, Ray Bans and the foil on chewing gum packets, one can only guess . . .) In fact, the women aren't even *called* women. They're ladies.

While the queue-less sari-clad ladies glide through their clandestine curtain check, we men (who outnumber our gender counterparts in this terminal by at least seven to one) shamble ignominiously to our communal and very public moment with security. There are several doorway security machines; once we pass through this initial check we are confronted by a uniformed guard with the handheld – beeping – detecting machine. At this point we are offered a small raised dais in order that we may elevate ourselves for our body check. This may be to save the strained backs and injured vertebrae of the security staff. It could be, but it feels much more as though they simply want the rest of the terminal to have a good view of us, legs apart, arms outstretched, in a pre-star jump pose.

I await my star-jump moment. Ahead of me I see the drunk man. He sways upon his dais. It's a minor victory that he managed to uplift his lanky six foot three physique up to what (for him) is a challenging height. He is further impeded by the fact that the overwhelming majority of his six foot three frame would appear to be almost exclusively legs, clad as they are in static-garnering beige-coloured slacks. (So long are his legs I wonder whether he holds some junior ministry amongst those with silly walks.) Baby giraffe-like he steadies himself, as if unused to the world. He places his feet together, arms outstretched, perhaps more in an attempt to steady himself rather than to facilitate this particular security check.

The drunk man empties his pockets, and the small change, tissues and detritus of drunkenness spill and crash into the small metal dish. Very deliberately he returns his arms to their outstretched position. The irony that he looks like a three year old pretending to be a plane is somewhat lost on him . . . The most cursory of checks reveals nothing remarkable. His boarding pass is stamped, in the best traditions of Indian bureaucracy, and he is invited to alight the dais, the queue behind him heaving noiselessly in anticipation.

Trying his very best to maintain all the dignity that a lunchtime drunk can muster, he tries manfully to retrieve his change, his tissues and his detritus from the small metal dish. The height of the dais further accentuates his already accentuated sway. Coin by coin, rupee by rupee, tissue by tissue he retrieves each item, steadying himself as he places each into his pocket before attempting to replace the next. This is clearly going to take some time. The duty sergeant loses his patience, although given the taciturn look he had fixed on his face, this was no great loss. The sergeant grabs the dish and empties it into the surprised hand of our drunken friend. Miraculously all but one of the coins lodge themselves in his skinny-fingered hands. All but one.

As I walk through my own security check the last thing I see is the drunk man, his face a portrait of concentration, trying to collect his single, stray coin from the floor of the dais.

Cricklewood to Cochin. Welcome to India. There's something very satisfying about starting a journey at the very tip of a country. Kovalam is an India I would have never visited had I not undertaken this journey. It couldn't be less like the India I know. The heat is oppressive, even in the winter. The food is utterly different and the vistas are tropical. In a few weeks time I will have zigzagged my way, east then west and finally north to the other tip of the subcontinent, Kashmir and Srinagar, some two and half thousand miles away.

But I'm not quite there yet. It was all going so smoothly. Too smoothly. From north-west London to almost the southern tip of India. It's that 'almost' that is so very crucial. What any sensible traveller would have done would have been to fly directly from Bombay to Trivandrum, an hour's flight, but where's the fun in that? Having taken a flight to Cochin, I thought that it would be a shortish cab ride from Cochin to Trivandrum (now called Thiruvananthapuram, at least by the Indian government; it's just far too many syllables for me).

What I had failed to check in my haphazardly 'creative' way was the distance from Cochin to Kovalam: 260km. I am faced with a stark choice. A charmingly helpful gentleman at the pre-paid taxi desk tells me that a cab from Cochin to Kovalam will cost me about fifty quid and take five hours. Now what you have to realise is that in the UK we have great motorways which means a 260km journey, approximately 150 miles, can be executed in two hours or so. In India however no such roads exist. If it was early morning I might consider the cab ride, given that daylight brings an enhanced degree of safety on the roads of India. The fact that it is just past three o'clock in the afternoon mitigates against a journey that would inevitably end under the canopy of a chaotic Indian evening.

Thankfully there is a flight to Kovalam – in seven hours' time. It transpires that it will cost the princely sum of seven good British pounds. I have to wonder why the price of a flight is so cheap. In India, given the massive differential in exchange rates, there are two prices for everything: the Indian Price and the Tourist Price. I suspect that the small airline from which I have purchased my ticket has mistaken me for an Indian, a proper Indian rather than a British Indian interloper. And why wouldn't they? This is the south. No one really speaks Hindi here; they speak Keralan. I have only just arrived in India and I am already being mistaken for an Indian. But I have a decision to make: fifty quid for a five-hour cab ride or a seven-hour wait for seven quid? The sevens have it.

With hours and hunger to kill, I realise I have more than enough time to travel into town, look around, eat and come back. I hail a cab for Port Cochin to a place called the Chinese Fishing Nest. Intriguing.

Once in the cab I realise that my decision to fly has been vindicated. The cab is older than me. In fact, older than me and the driver combined (which is saying nothing since he is but a boy). This boy at the wheel of an ancient white Ambassador has yet to be bothered by the complexity of a multi-blade Gillette razor; he is blissfully ignorant of a contour-hugging shave; he has some years to go before truly appreciating 'the best a man can get'. Having said that he has freakishly hairy arms. Hirsute arms and a baby-smooth face: my first close-quarter encounter with a man of Kerala.

The Ambassador spirits its way through the traffic. That's the thing about a country as deeply spiritual and religious as India, there is a strong investment in fate. It is their constant daily beacon through this life, as it has been through past lives and future lives. This unstinting belief in the Kismet Code by extrapolation surpasses any requirement for other codes, particularly the Highway Code. They drive like nutters. They seem to believe, quite seriously, that if fate dictates your time is up, then your time is well and truly up. Bad driving per se will not attract death; only the eternally pre-written event of your death will lead to your death. This renders lane discipline meaningless.

They laugh in the face of oncoming traffic, coming on from every side and angle; people, elephants, carts, bicycles, oxen, buses, children, goats, cars, lorries and a white Ambassador taxi all exchange space in the potential explosion of metal on flesh. The one thing about north and central India is that the cow is sacred. In the hierarchy of Indian highway management the bigger you are, the more right of way you possess; unless you are a cow, in which case you trump even the largest of military vehicles. This however does not apply in the south. There are more Christians than Hindus here and so the sacredness of the cow does not apply. And while the pandemonium of the north and centre is bizarrely regulated and calmed by random bovine acts, there is not this freakish cow-based control on Keralan and Southern Indian traffic.

Having reignited my own belief in the Almighty, based on the age-old premise that an inability to beat the belief system is reason to join the belief system, we weave and brake and hoot and horn and eventually make our way into Port Cochin.

The Chinese Fishing Nest turns out to be Nets. The vagaries of Indian–English road signs. But, Nets Shmets, I have come here to eat. Cochin is the centre of Kerala's tourist trade, the gateway to the lush and verdant backwaters or, as I have planned, further south to the sea resort of Kovalam. Given its prominence on the Arabian Sea, Cochin has become a conduit for commerce throughout India and has a multi-faceted and somewhat chequered colonial history. The Portuguese first visited in the fifteen hundreds, closely followed by the Dutch and British. It boasts India's first church and also a synagogue. Wandering around I discover a restaurant called Menora, with the image of a Menora, rather aptly, painted on its doorway. I rather excitedly enter assuming they would offer me fusion Indian–Jewish cuisine. But alas, it is but a ruse to pull tourists in. I leave empty of stomach. I wander around the small garden square by St Francis Church and up to the children's park. Daytime is considering its position as evening suggests resignation, and families have gathered around the pretty park, the noise of the ice cream vendor's generator sporadically punctuated with the laughter of children. Here I find a smart little terraced restaurant a hop, skip and a jump from the sea front.

There seem few more picturesque places to start such a journey as mine. India is a country of great and varied beauty; I suppose it's a beauty I have always taken for granted and perhaps a beauty I have not always readily seen. Friends of mine, white friends, would come back from a few weeks or months in India and regale me with stories of stone-carved temples and white-sand beaches and mystic men with flowing beards. They would talk of the stunning natural beauty, the wild jungles and amazing architecture. I didn't recognise the India they spoke of. If they had chatted about the dusty street in the Punjab where my grandfather's house was, or the utter pandemonium of trying to get to the Golden Temple on a Sunday to pray, or having to use squat toilets while enduring a bowel-thinningly bad dose of diarrhoea, then perhaps I could have engaged with them. It felt like the beautiful India, the mystical and magical India had always belonged to someone else. Until now. Now, at last I might be able to experience that place for myself.

I settle myself at a terrace table with a front-seat view of a descending Cochin dusk: magical and mystical. Unlike the restaurant's staff who take ten minutes to be alerted of my presence as the lone customer in the place, and a further five to bestow a menu upon me. Soon after receiving the menu I am joined by another two diners, swelling the custom base to a modest three mouths. They are a couple from Sheffield called Sarah and Paul. They are three weeks into their month-long Indian escapade, which itself is a quarter of their four-month South-east Asian extravaganza. They have both finished their first degrees; she is returning to read Law – I try my best to dissuade her – Paul has completed a degree in marketing but isn't sure what he wants to do. Irony of all ironies: the marketing department of a university doesn't market a career in its own subject with any amount of success. I am glad of some British company, yet being with Paul and Sarah I feel like a tourist. Which I am. I'm struggling at this point to know quite how to feel or how to act. I always dislike British Indians who go to India and act like they're white tourists, speaking English loudly and slowly. They seem to lack any empathy or indeed humility. I'm worried that I might come over like this. Yet, I realise that I am effectively a tourist; I'm from Glasgow.

My waiter comes and I have a thirst on for beer. Cold beer. But this is India. Nothing is straightforward. They can't serve beer until 'later on'. 'Later on' is a phrase I am to hear lots of this evening, but more of that 'later on'. Paul sidles over, his empty rucksack on his back and kindly offers to hunt down and bring back beers. I give him a hundred rupees and bid him a swift and safe return. Meanwhile the waiter comes to take my order. There is only one thing I would be eating in this part of India, a dish rarely seen outside the non-Christian south. Pork vindaloo. Given the 120 million Muslims in India, as a sign of secular respect pork is very rarely served in any region where there is a discernible Muslim presence. But the south is so heavily Christianised that this restriction does not apply. The waiter couldn't be less enthralled by my order.

'Ready later on,' he says.

'When?' I enquire.

'Twenty-five minutes,' he proffers. 'Pork still boiling.' He fails to make eye contact.

Very precise, I think and with a reasonably accurate explanation for the delay. This must mean he knows what he is talking about. After all, I am here with time to kill. Twenty-five minutes would be a useful bridge to the next hour I have to spend before my flight to Trivandrum.

'Fine,' I say.

He glowers at me, as if somehow trying to summon an eloquent English language diatribe. Glower over, he skulks off. He would be back 'later on'.

As I sit and wait I ponder my vindaloo. Vindaloo relates directly to India's Portuguese heritage. As I've mentioned, it is said the Portuguese brought the chilli to India, and it is this very chilli that forms the basis of the vindaloo. The 'vin' prefix refers to vinegar and I suppose the '-daloo' might be a version of a translation pertaining to 'of water'(I'm guessing that, though). What is so very interesting about the preparation of a Vindaloo is that unlike most other Indian curries, where the onions and spices are fried in tempered oil, the vindaloo grinds the chilli, vinegar and spices to form a paste or masala, which is then added to the fried or boiled meat. This paste reduces and cooks, cooks and reduces, and provides the most complex of astringent, chilli and spiced sauces. A true vindaloo is a million miles away from the unsubtle British version that is served in restaurants on a Friday night, only to be re-served to some pavement or toilet the following Saturday morning.

My Yorkshire hero Paul returns with a rucksack that now clinks with the music of beer. A big bottle of Kingfisher each, wrapped in yesterday's newspaper; not quite cold enough but hey, it is beer and it isn't warm. The restaurant is not fully licensed so we are offered opaque coffee mugs to drink our beer out of: anything rather than betray the true nature of our beverage. My mug has images of American Football Stars on it, with the word 'Stamina' printed on the handle. Little do I realise the prophetic promise of my mug.

A further twenty-five minutes pass, over and above the initial negotiated twenty-five minutes. Still no pork vindaloo. The beer is warm now but thankfully almost finished. I look at the American Football mug. 'Stamina'. I wish I had more. My surly moustachioed waiter shuffles back almost noiselessly to inform me that there is no pork vindaloo, because there is no pork. There has never been any pork. The restaurant is officially pork free. He has been lying to me, and so early in our relationship. He could have easily crossed the road to one of the many pork-abundant restaurants and passed the dish off as his own. But no. There is to be no spicy vinegar pig for me. I am too tired to fight and his English is nowhere near robust enough for my multi-clausal reasoning and contingent arguing.

Instead I order squid in coconut. And a watery vegetable curry. It comes, I swear, I conquer. This is my first Indian meal in India. It doesn't augur well for the journey ahead; it isn't the most delicious of meals, but even so it makes me realise the vast chasm of flavour and taste that exists between our food in Britain and the food of India. If a palate is so very accustomed to spice-tingling sensations, sensations that occur even in the most average of curried squid dishes, it is difficult to promote the comforting warmth of mashed potato and stewed lamb. Sausages in Yorkshire pudding batter will inevitably seem bland when compared to a dish that requires eighteen spices and five flavourings. Even though my first meal on my quest has been a very average Indian meal, would this average meal be more flavourful than even the finest British food that I could conjure? It's not rocket surgery to work it out. Even if I managed to pull off the finest shepherd's pie ever to be created outside the western world, with the creamiest, richest mash atop the most delicately cooked and adequately seasoned lamb, replete in its own earthy and enriched sauce, I could still very easily fail. Miserably. I banish such thoughts and haul myself back to the airport. I have a plane to catch, some food to cook and myself to find. It's time to start my journey in earnest. I have landed but I have not yet arrived.

❧

Food is a massive part of my life. When I'm not cooking it, I'm eating it; and when I'm not eating it, I'm thinking about it. I plan my life around meals. I will schedule meetings in certain parts of London to enable me to slip into a specific café or restaurant for a specific meal. I love food; and for its sins, food loves me. There is no one event, no one occurrence that I can look back on and use to explain the prominence of food in my life. When someone once asked me why I was so obsessed with food, I thought a moment, struggling to find a coherent answer. And then it dawned on me; it had only taken me thirty-eight years to realise that, as a child, the only aspect of being Indian which wider society seemed to celebrate was our food. To say Glasgow likes Indian food is inaccurate; it doesn't like it, Glasgow loves it. And my experience of this love as a boy in Glasgow seemed to be true of life in every other British city. It's bizarre when you think about the impact Indian food has had on British culture. The smallest town or village more often than not has a little Indian restaurant or take-away, often run by the only Indian family in the area. Even the racists who hated the fact that my parents' generation had come to Britain still liked our food. It was the only aspect of being Indian that garnered any positivity.

Ironically, despite this plethora of restaurants around us, we never ate out much as kids. We were the offspring of immigrants. The single biggest expense in my parents' house was school fees. Still, to this day, I have absolutely no idea how my parents ran a house, fed us, clothed us, took us on holiday and paid the mortgage. And paid the school fees for three boys. Randeep, more commonly known as Raj, is my elder brother. My younger brother, Sanjeev – Sanj, Sniff, Yich, Barbecue Fingers – has a myriad of nicknames and a heart of gold. And I was the tricky second child; the difficult one. The prima donna. They have a phrase for it in Hindi: '*beech wala*'. It translates as 'the one stuck in the middle'. And I did feel very much stuck in the middle. I was not bestowed with the gifts and love that a first-born son enjoys in an Indian house; neither was I the cute, good-natured baby, the son that they really wanted to be a daughter. I was the misunderstood, James Dean-like presence in the progeny. I was also, admittedly, a right pain in the arse. I was intransigent and eloquent. There's nothing worse than a snotty child with the linguistic dexterity to give oxygen to his irrationality.

None of my failings, innumerable though they were, changed the fact that my parents would marshal their very limited financial resources and were able somehow to make them go a long way. Both my parents worked: my mum in the shop; my father long and irregular hours as a teacher in a List D school (the D stood for Delinquents). It was a glorified borstal. His days and evenings, weekends and public holidays were spent whiling the hours away with rapists, armed robbers and murderers, all of whom shared one single defining quality: they were under the age of eighteen.

And yet, even though we didn't cuddle up in the lap of luxury I never felt that I went without. We had what we needed. And what we didn't need, thanks to the fiendishly fiscally astute way my mother planned weekly meals, was anything more than one night of dining out a year. So that's what we got. A little tandoori restaurant in Elmbank Street in the heart of Glasgow, the same street on which years later I would meet the woman who would become my wife. The name of the place escapes me. Glasgow in the seventies was only just starting its love affair with Indian food, a love affair that would blossom and burgeon into a full-blown, lifelong romance. And it all seemed to start at this anonymous little place just off Sauchiehall Street.

We would never have gone out to eat food that Mum could have made at home. That would have been pointless. Why pay over the odds for home food? But Mum didn't have a tandoor and no matter how good her spicy yoghurt mix, no matter how well she balanced the chilli and the lemon, no matter how infused her chicken became, it never ever tasted like it had come out of a clay oven.

So we went to this little place and gorged on tandoori food. I remember it being delicious and my father being very excited about it. I didn't quite understand why he was so happy eating red chicken; it was only years later that I fully comprehended how much my dad missed the food of the Punjab, the food of his home. We ate there every year on my dad's birthday for a few years until the place burnt down. Perhaps the victim of over-eager cooking.

⁍

Sauchiehall Street was very much in my mind as I arrived in Trivandrum late at night. It's another twenty-minute cab ride from the airport to the hotel in Kovalam. The contents of my mind could not have jarred more dramatically with the scenery around me as I walked across the runway to the terminal building. I was entering the tropical heat of southern India with its palm trees and sand, while in my mind I saw the postcards of palm trees and sand behind the bar of that small restaurant in Elmbank Street. The plane had started its journey in Bangalore, a place I would be visiting at some point soon, and had stopped at Cochin to fill up with more passengers all heading for the final stop, Trivandrum. Even though night was upon us, the temperature was only one notch below oppressive. I wonder how one deals with such heat all day and all night long?

This was the beginning of my quest. Once my journey started, I would have to give myself over to the complete travelling experience. I would have to make do with whatever mode of transport, whatever accommodation and whatever people were available. I realised that this was the last moment I had total control. I could parachute myself into deepest darkest India to test my culinary resolve in the most unforgiving of circumstances, the most intense of arenas: a small rural village a dirt-track away from western civilisation where ancient Indian cooking traditions have developed over millennia; a verdant cove of Indianness, untouched, unspoilt, unaccustomed to the strange vagaries of the western palate. I could have done that. Or I could have booked myself into a glorious five star Taj health and wellness spa. Guess what I did . . .

It seemed strange all those years later to be in the Taj Green Cove, a five-star hotel in India, when little of my childhood was spent anywhere but at home. And this hotel was a rather extreme version of opulence. Set in acres of tropical forest the accommodation was a series of chalets, nonchalantly scattered over the side of a small hill, overlooking the azure blue Arabian Sea below. This was one of those places where one forgets one is in India and is sure to have entered paradise. Perhaps this was the new India, the international globe-trotting hedonists' India?

One of the main reasons I came to this hotel was because they offered a *Sadhya* meal, a 'Big Feast'. Nothing too subtle in that translation. It originally offered sixty-four courses of vegetarian food, eight varieties of eight different curries. Sixty-four. And then a further eight desserts. Nice. Traditionally served on a banana leaf, dishes are served with almost mathematical precision, each area of the leaf having a designated curry type. One is meant to sit cross-legged on the floor to eat. As the maître d' and head waiter and sommelier accompanied me to my table, I felt a little self-conscious at the thought of my oversized arse having to somehow negotiate its way floorward. Luckily the hotel had dispensed with that requirement of the

Sadhya meal and I allowed the waiter to lay my crisp, white linen napkin across my lap. I appeared to be the only diner in the beautifully appointed dark-wood dining room. The smell of jasmine drifted on the air.

A banana leaf sat before me, nearly three feet wide and eighteen inches in depth. It had already been adorned with mango pickle, mango chutney, salt and a banana. It was like the start of a surrealist food gag. Then the onslaught arrived. Wave after wave of rice, daal, vegetables, more rice, papads, daal, yoghurt, coconut rice, more papads . . . I don't know about you, but I can eat loads. Really. Within an hour and a half I was languishing under my own body weight in lentils, yoghurt and vegetables. Languishing, but not yet happily full, not yet content in the stomach department. Finally dessert arrived. Only three of these, each sweeter and richer than the other. I was replete. Good and proper.

I stole myself off to my room. I had planning to do. I had to decide on a meal to cook for the executive chef, Arzooman, and his crack team of sous chefs. I lulled myself off to sleep that night with thoughts of beautifully roasted chunks of lamb in an anchovy and garlic sauce and found myself dreaming about creamy, buttery mash and perfectly seasoned broccoli with a tangy hollandaise sauce.

The following evening I wandered through that same dining room, nodding familiarly to the maître d', the head waiter and the sommelier. This time I continued past my table and beyond the door that separates the world of the guest from the world of the kitchen. I had been told that I had the run of the kitchen; it was a massive hotel and having read through all the various menus for all the various restaurants and clubs I had appraised myself fairly well of the ingredients available. I couldn't help but feel nervous. I had no excuses, nowhere to hide. Arzooman knows what good food tastes like. And the thought of being back in a commercial kitchen was both thrilling and terrifying, hampered as I was with English as a first language. That and the fact that I knew all the staff would look at me like some freak of nature.

'Why does the slightly overweight Sikh man from Britain want to come and cook British food in our kitchen?' I could almost hear them asking.

I didn't have a ready answer.

For a moment I'm genuinely not sure why I am here and what I am doing. What do I seek to achieve by cooking for these people? Are they any more likely to understand British life after a plate of my food? Did Glaswegians feel any more knowledgeable about the history and culture of India after a chicken bhuna and a peshawari nan, with a side order of aloo gobi? And it's not like the food I am cooking will be anywhere near the standard of the food Arzooman cooks. I steel myself, reminding myself that it's only food. What have I got to lose apart from my credibility, my reputation and my way on a journey that has only just begun. That calms me right down. I head down to the kitchen.

I'm handed a purple apron that clashes terribly with my pink kurta top. My attempt to articulate this fashion faux pas is greeted with stony silence by one of Arzooman's sous chefs. It's going to be a long night. And suddenly I realise that Arzooman has dedicated his entire continental kitchen to me: a kitchen completely open to the public gaze, a kitchen where my every mistake can be publicly witnessed. Marvellous.

I remind myself that if this evening goes badly and I manage to cock the whole thing up, lose a finger and poison a commis chef, then I am entitled to plead the defence of valiant failure, repack my wheely case and return to Britain. I explain my quest to Arzooman. He understands that I want to travel the country of my forefathers, that I wish to explore my heritage and free my mind of the preconditioned opinions I had of India as I was growing up. He is also very acutely aware of the tension that exists in my dual identity, but seems perfectly comfortable with my sense of Britishness and Indianness. Perhaps that is because he has travelled much of the world; he trained in Chicago and Switzerland. He knows something of being an outsider. The only thing he doesn't get is my desire to cook British food.

'It's bloody hilarious, man!' he says after I poke and prod my way through his superficial politeness.

'Why?' I ask.

'Listen, man,' he explains. 'These guys, Indians, are obsessed with food, but only Indian food. I cook hundreds of meals here every week and they are mostly eaten by foreigners. Indians rarely come and eat here. Which is fine because we are an international hotel.'

I take a moment and look around the restaurant. It is early, he is right. There are very few Indians eating; and those who are here seem to have ordered from the Indian menu. I'm in trouble. Deep trouble.

This is my first dish in what promises to be a long and winding road through India. The Indians are not well acquainted with British food, less so Scots food. But I have decided that my opening foray into the education of the Indian palate should be something straight out of the heart of my childhood; a plate of food that by its ingredients and history alone tells the story of where I come from, the story of Scotland. I need to be bold, uncompromising, resolute. I must embrace my quest and deliver to Arzooman and his chefs a dish that epitomises all I am, all I hope to be. I will give them stovies.

You've probably never heard of stovies. They are utterly delicious – delicious and quintessentially Scottish. It is a peasant dish, said to have come from the gentry handing leftover meat from Sunday lunch to their workers. The workers would then combine this meat with potatoes and onions, frying the mixture in dripping, thereby creating 'stovies'. This would last them the week, until the next Sunday. Much like my mum and her two pot method. Every Sunday night my mother would cook one pot of meat or chicken and one pot of daal or vegetable. By Wednesday of that week both pots would be almost empty. So on a Thursday evening both pots were combined giving us innovations such as lamb and cauliflower or chicken and daal. This was the two-pot method.

The stovies I grew up eating were mince stovies. Another common thread between the Punjab and Scotland is the combination of mince and potatoes. The Punjabis have keema, curried mince with quartered potatoes, the floury potatoes mashing down into the rich, spicy, minced lamb which would then be enveloped in a hot buttery chapatti. The Scots love their mince and tatties. We got stovies at school, once a week on a Tuesday. It was my favourite meal of the week; it was also my elder brother Raj's favourite meal of the week, because it was the only lunch that was bereft of vegetables.

So I feel stovies somehow speak from both sides of my heritage. And if I am to find myself on this culinary adventure around India I must be bold, uncompromising and resolute. I must be ...

But suddenly I am meek, compromising and irresolute. I can't cook a plate of stovies in a five-star hotel for an internationally trained chef and his team. It would be mental. How could I possibly convey to them the myriad reasons for what is effectively a plate of carbohydrate-heavy brown sludge that tastes of comfort? I can't do it. So instead I choose to cook something really poncy and European.

I pitch the idea of an Indian pesto to the not-altogether-convinced Arzooman. I explain that while it seems part of my culinary journey is bringing Britain and Europe to India, I am also trying to take a little of India back to Britain and Europe. I choose not to even mention stovies. Instead I suggest a pesto with coconut, coriander and paneer.

'Coconut, coriander and paneer?' The stress is all on the question mark. His face is deeply quizzical.

He thinks for a moment.

'Not paneer, man. It's too . . . grainy. Not smooth enough for a pesto.'

'Oh,' I respond, trying my hardest to look simultaneously unflustered and knowledgeable. 'Yeah. Paneer. Too grainy.'

The usual cheese used in a pesto is either pecorino or parmesan. Arzooman doesn't use pecorino, parmesan is limited and expensive, and I don't want to use such a precious kitchen resource. And as I stand face to face with Arzooman I suspect that I may be close to tears. His eyes light up.

'You can use strained yoghurt, man.' With that he rushes into the kitchen.

Strained yoghurt instead of cheese? I try hard not to look confused. Confused and ill. This yoghurt strained through muslin sounds similar to something my mum used to make when I was a boy: paneer. My mum would boil milk and then split it, with the addition of distilled vinegar. There's nothing quite as repulsive as the smell of split milk. Actually there is: split milk solids tied up in muslin. That's what my mum would do. Once the milk was split, she would pour the entire mixture into the largest piece of muslin I have ever seen, the solids being caught in the muslin and the water draining away. She would then tie the muslin to the tap in the sink and allow every last drop of liquid to escape. Later the paneer would then be chilled and cut into cubes or grated, with its mince-like consistency. Paneer. I often think of this bulging mass of cloth dripping smelly cheese-water over the kitchen sink. And she wondered why we were less than keen to eat it? The fact that the stink of the preparation bore no similarity to the delicious taste of paneer was lost on us children. We simply refused to eat it. And she would shout at us to eat it until we cried. As children we cried over split milk. As opposed to spilt milk.

Thoughts of my mum lead me uncomfortably to thoughts of my dad. I'm fairly sure that if he were with me in this kitchen he would suggest I put down my cooking implements and return to my room for a wee lie down and a gentle thought-regathering session. But alas, my dad is on the other side of the world, the Indian man in Britain while I, the British man in India, am attempting to bluff my way through.

Arzooman is back clutching a small, golf-ball sized white package. 'Strained yoghurt, man. Use the good stuff.' He nonchalantly throws the cling-film-wrapped soft yoghurt ball over to me.

I catch it with both hands. 'Great!' I say, again trying that simultaneous look of unflustered and knowledgeable. 'This'll be great.'

The chicken breasts are slit and a cavity fashioned within them. The breasts are skinless. Ordinarily I would have preferred skins to have remained intact; the skins have so much flavour and they take much more colour than the naked flesh, but ho hum, skinless it is. At the continental cooking counter, visible to the entire poolside restaurant crowd that has slowly started to filter in, I am furiously chopping coriander and grating fresh coconut. Time to blend my Indian pesto. It seems only right and proper that I use coconut, so ubiquitous in Kerala that it featured seven times in seven different dinner dishes from the Sadhya feast the day before. The coriander is fine; my only concern is this strained yoghurt thing. It is like ricotta but less rich and more tart. I would have to balance it somehow.

The pesto is whizzed and turns out to be quite delicious. I try hard to hide my surprise from Arzooman. He tries less hard to hide his from me. I delicately stuff my breasts and close off the holes with toothpicks. The last thing I want is pesto spillage; that's ugly and unnecessary. My plan is for the breasts to fry and then roast so that the ricotta, the coriander and the coconut will meld and merge and set slightly within the cavity. Generally that's another good reason for resting the chicken, apart from the fact that rested meat is tastier for allowing the juices to settle back into the flesh.

Meanwhile I have my stock reducing. I pop the skinless chicken breasts into the frying pan, adjusting the timing for absence of skin. As they fry away, I add my wine to the chicken stock. Arzooman has gone away to talk to someone about a banquet for 500 and I ask the humourless sous chef he has given me where the oven is. I've turned the chicken and need to finish it off. He points at a microwave and grabs my breasts, so to speak. I have images of exploding pesto bombs and manage to wrestle them back from his over-zealous hands. Arzooman returns and chastises the sous before sending him off with them to the oven.

The breasts spend a few minutes luxuriating in the heat of the oven. I spend the time watching my stock, willing it to reduce. Because that really works: pot watching. Stovies would have been so much easier. They would have had no expectations of stovies. I could have added a handful of chopped green chillies, a soupçon of ginger and a smattering of garlic, and convinced them that it was traditional Scottish fare. When it comes to a stuffed and pan-fried chicken breast with a white wine sauce, there is nowhere to hide.

Plating up time. In a proper kitchen there is a certain presentational pressure. Food has to look good. I gently place my perfectly cooked chicken breast, even if I say so myself, on the centre of the plate. The white wine and chicken stock reduction has been enriched with wonderfully sumptuous Indian butter which surrounds and elevates the chicken. I serve the chicken up to Arzooman and his chefs, not confident to send it out to paying customers. I watch them tuck in with grunts. Since it is nigh-on impossible to distinguish between grunts of approval and grunts of derision I err on the side of optimism: they are grunts of approval. As they eat my chicken stuffed with Indian pesto I ponder what their reaction might have been to a plate of mashed potatoes and mince.

That night I lay in bed worrying about whether this whole trip was a good idea. I had managed to pan-fry a chicken breast and reduce a white wine sauce in a state of the art commercial kitchen with an entire team of chefs on hand and the finest ingredients one could fly into India. These guys ate and cooked, cooked and ate European food every day. And what I had cooked could never really be described as British; it was the bastard child of French and Italian cuisine with a misplaced Indian influence. This was no sort of challenge. I felt indulged by Arzooman, a nice man and a talented chef. I had thought my dish would impress him, I had hoped my quest would inspire him. But he really didn't get the idea of me bringing my food to India. Maybe this trip was much less about what I was taking to India and much more about the impact India would have on me. That night I can't say that I didn't consider packing my bags and going home, the words of my father ringing in my ears: 'Son, if British food was all that good, then there would be no Indian restaurants in Britain.'

The fact that there are more Indian restaurants than almost any other in the UK did not mean anything as I faced the next stage of my journey. I was leaving the cosseted comfort of Kovalam and heading for the antithesis of five-star India.

The next morning I took my wheely bag and my desire to cook up towards the north-east, to Madras on the way to a small fishing town and a fisherman.

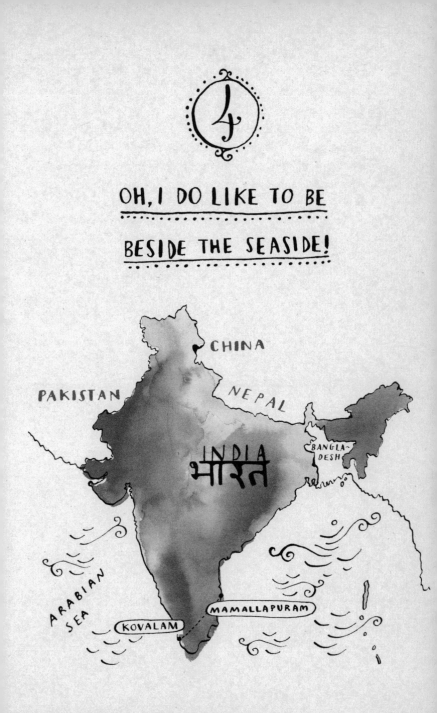

It was an easy car ride to the station from the luxurious elegance of the Taj Green Cove. I may have left behind Arzooman and his kitchen, but his words mixed with my father's and reverberated around the inside of my quickly emptying head. What was I doing? I had a choice. I could simply take a train to an airport and write a book about gardening. Or I could knuckle down and embrace this journey of self-discovery. (So far all I had discovered about myself was that I had a lot of self-discovering to do.)

Trivandrum train station was possibly the quietest railway station I have ever visited in India; I am, however, not complaining. It was lunchtime; the sun beat unrelentingly, no doubt worn out from its day's shining. All of the eight tracks in the station were full of dark-blue and sky-blue painted trains. Latent expectation filled the air. This felt like my first proper foray into India. The airports had been unreal nexuses into the country and the briefly snatched beauty of Cochin had a slight dreamlike quality about it. Trivandrum felt real.

I couldn't come to India and not go to Madras. All my childhood I thought Madras was solely the description for a curry. Some chef somewhere had decided that naming a dish after Madras would be a good idea. It could so easily have been a chicken delhi, or king prawn bangalore, or lamb pondicherry.

But madras it was, so the name went down in culinary legend: the city that gave us a mild curry. And to be honest, the mild curry is about the most interesting thing about Madras. It would appear to be a quite unremarkable city, given its status as India's fourth largest city. No one ever raves about how amazing Madras is; there are no stories relating great temples and amazing sights. It is the capital of Tamil Nadu, the state that stretches down the south-east coast of India, subsuming the tip above Sri Lanka. But while Madras holds no great intrigue for the traveller itself, it is a conduit to those ancient temples, stone carvings and spiritual experiences of India. This is the side of India the westerners sought. This was the India that seemed, inexplicably, to answer the questions that these travellers carried with them from thousands of miles away.

My plan was to venture to a small fishing town south of Madras, a place called Mamallapuram, or Mahabalipuram, to give it its proper Tamilian name. Mamallapuram is home to some of India's most photographed monuments and is a town over-endowed with architectural and religious beauty. It is also a place that was devastated by the tsunami of 2004, the first disaster in modern Indian history when the nation of India refused external aid and attempted to repair itself. As a child the overwhelming images I saw of India on TV were of a nation bent and broken by famine, poverty and natural disaster. India seemed forever to be asking the rest of the world for help, for aid, for understanding. And one might have expected that such requests would have been made after the devastation of the tsunami, the shocks of which were felt on the east coast of India. But this time, India decided that it had the economic prosperity and infrastructural wherewithal to sort out its own problems. India politely refused the aid of the international community and set about saving its own people. Whether India succeeded in its self-sufficiency is a moot point; the fact was that it felt able to make such a stand. This was modern India looking after itself. I wanted to see it for myself.

Break of Journey Rules
Trivandrum Train Station

Passengers holding single journey ticket can break their journey at any station en route after travelling 500km from the starting station. However break of journey will not be permitted short of the station up to which the reservation has been made.

If a passenger seeking a reservation on a through ticket asks for a break of journey en route he must clearly indicate on the requisition form the names of the stations where the break journey is requested.

Reservation in this case will be done up to break station only. One break journey is permitted for tickets up to 1000km and two break journeys are permitted for tickets of 1000km and above. During the break of your journey you can stay two days at the intended station excluding day of arrival and the day of departure.

My train is the 12:30 Anatpuri Express from Trivandrum Central to Chennai (Madras). It may not be significant, but this train seems to be sporting livery of orange, white and green, the selfsame colours of the Indian flag. It looks clean and comfortable. Not so much the lap of luxury but certainly leaning comfortably into the shoulder of luxury. The train seems almost suspiciously quiet. I worry that perhaps there is information that has not been shared with me, some conspiracy that has seen this train cancelled with all the passengers tiptoeing off, unseen, to board another, better, faster train to take them to Madras. Paranoid? Me?

> **PLEASE PULL UP BACKREST-CUM-BED DURING 6 A.M. TO 9 P.M. TO AVOID INCONVENIENCE TO SITTING PASSENGERS**

On checking the itinerary list chalked on the side of one of the carriages I soon realise that this is the slow train to Madras; it will stop many times and bite off a fresh load of travellers. Rumour has it that we will arrive on the east coast of India sometime around 2 p.m. the following day: just over a day away. I make my way to carriage A1, seat 14, UB. UB stands for upper bunk. This is the sleeper train. I will be sleeping on this train. Hopefully. It will be the first time that I have travelled in an Indian sleeper train since my childhood.

When I was a boy, between 1977 and 1983 my dad brought his three sons to India every other summer. The first visit was whistlestop to say the least. We came for my uncle's wedding. Time was of the essence. Much of that holiday was a blur. But what I do remember is the train journey.

It was 1979. My family were a family of meagre means. So when it came to flying we had little choice in terms of prospective airlines. In fact for 'little' choice read Hobson's choice: Aeroflot. Even all these years on the name fills me with stomach-curdling dread. Aeroflot was the national airline of the then pre-Glasnost USSR. There are many words to describe the Aeroflot experience, but in my father's context there was only one epithet worth concentrating on: cheap. And Aeroflot was cheap; substantially cheaper than all the competition, because of course, in Soviet Russia there was no competition.

We flew Aeroflot from London to Delhi, having first schlepped ourselves and our not insubstantial luggage down to London on the coach. That's the other thing you need to bear in mind about travelling to India in the 1980s. India was a closed market, an epoch away from the vibrant free-market booming economy of today. You couldn't get anything in India. So whenever a relative from 'Velat', the west as they call it in the Punjab, came visiting they were compelled to bring gifts, gifts to show how successful their lives had become since leaving India. (There is no irony in the fact that many Indians who left enjoy a marginally lower standard of living outside India than they might have enjoyed had they stayed.) I remember that we had packed our luggage full of chocolate to take to our cousins. My mum had also bought us loads of new clothes to wear. Fancy jumpers, smart trousers and kung fu-style pyjamas. I loved those pyjamas. I still do.

So there we were, our flesh and bone far outweighed by our luggage full of gifts, alighting a plane in Delhi, having spent the entire journey not being able to communicate with the Russian-speaking stewardesses; the only phrase my father knew in Russian sounded like: 'caca familia?' which appeared to mean: 'what is your name?' A conversation opener no doubt, but rather useless when the stewardesses wore name tags.

That year my dad, Raj, Sanjeev and I – Mum stayed at home to run the shop – landed in Delhi a few days before Christmas and headed straight for a taxi to catch a train to the city of Ferozepure in the heart of Punjab. The Shatabdi Express would ghost us through the night and deliver us home. Home. There's that word again. My father's home; my grandfather's home. As kids we had rarely travelled on trains; in fact prior to that sleeper journey in India, I have no previous recollection of ever having travelled on a train. Not that any other train journey could have prepared me for the Shatabdi. The Shatabdi Express is my dad's favourite train in all the world, a train lodged in my father's folklore, a train that carries the Punjabi masses home from the capital to their families in the towns, villages and farms. The Shatabdi Express is the locomotive equivalent of a Sikh: proud, fierce and a little lumbering. The exterior livery of these seemingly massive trains was navy blue with a sky-blue stripe across the lower third. The sky-blue colour motif continued within the interior of the trains: sky-blue vinyl seats, sky-blue floor, sky-blue curtains. We had entered a sky-blue world. The carriages were laid out in two sections. Along one side of the train two benches faced each other, the other side of the gangway had two single seats face on. This was the daytime arrangement. At night the sky-blue world became even more sky blue as the seats morphed into bunks. The eight seated travellers soon became eight supine travellers.

There I was, a ten-year-old boy, more excited than excitement itself at the notion of an all-night train journey, a journey that involved a secret fold-down sky-blue bed. The four of us filled our section of the train with anticipation, as it trundled us along to my grandfather's house in my grandfather's town of Ferozepure.

For us it was the most amazing adventure. Even adults find train journeys in India exhilarating. Imagine how my brothers and I felt.

We were jet-lagged and found ourselves, almost by default, in a sleeper carriage at New Delhi train station, having fought our way though the hordes. I could see my dad trying his best to contain his excitement. He hadn't been back in India for over ten years; since he had left his father had passed away. And now he was going home. I remember vividly being transfixed by the country that slipped by the grated window. I clung on, pulling myself closer in the descending gloom, trying to see more than the light would let me. And later trying in vain to sleep. The noise of people alighting and boarding; men selling snacks; babies crying; friends laughing; old women gossiping. And then morning came, a hazy, grey morning, a morning somewhat unsure of its own credentials. A mist lay upon Ferozepure as we unloaded our luggage from the train, only to reload it on the back of an ox-drawn carriage.

This was the India I first knowingly laid eyes on; a very real India, an unpretentious India. And I think I fell in love with it without even knowing.

Twenty-eight years later I sit alone in an almost identical train compartment, missing my father and missing my brothers. I am joined by a sweet young family. The good-looking young husband stretches his feet across the benches as his wife reclines with someone I assume is her younger sibling; the younger sibling sitting cross-legged atop the bench provides a makeshift pillow for her older, more amply endowed sister. The children sit and play on the top bunks of the adjoining compartment.

At 16.21, nine minutes *before* its designated time of departure, the Anatpuri Express reluctantly pulls out of Trivandrum train station. Fifteen minutes later we have stopped for no good reason. But this is India; you never need a good reason for anything. You rarely need a reason at all. The hiatus is filled with an army of shabbily uniformed, pungent young boys singing their wares, offering tea, coffee, snacks and sweets.

Then, with an almost mechanical unwillingness, the train is moving again and the chai boys are replaced with equally shabbily uniformed train staff who hand out freshly laundered white sheets, pillows and grey, scratchy-looking blankets. This is the first stage of the metamorphosis of a day train into a sleeper, the entry into the white-sheeted world of night.

Kerala has become Tamil Nadu much sooner than I had thought. I realise this because a message appears on my phone display with a beep, welcoming me to Tamil Nadu. If Kerala was verdant, then Tamil Nadu is no different. Even in the final embers of daylight I can see the coconut tree jungles that line either side of the railway tracks. The Tamilian sky seems a little angrier than the Keralan one. We cross a beautiful lagoon cut into the red clay earth; it's almost like civilisation hasn't happened as the deep, feral-red clay vies with the sparkling, azure-blue water for prominence.

We stop just a few yards ahead at a small local train station, an afterthought of a place with no more than a hut and a tree suggesting a place to stop. There is the usual all-too-frantic coming and going, which in itself would not be a problem if it weren't for the fact that those who want to come and those who want to go seem to want to do it at exactly the same time, which is the perfect recipe for pandemonium. Amongst those joining our happy band of travellers is an old, yellowed-eyed man with a matching yellow shirt that once was white. His skin has been sunkissed on a daily basis and is now so dark it is almost black. His thick, white hair makes his skin look darker still and he possesses the most vacant of expressions. He carries a shoulder bag, a suitcase and a large sack of mangoes. Quite why he has decided to transport mangoes manually no one knows. This is after all India; mangoes are in plentiful supply. He pauses a moment and looks blankly at me and the young family. He mutters something inaudible to himself and takes himself and his mangoes further down the carriage. There is an unspoken sense of relief shared between the young family and me. Although there is space for another passenger in our compartment, we would be all too happy to travel as we are and enjoy the extra space – space that would have been further compromised by a sackful of mangoes.

Our relief is premature. We are joined by a short neat man with large glasses and a fulsome beard. At first I mistake him for one of our Muslim brethren and I quietly enjoy the multi-faith microcosm that this carriage represents: the Glaswegian Sikh, the Hindus and the Muslim. But he's not a Muslim; the short, neat-bearded man starts talking and informs us that he is a Christian pastor. No sooner has he established his theological credentials than he has a laptop out, unremitting in his desire to save souls for Christ's sake. I have to say the phrase 'Christ's sake' sprang to mind quite often during this journey.

The pastor has a kind face and matching eyes, but he does look tired. No doubt God's work is never done and requires significant overtime. The contented quiet that I have happily shared with the Hindu family has now been hijacked. Within the next few minutes we have been told that he has just completed his fourth degree, adding to his PhD in Religion (no surprise there, then). He works for Church hospital groups, raising funds and helping with administration. He has been to Trivandrum for a seminar on clinical pastoral care and is now heading back to Chennai. He starts talking to the young family, which it soon transpires are no ordinary young family. The man is the heir to the Indian equivalent of John Lewis. His family owns eight massive stores all over India, stocking everything a middle-class Indian home could want. I joke with him that like a dentist has bad teeth, he probably has a broken toaster. I don't think the British ubiquity of toasters is the same in India. He looks at me curiously, without laughing. Not only is he the heir to a multinational department market chain he also seems a little anti-religion, which makes for fun in a carriage shared by an evangelical Christian pastor with a laptop and four degrees.

I feel it a good opportunity to explore the carriage. I extricate myself and wander. I see a family of short people who have set up a conveyor belt of sandwich-making. The father hands the mother a slice; she butters; the daughter jams and the younger son brings the slices together in sandwich form, and eats. Beyond them a skinny girl faces her mother, both sitting cross-legged. On their newspaper plates they feast on idli and chutney; nothing could be simpler, nothing could be more delicious. An idli is a steamed dumpling made from a paste of ground rice. The idli itself has no great flavour; it is light and airy, but it is a fabulous conduit for flavour, and when combined with a rich coconut, chilli chutney can elevate the eater to another place altogether.

I return to my compartment hungry. As if by magic, Mr John Lewis offers me a local delicacy: battered and deep-fried plantain. He can't be aware of this most beautiful, most circular of ironies that I, a boy from Glasgow, should find myself on a train in deepest, now darkest south India on a train eating something battered and deep fried. Alas, the plantain only serves to accentuate my hunger and I am more than a little relieved when the porter comes to take our food orders. There seem to be a number of dishes on offer, but I fail fully to comprehend the porter. Mr John Lewis steps in gallantly and translates for me. There appear to be three meals to choose from: a chapatti, a paratha meal or vegetable biryani. Embarrassed by my inability to understand the porter's Hindi and fearful to ask for a more detailed explanation of what a 'meal' entails, I opt for the biryani. How can you go wrong with rice and vegetables?

While we are waiting for the food to be served, the pastor, who has failed to say anything for a few minutes, rediscovers his calling and fires up his laptop. He decides to show Mr John Lewis an image he had stored on his computer. Having shared the image with him he spins his laptop round so I too can be privy to the visual feast. It is a photograph that the pastor has taken in Bangalore airport around one of the food kiosks in the departure lounge. The image shows a medium-sized rat nestled inside an otherwise exemplary glass-topped display of food; the rat is nibbling away at an aloo boondi, a spiced mashed potato ball, battered and deep fried. Obviously it's the sort of dish loved by humans and rodents. Let me be clear: this food kiosk is not a shabby, side-of-the-road type of affair. It's a beautifully clean, modern Indian food outlet. It would not look out of place in Heathrow airport, save for the rat.

Quite why the pastor has the image on his laptop soon becomes apparent. He is on a crusade against big companies squeezing small businesses out of existence. And Mr John Lewis is big business personified. My holy friend tells me that this 30-rupee boondi sells for a sixth of the price in a street stall, yet people feel that street stalls are less hygienic. They are willing to pay the 25-rupee difference in an airport, yet the food is no less unhygienic.

It's a valid point, but I still feel that having a screensaver of a rat eating an airport snack is more than a little weird. Mr John Lewis looks so angry he may explode at any moment with rage. He was not best pleased with the pastor prior to his rant on big business; he is decidedly less well disposed now.

The awkward post-rat silence is broken by the food arriving. I appear to be the only diner. The pastor seems not to eat and the John Lewises have packed a lovely meal of parathas and chutney. My vegetable biryani is surprisingly bland: a massive helping of rice with carrots and peas and the very occasional guest appearance made by a floret of cauliflower. It is accompanied by a thimbleful of onion raita. Rice for Goliath, raita for David. But I eat, uncomplaining and grateful for the sustenance.

Then it is time to lower bunks and make beds, all of which happens noiselessly and surprisingly efficiently on Indian trains. Passengers become automatons for those few minutes as sheets are spread, pillows placed and blankets unfurled. Individuals exchange places in the cramped space as if choreographed by some unseen director. At times it is almost balletic.

It is a strange night. I drift in and out of a fitful sleep. The constant motion of the train lulls me off into a gentle sleep, then the infuriatingly frequent stops allow new blood on the train: loud, awake people who fill the lower bunks in other parts of the carriage before themselves drifting off to sleep.

Having started my journey some twenty-three hours earlier we finally arrive in Chennai. No matter what the clocks in the station tell me, my body seems to refuse to accept that it's three o'clock in the afternoon. More asleep than awake, I haul myself out of the train and make for the front of the station. I hope to catch a taxi the remaining 60km or so I need to travel to reach Mamallapuram. I find a decent-looking man outside the station, who ushers me excitedly towards the car park. My Hindi is terrible so I am blissfully unaware of the fact that my decent-looking man is not the owner of a taxi; he is an auto rickshaw driver. For the uninitiated, an auto rickshaw is a scooter around which is attached the paraphernalia of passenger transport. It's like a small covered couch being pulled along by a 75cc engine. The sides are open adding a certain vibrancy to the journey. They are invariably black with yellow hoods and are best described as rats on wheels.

I love travelling in auto ricks. You feel much more part of the city, hearing and seeing everything at first hand rather than from the back seat of a cab. Besides which, right now I have little choice, since there would appear to be a dearth of cabs around. I agree a price of 500 rupees with the driver. That would seem to be the only thing we agree, since I'm not altogether sure he knows exactly where we are going. It's not till much later on this 60km journey that I fully understand the implications of what I have agreed to.

We stop to check the destination with the local English speaker. This is a bizarre three-way conversation between me (who is speaking English), the rickshaw driver (who is speaking Tamil), and the local English speaker (who speaks both). The driver then refuels and checks the air in the tyres. 'Long journey,' he says to me and almost smiles. Long journey. I should have realised then ...

If you are unused to travelling by auto rickshaw, then a short journey around a city can be quite hair-raising and a tad bruise-worthy. I am not new to the auto rick experience, yet what I hadn't fully taken into account was the fact that Mamallapuram is not just 60km away. It's 60km down a broken, pot-hole-infested, sometimes non-existent road that would seem like an arduous quest even in a luxurious four-wheel drive.

I am bumped and thumped and thrown around the whining little auto rickshaw for the best part of two long hours. My already tired body soon aches with the unrelenting physical assault of the journey.

৹৩৹

Seven things I saw on my two-hour auto rickshaw journey

The shell of a white car with no seats or upholstery driven by a boy sitting on a yellow plastic bucket.

A fully grown man going off to work with a Spiderman lunchbox.

A mother with three children on a scooter.

A bolting cow narrowly avoiding a head-on collision with a packed minibus.

About eleven beautifully turned out and uniformed school kids in one auto rickshaw.

Two children dressed as clowns.

Three sari-clad ladies making themselves wet with a sprinkler, as if attempting to realise a Bollywood cliché just for me . . .

When I eventually get to Mamallapuram I am shattered. I set off from Kovalam nineteen hours ago. I feel defeated. This defeat is compounded by the auto rickshaw driver reneging on the deal we had struck when leaving Chennai. The 500 rupees we had agreed on has now escalated to 700 rupees. I refuse point blank to be blackmailed and after much haggling I pay him 650 rupees. As I walk away from his wronged rebukes I realise that I have saved myself a massive sixty pence. I try to convince myself that it isn't about the money: who can put a price on principle?

I check into Greenwoods Beach Resort and fall face first and fully clothed into bed. Which is a mistake because the mattress is the typically hard Indian type: great for your back, not so good for your face. But I sleep.

Three hours later the afternoon has become evening. I am woken by the sound of an errant child, bemoaning his lot in a language I guess to be Tamil. A day ago I was coddled in the five-star luxury of the Taj, and here I find myself in an altogether different world. A basic room with a (hard-mattressed) double bed, a dresser, an Igo TV set with an Onida remote control (which doesn't work), a small bathroom, no toilet paper, no soap. The only wall adornment is a row of four rust-coloured pegs; there used to be five. There is an AC unit, the noisiest AC unit I have ever experienced and of course it would have to be right over the head of the bed. But the room, such as it is, is clean and comfortable and it's home for the next few days. It has been more than twenty-four hours since I last felt clean. I need to feel clean. I wash the day's journey away with the only water that is available: dirty, cold water and I step out to examine the rest of the 'resort' that fatigue had blinded me to on my arrival.

Greenwoods is actually a very charming place. An old rambling house, it is built around a beautiful central garden, tended to and loved by the family that run the guest house. The garden is full of trees and flowers and plants and in the very centre of this fecundity sits a multi-coloured shrine to Lord Ganesh, the elephant god. It's low season so there seems to be more family that guests.

There is a terrace all the way around the first floor, looking in and down on the garden. The errant child is attempting to cajole an older female relative into coming and seeing something high up in a tree. She refuses to move. The child disappears out of view and returns with a long cane at the end of which is a home-fashioned wire hoop. The cane is perhaps three times longer than the grubby-faced boy, but when has endeavour ever stopped a four year old? He lifts the stick up into a mango tree and after a series of sharp, awkward movements, his bounty is released. A large green mango falls to earth. Enormous actually.

The green-fruited prize assuages his Tamilian moans, and he and his younger sister now work out how best to cut the bugger. The joys of childhood.

After this brief tour and the ad hoc circus performance, all seems right and proper in the world. I ask the older female relative for directions to the Fisherman's Colony. When Mamallapuram was hit by the tsunami and the seafront devastated, a lot of fishing families lost their livelihoods, which were fairly basic to begin with. The Colony took a year to rebuild. I have arranged to meet one such fisherman, Nagmuthu, son of Mani. He sounds like a character from either *The Lord of the Rings* or the *He-Man* cartoons that used to run on ITV on Saturday mornings.

I would like to say that I had found Nagamuthu, son of Mani, by writing a letter to a cousin's friend who knew a man at the local newspaper who searched the local records and spoke to local people and found a likely candidate. But I actually found Nagamuthu's email address via a website about the events surrounding the tsunami. Why him? Well, he seemed able to communicate in English and he was very happy to let me come and cook.

Greenwoods was telling the truth when it referred to itself as a 'Beach Resort'. It's barely minutes from the sands. On walking to the sea one soon realises how tourist driven Mamallapuram truly is. Trinket shops, cyber cafés, massage centres, guest houses – it's an unending line of consumer-driven businesses. One of the little stalls sells but three types of produce: cigarettes, cold drinks and toilet paper: surely the distillation of the western tourist's needs?

Soon I'm off the hot tarmac and have the sand between my toes. There are a handful of beach-fronted shacks and I have yet to see anything that looks like a fishermen's colony.

Two boys play cricket on the beach; one is wearing what looks remarkably like an Arsenal football top. As I draw closer I realise that it is an Arsenal football top. As an Arsenal fan myself, I consider stopping and chatting to him about the fragility of our midfield last season, to ponder as to whether the back four is less well suited to the offensive component of the modern game and discuss at length the options for an 'in-the-box' striker; but I think better of it. Instead I ask him where I might find Nagamuthu, son of Mani. It would appear that I am standing right outside his shack, the Fisherman Restaurant. I should have guessed.

Mani's shack is little more than a lean-to covered in bamboo. A new concrete wall raises the restaurant floor a couple of metres off the sand, and steps welcome you in. It is sweet, with half a dozen tables, each with a pretty coloured lightshade above. At the back is a small concrete building, the kitchen I'm guessing. There is an old man asleep on the floor and something stirs in a hammock slung between the two central supports of the empty restaurant. The stirring is Nagamuthu; the old man is Mani. Nagamuthu, son of Mani, is asleep in his hammock. There's no way he's going to overthrow Skeletor and win back the Enchanted Forest with mid-afternoon siestas. No way.

He greets me warmly as he rubs sleep out of his eyes. He is a short man, under five and a half feet with Dravidian dark skin. He is stocky and strong, with the sort of musculature that comes from repetitive hard work rather than a gym. He shows me around the kitchen, which is basic. Three steps deep and five paces across, it's small; he has a two-ring burner and a single fridge. I'm now slightly panicking inside; what am I going to cook? Nagamuthu suggests we go to his nearby house to relax and chat. We walk up the hill behind the kitchen and the colony becomes apparent. Nagamuthu tells me that at the time of tsunami, although they lost all their beach-front businesses, luckily their houses were protected. Had it not been for the beach-front shacks . . . His voice tails off into uncertainty.

Outside his house there's a discarded fishing net and a motor boat engine. We enter his house.

There are times in one's life when one realises how others live, the bounties that have been bestowed on us and the hardships afforded to others. For me, this is one of those times. Nagamuthu's house is a single room, smaller than his kitchen at the shack. It has a mattress on the floor, a fan and a TV set. The walls have been painted a moss green, the colour now distressed and peeling with time. One room. That's it. Real life. Prone on the floor in the midst of watching a Bollywood song and dance number is a woman I later find out to be Nagamuthu's sister. She hurriedly collects herself and some clothes and vacates the room, killing the Bollywood soundtrack as she goes. Nagamuthu pulls up a stool for me to sit on while he sits cross-legged on the floor.

I ask him about his life. His father is a fisherman, his grandfather was a fisherman, as far back as he can remember or anyone else in his family can recall, the men would fish. He too is a fisherman, but less so these days. He devotes more time to cooking and running the Fisherman's Restaurant. The tsunami hit the village hard. Mallamapuram always had a strong tourist sector. The beautiful carved temples saw to that. The fishermen had become used to a ready market for their catch, many opening shacks like Nagamuthu's. On the day itself he recalls that he and his father and a few other fishermen had been out laying nets at 3 a.m. Their routine was to return to harvest the nets some four hours later. This they did. By 9 a.m. they were back on the beach. They saw the wave coming. There was obvious panic amongst the fishermen. They knew this was neither a full moon nor a black moon. There could be no explanation for this tidal wave approaching . . .

For seven months they couldn't fish. For that they were grateful; at least they had escaped with their lives while others still searched in vain for the bodies of loved ones. Although they were alive, one wonders about the quality of that life, relying as they did on charity handouts. The restaurant was destroyed. Sitting where I am now it is difficult to imagine the sense of fear that must have overcome those in the colony. India is a highly superstitious country; my own beloved mother has her superstitions that I will always carry with me, as if they were transmitted in the very milk she fed me. But here in this uncomplicated community, superstition is a way of life. Far fewer men now go to fish, which is in itself a good thing since stocks seem very low. Perhaps another by-product of the tsunami? In the old days, Nagamuthu tells me, regardless of the weather the fishermen would venture out, sometimes for days on end. They felt at one with the sea, attuned to its motion, a human extension of its watery being. Now they harbour suspicions. Should a stiff breeze escalate any further, many refuse to fish. Nagamuthu puts it beautifully. Pointing at his heart he suggests that that is where the tsunami now exists, within the fishermen themselves.

He offers me some lunch before taking me around the temples of Mamallapuram. Of course I accept; I love food. We wander back down to the restaurant. Sitting down at the table closest to the sea I take in the view, concentrating on the sounds of life around me rather than the hubbub of unanswered questions in my head. Mani, the father of Nagamuthu, sits at an adjacent table, noiseless. What thoughts is he pondering? I wonder, as he gazes out to a sea he has gazed out at for half a century. We are joined by the occasional crow whose ugly squawks make mango boy's moaning seem like the sweetest of poetry. So clever are these birds that Mani needs only grab a nearby catapult in his gnarled hands and they are off, with cries of derision.

I am overcome with the complete sensory power of the ocean. The salty taste, the smell of seaweed, the cooling breeze on my skin, the sound of crashing waves and the sight of the metamorphosing seas as they turn from green to wake white and then retire to consider a similar change in a few moments' time. Much as we pollute, abuse and use the seas, we have by no means got their measure. There is a certain self-confidence about the way in which the waves collide constantly into the land, a reminder that the seas control us, not we the seas.

My daydream digression is broken by a cornucopia of seafood. Nagamuthu has been busy in the kitchen: fish curry in a rich tomato and onion sauce tempered with curry leaves, mustard seeds and chilli, cooked to perfection; king prawns in a sweet tomato sauce, finished with a little lemon juice, succulent and fresh; and shrimps, fried in chilli, salt and pepper. All served with plain white rice. It's absolutely delicious.

The only sort of non-Indian fish we had in Glasgow was battered and deep fried. I can only ever remember one occasion when the fish cooked in our house was breaded in the finger form. That was an utter disaster. There are some things that you will have probably realised by now and others that you will shortly learn. I am the way I am about food because:

1. My mum is an amazing cook of Indian food.

2. My dad has a deep desire to experiment and try new things (so long as they don't contain vinegar or tamarind, both

of which in his later years seem to bring him out in a coughing fit and generally allergic reaction).

There is no story more indicative of my father's desire to experiment with food and try new things than his rather doomed adventure into the world of slow cooking. As most immigrants can testify, being a newcomer to a country more often than not requires a dual income, since each individual income earned is insubstantial. Yet my father was evangelical about his kids eating good, freshly cooked food every evening of the week. This presented obvious challenges when set within the fiscal context of both parents working. That is when my father's discovery of the slow cooker seemed, for a week in the early 1980s at any rate, to revolutionise the world of food in our house.

The slow cooker was the perfect invention for any immigrant family. I remember the first day it arrived. Dad unpacked it and filled it full of pulses and onions and lamb and saffron and prunes. The excitement was palpable. We all saw this selection of raw ingredients enter the terracotta dish of the slow cooker but we could only imagine the flavours that would result. As dad set the machine to cook through the course of the day, he extolled the virtues of the process of gradual cooking, allowing time to pass as the juices from the meat mingled with the sun-sweetened prunes and the deep, earthy saffron, in amongst which the pulses were plumping and cooking. We left for school, our heads full of fanciful flavours and our hearts brimming with hope.

We returned that evening expecting the house to be permeated with the most exotic of aromas, the table heaving under the weight of Dad's new slow-cooked feast. It would have been a feast indeed had he remembered to actually turn the thing on. It was as if time had stood still in that kitchen in Bishopbriggs.

These minor setbacks never held my father back. Knowing how adept my mum was in the kitchen he nevertheless continued his adventurous escapades into the world of food. No single incident combines my father's sense of gay cuisinal abandon and my mother's skill at cooking than the following story.

Every week my father would return home with produce from KRK. KRK was, for all Indian and Pakistani immigrants in Glasgow back when I was a boy, a lifeline of food and produce. KRK was the only place you could get spices and lentils, Indian style meat, fish, chicken and mangoes. I had not visited a traditional Scottish butcher until I was well into my twenties. If you couldn't afford an airfare back to the subcontinent all you needed to do was pop down to KRK on Woodlands Road and buy a couple of mangoes and an eight-kilo bag of rice; it was the next best thing.

You couldn't help but be curious about food in our house. My dad was forever coming home with random produce. I can have been no more than twelve years old but I was already gaining curiosity about food. I remember him on numerous occasions placing yet another bizarre-looking fruit on the counter at home.

'Cook this, Kuldip,' he would command.

'What is it, Ji?' asked Mum.

'No idea,' he would respond as he wandered off.

But my mother would invariably find a way of cooking it. And invariably it tasted delicious. In later life I realised how instinctively talented my mum is when it comes to food preparation. I have witnessed her smelling, sniffing, cutting and chewing the plethora of weird objects my dad has brought back from numerous visits to KRK. I sometimes think they see him coming and bring out their most freaky-looking vegetables and fruits, knowing that Mr Kohli with his indefatigable sense of adventure will purchase it and make his long-suffering wife find a way of cooking it.

This particular KRK trip was perhaps the most famous of all the KRK trips. Or the most doomed, depending on how you look at it. In amongst the uncontroversial staples of tinned tomatoes, moong daal, coriander and the like lurked a rather pungent paper bag. Triumphantly my father raised the bag and handed it to my mother. Somehow, lifting the bag reinforced the stench and we were all forced to take a step back. Mum asked what it was. Bombay duck, Dad replied. It would appear they only had one in the shop and he'd snaffled it. Right then no one could quite work out why he had bothered, least of all my mother.

Let not the name confuse you. Bombay duck is no sort of duck at all. Oh no. It is a fish, and I doubt if it even comes from Bombay. It could be called Bhopal lamb or Dundee cake for all the relevance the name bestows on the produce. And the version he'd brought home was dried; dried and very stinky.

'Apparently,' my father related, 'it's quite the delicacy in South India.'

'That's great,' my mother muttered. 'But we live in north Glasgow.'

But, such was the patriarchal system she'd married into, Mum tugged her metaphorical forelock and put the deep fat fryer on the stove. Now, I'm not sure if she was going to fry the Bombay duck because that was how you were meant to cook it or if years of a Glaswegian culinary lifestyle had rubbed off on her to the extent that her default with all things fishy was to deep fry; but frying deep she was. We had to leave the kitchen to escape the smell of the dried fish. The lounge was no better as the acrid aroma permeated its way through the house.

Basic rule of cooking no. 1: A thing that smells before you cook it rarely smells better after you cook it. It's self-evident. The heat accentuates the smell. Fair enough? Good.

Our house stank for months after my mum cooked that bloody Bombay duck. And I mean months. The curtains, the sofa, the carpets; no doubt even we had more than a faint whiff of the duck from Bombay about us. It was really bad. Much as I am prone to the occasional comedy hyperbole, really and truly we were constantly reminded of that fateful afternoon well into the next calendar year. To top it all, the Bombay duck didn't even taste nice. It was rank.

Basic rule of cooking no. 2: A thing that smells foul generally tastes foul. The single and notable exception is the Malaysian fruit durian. My favourite cousin in the whole world, Teji, loves durian. He admits it smells of a teenager smeared in rancid seal oil, but if you can get beyond that, the white flesh is sweet and unctuous.

Bombay duck-gate aside, my experiences with home-made fish dishes were generally positive. Fish curry was one of the first Indian dishes I ever learnt to cook. There's no great tradition of seafood in Punjabi households. There is of course Amritsari fish, but I have never seen that anywhere beyond a west of Scotland Indian restaurant. But what I am about to share with you is a dish borne out of economic necessity, a dish behind which is the story of a work ethic and of running a family on a limited budget. The story of Glenryck mackerel fillets in tomato sauce.

Glenryck mackerel fillets in tomato sauce did exactly what it said on the tin. They were precooked fillets of mackerel in a tomato sauce; and they were made by a company called

Glenryck. Per se they were nothing special. But when my mum made her special masala and then added the fillets, the mackerel was somehow elevated to another place altogether, to a taste nirvana. I loved watching my mum cook. To this day I doubt there is anything that woman cannot rustle up. Show her how to pan fry foie gras once, and she will improve the recipe and manage to feed eight more mouths from the same helping.

I loved watching my mum cook because I loved eating. And it's the only time she never told me to do my homework. For this dish she would slice onions, which was unusual because she almost invariably diced for every other curry. A fine dice allowed the onions to fry away to nothing and form the curry sauce. But, in this case, the slice made a feature of the onions. She would temper the oil with whole cumin, waiting till they stopped popping in the hot oil; she would then add her other whole spices: cardamom, cinnamon, bay and whole peppercorns. A little turmeric, a pinch of salt and a touch of paprika. A finely chopped chilli joined the pot and then the moment of truth: I would get to open the tin of mackerel. Always Glenryck, always fillets, always a tomato sauce. They would be poured into the pot and once the fish had heated through, dinner was served. Mackerel curry on a bed of white rice. I seem to remember that by the age of twelve I was cooking it myself. My mum always told me to experiment, to try more of one spice and less of another and work out how it tasted. If you ever asked her for a recipe she would be at a loss. She had no idea what she was doing until she was doing it. And every time it was delicious.

෧ᨰᨭ

Life seems to have turned full circle; the first curry I learnt to cook was fish in an onion and tomato sauce and here I am, thousands of miles from Glasgow, hundreds of meals later, decades forward in time, and I am eating fish curry in a tomato and onion sauce on a bed of white rice as I watch the waves of the Indian Ocean crash against the sun-beaten sands.

Dusk is descending. It is time to prepare dinner. I thought fishcakes would be the thing to do, given the preponderance of them in the area. I always think of fishcakes as very Scottish. I suppose anything in breadcrumbs that is fried has an innate sense of Scottishness about it. Fishcakes with a parsley sauce. Smoked haddock fishcakes. Salmon fishcakes. Fishcakes are great.

Nagamuthu seems nonplussed by the idea, but I have to push on and open his mind to the new possibilities of food. Having said that, he caters for an international tourist crowd, so he's not exactly limited in his applications of seafood. Mani, the father of Nagamuthu, is at the sink in the kitchen, cleaning fish and prawns in preparation for our culinary adventure. A lone couple sit outside, not eating, just drinking a little sweet lemon and soda. That can't provide much of an income in the low season.

I get down to peeling and boiling the potatoes. Nagamuthu says I am his guest and that I should sit and instruct him as to what needs doing. I succumb at first, but it seems unfair and not quite in keeping with my journey that I have him sous for me. I let him peel one potato. He then has to rush out and get more lemons for the sweet lemon soda couple. I peel the other potato and both are chopped and put in the water. Ideally they should be left with skins on to keep the moisture out of the potato. I rifle through his herb selection. Mint, coriander and the ubiquitous curry leaf. I'm tempted by the curry leaf but am also aware that it is a big flavour, akin to adding sage: it has a tendency to overpower a dish if not offset by similarly strong flavours; strong flavours I wish to eschew in favour of sweet seafood and fluffy potato. I opt for some mint and coriander; the mint isn't too minty and the coriander is equally mild. I can't resist chucking a chilli in. When in India . . .

I chop them up fine with a small onion. I might soften the onion at home, just to take the fierce edge off it, but the onions here have a certain sweetness and the bite will be a familiar flavour for Nagamuthu, son of Mani. Nagamuthu returns and he asks me how I would like the seafood prepared. I notice that there are some crabs sitting on the table, looking spare and useless. They are in fact spider crabs; small and delicious but next to impossible to remove the flesh from. But they might be lovely to eat alongside the prawn fishcakes. The prawns are huge and juicy. And there is also a fish called a coconut fish. It's a scale-free, shiny-skinned fish that, like the crabs and the prawns, was in the Indian Ocean some hours ago. So fresh. The flesh is a cross between mackerel (coincidentally) and grey mullet. It's firm and looks like it should taste good. I decide that we will have prawn and coconut fish fishcakes. I'll boil the crabs and they can act as a garnish. Decadent or what?

Mani fillets the fish beautifully, effortlessly, instinctively. As he shells the prawns and cracks the crabs I realise that these wizened, tired hands have been filleting, shelling and cracking for over half a century. He could do it in his sleep. He hands me the prepared seafood. I cut the prawns and fish up into the requisite chunks. I'm sweating so much. It's eight o'clock in the evening and it's still in the thirties. The potatoes are done. I combine the chilli, herbs and onion mixture with the mashed, salted potatoes. I throw the fish in. I ask Nagamuthu what he uses for breadcrumbs. He produces two bags of sweet rusks, the sort of thing my dad loves to dip in his tea and chew on. I crush a few up and add them to the mixture. He crushes a few more as I start forming the patties. Egg dip followed by the smashed rusks. Onto a pan of oil. I throw together the tomato and mango salad and before you know it Nagamuthu and I are sitting at a table with our fish and prawn cakes in front of us.

I think he likes it because all I can hear is the sea crashing against the beach as he chews on the last crab claw.

Tonight seems like a million miles away from Kovalam and my crisis of confidence with my chicken stuffed with pesto. I want to phone my dad and remind him of the Bombay duck story and the incident with the slow cooker; I want to hear him laugh. I want my mum to roll her eyes the way she does, a half smile on her face letting me know that she loves my dad in her most Indian of ways. I feel that they are with me on this journey. With Arzooman in Kovalam I had no idea who I was and how I felt. On paper you would think that Arzooman and I would have a great deal in common. He is a middle-class Indian, skilled in English having travelled the world. We conversed fluently about food and shared a few jokes. But here I am with a man with whom I have very little intersection, a man whose life could not be more different to mine. Yet we sit in happy silence. What binds us is the fact that we are men. Ordinary men. And as ordinary men we sit and crack on crab bones and let the darkness envelope us.

୧ৠᎧ

I had found some genuine solace in Mamallapuram in the most unexpected of places. Nagamuthu, son of Mani, seemed happy to accept me for who I was. He accepted my food for what it was, although it wasn't perhaps the most authentically British of dishes. On the golden beach in front of his shack I felt at once at home, at home within myself. But I had barely started my journey. To make sense of Nagamuthu and my Mamallapuram experience I needed to move on, to experience more. If I had given up after my chicken breast and Indian pesto incident with Arzooman, I would never have experienced the idyllic contentment of Mamallapuram. It was only the sense of impending failure that I had felt at the Green Cove that made the sense of accomplishment here so much more worthwhile. Similarly I would have to move on from this experience and test myself further.

It was like leaving our flat on the Great Western Road. When my family first moved to Glasgow we shared a flat with my maternal great-uncle. The flat was in Glasgow Street. Ironic really that the new immigrants lived in Glasgow Street. We eventually bought a place on the Great Western Road, in a red sandstone tenement block. The Great Western Road is not so much a street as an infrastructural institution. It stretches aorta-like from the heart of the city heading westward through Kelvinbridge and into Hillhead. Metamorphosing, changing and developing, the road reaches out all the way to Anniesland Cross. It is Glasgow's straightest and longest road. My parents bought a rundown little two bedroom flat above a fabric shop, aptly called Fab Fabrics. 605 Great Western Road was the first property that my parents owned in Glasgow and it was the most amazing flat in the world to grow up in. It was on the first floor of a four-storey close and out back we had a crappy little communal, dark and considerably scary garden. At the back of the garden was a giant Victorian bird cage, for no apparent reason. This flat, this garden and these streets were the most exciting playground a child could hope for. Tenements were best described by Billy Connolly as vertical villages. That is exactly how they felt.

But of course the aspirations of immigrants meant that a flat in a block was not nearly enough. My father wanted a house; a house was a statement of success, it showed that the immigrant had made it. A house had an upstairs and a downstairs, it had no communal parts. And it had its own garden. So, having settled in the idyll of Hillhead, at the tender age of six I found myself dislocated to the heart of Spam Valley, Bishopbriggs. There is a distinct lack of charm in a 1960s Wimpey house. I remember a real sense of loss for our old tenement block in the heart of the West End of Glasgow.

The first flat I ever bought as an adult was a tenement flat in the heart of the West End of Glasgow. It was kind of karmic. And this same sense of karmic completion gave me the feeling that my brief episode of calm with Nagamuthu, the very sound of the Indian Ocean crashing quietly on the sandy beach would make some sense and grow in significance only after I had left.

I knew that something significant within me had altered. I was, as yet, unable to quantify or clarify what exactly it was. Like the sense of anticlimax I felt leaving 605 Great Western Road, arriving at Bishopbriggs made sense of it, and every house or flat I have lived in since has made sense of the experience that preceded it. I was sure that the knowledge I had garnered from Mamallapuram and Nagamuthu would unfold from within me, as my journey itself unfolded further.

I had seven more cities to visit and seven more meals to cook. I felt like it may well end up being seven more lifetimes. Maybe that hippy in the pastry shop on Byres Road was right.

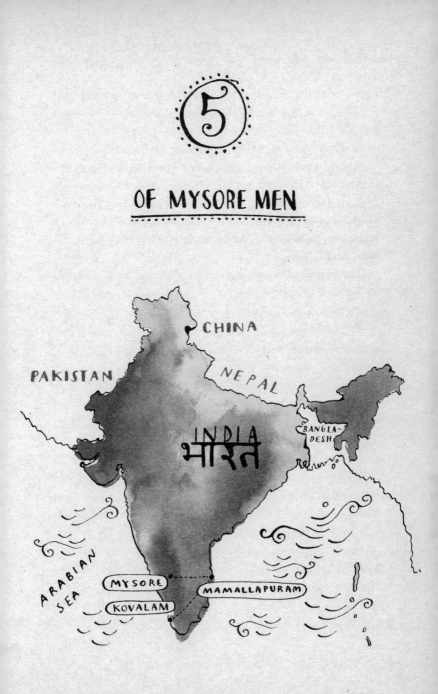

5

OF MYSORE MEN

'Your kind attention, please. Train number 6222 Mysore Express will leave platform three at 21.30 hours.'

'Welcome to Chennai Station. Please do not sit on the floor.'

The faux-welcoming voice of the slightly snotty lady on the prerecorded tannoy is the first thing I hear over the dull roar of life that seems to be sucked into this building. And what a building! A massive marble structure with unfeasibly high ceilings, it seems that all of humanity have a train to catch from Chennai station tonight. The few seats that were available have long since been claimed, and old, sari-clad ladies lay sleeping peacefully on the floor of the concourse, flagrantly disregarding the tannoy'ed request, waiting for a train from nowhere to take them somewhere. There is a buzz about this place, the sense of constant movement, permanent transience, an indefatigable energy. Music blares from speakers, people blare at each other and TV screens blare heroines miming to the latest Bollywood hit. The station is open on three sides and from these three sides they come and they gather, expertly orientating themselves around and into the ever diminishing gaps between brown flesh.

This can't be more different from my first train journey. Chennai Station is much more akin to my expectations than

Trivandrum was; in Chennai the only expectation is how many extra bodies can be crammed onto already full departing trains. This sense of chaos around me only makes me feel more smug about my prearranged ticket.

I saunter amongst the pandemonium. I am worry-free; what shall I do first? Shall I check on the status of my train? Why ever should I do that? I have aeons of time. Protocol suggests a small, sweet Indian coffee from one of the scores of coffee shacks on the periphery of the concourse. A sweeter, more delicious coffee I have yet to taste in India. Shall I check the status of my train now? Are you insane? But the last thing I want is a panic. Which is exactly why I had prebooked a slightly more expensive air-conditioned white ambassador car to bring me to the station. He had arrived quarter of an hour early and my wiry dark-skinned driver with his impossibly full moustache had spent the extra minutes buffing an extra sheen of whiteness on his already gleaming car, a whiteness sadly lost to the inexorable gloom of night. As I skipped out of Greenwoods, my trusty wheely bag by my side, I reminded myself that I had given myself a clear two hours to make the journey, recalling the words of Thom Yorke from Radiohead in the song 'No Surprises'.

The cab journey had been generally smooth. Now I have a full hour before departure. I amble carefree to grab a couple of pyramidical samosas, noting a banana vendor on my way, making a mental note to purchase a bunch on my journey back to the as yet unmolested departures board. Having smugly dawdled the first thirty-five minutes away I should have sensed the initial stages of hubris gathering within me. The train to Mysore is at platform three. It is an enormous snake of carriages falling away to a train-like dot in the platform distance. I reckon it would take Sebastian Coe, at the peak of his powers, at least two minutes to run its length, with a feisty Steve Ovett kicking hard behind him. I finally look at my ticket. I have never in all my life seen a single train ticket that conveys so much information. It declares the distance to travel; whether I am an adult or child; gender specifications; age details; ticket number which is different from a booking number which in turn varies from a reservation number; the class of journey; some other random but rather official-looking numbers; coach number; berth number; seat number; ticketing authority; concession status, rupee fee. It even has a note on the side suggesting a 'Happy Journey'. It's astonishing really. This single ticket has more information than some novellas I have read. And the information is truly inspired if you know what to do with it, if you know how to decode it and make the information work in your favour. Such decoding is lost on me.

I know I am at the right station at the right time; I have been reciting it in my sleep for the last two days. My gender is correct and I have to thank them for making me three years younger on the ticket than I really am. What is vexing me are the details of my carriage and berth number: carriage WL/17 and berth WL/05. There seem to be no such carriages; more worrying still, there seem to be no carriages even close to that description.

I have very limited experience of Indian travel as an adult, but one thing I can be sure of: whatever else one might say about the trains here, the seat numbering system is exemplary; never in all my train-travelling experience has there ever been confusion or fuss about where exactly on the train I should sit. Never. So you can understand my confusion and fuss at being asked to locate a carriage that simply doesn't seem to exist.

Having perambulated the entire length of the train I am none the wiser and still unseated. Luckily for me, or so I think, each carriage has a printout plastered on the side listing names and seat allocations. The only carriages that don't provide such information are the third-class compartments. These are already full of people, boxes, bags of rice and the odd chicken. They are euphemistically referred to as 'free-seating areas', a.k.a. first come, first served. I walk carriage lengths at a time, samosas and bananas in one hand, case and ticket in the other. My nervousness grows exponentially as each printout draws a blank. It seems that every conceivable anagram of the five letters K-O-H-L-I appears save for the correct spelling of my name. I scuttle past another third-class carriage, catching myself thinking the worst. Is this where I will have to sit? Having checked every carriage, every list twice I end up back at the head of the train, none the wiser and a great deal wearier. My name appears nowhere. Not in type, not in biro, not in chalk; not even in my own imagination. It is like I have ceased to exist. I have been air-brushed out of Indian railway history in some sort of Stalinist manoeuvre to revise my very being. (As you can see I wasn't taking this experience too personally.)

I look at my ticket again in the vain hope that the 2km hike up and down the train might have imbued me with some new power of Indian Railway Ticket Understanding, or IRTU as I will now and for ever call it. Alas, my IRTU is still at novice level. My IRTU has got me to:

a) The right station
b) The right platform
c) On the right day
d) At the right time

Thereafter my IRTU has failed me. Spectacularly. As I hopelessly flounder, examining my ticket for the thousandth time, the lone Indian Railways official policing this platform walks past. Seeing me obviously confused, he ups his pace in an attempt to avoid close questioning. I manage somehow to trap him as I spread myself and my case and my samosa and bananas as wide as I can. He barely looks at my ticket and instructs me to board any old carriage and let the omniscient conductor sort out the fine detail.

It is 9:24. I have six minutes to make a decision. Time being of the essence I jump into the final carriage, a first-class carriage I have intimately examined four times thus far this evening. I find the first available seat and sit down. And I wait. Time is best killed in the pursuit of eating. I eat my samosas, knowing full well I am an interloper sitting in the wrong seat, trying to use the eating of a pyramidical Indian snack as some confident cover for my crime of seat theft.

Conscience gets the better of me. I decide to move to a different seat moments before a family of three crowd around my samosa-crumbed seat and seek refuge. The train has pulled off, a detail that has passed me by. I search in vain for a seat called WL5. I settle on another seat, a seat that very roughly approximates to some of the numbers on my ticket. It isn't seat WL5, but it is *a* seat 5 and it resides amongst some jolly young student types. I brush samosa crumbs from my mouth. I hold my case, my bananas and my breath. I close my eyes and hope that sleep will offer some solace and shelter from my seat-less existence.

No sooner have my eyes shut than images revisit me of the mayhem in the third-class carriage; my imagination runs riot. I dream of tooth-free, wrinkled grandmothers in skimpy cotton saris tempting me with newspaper-wrapped food, the provenance of which could not be guaranteed; their long, bony brown fingers ushering me forward, nothing but darkness behind their cold, uncaring eyes. My sleeping mind transfixes on an insolent, big-eyed child, a girl who has, so early in her life, developed anti-Sikh tendencies, eating a rotten mango and offering me nothing but hate. And that chicken, now the size of a small man clucking straight at me, questions my very existence with every juddering movement of its overly large head. And I feel myself being inexorably pulled towards this unreserved, third-class dystopia, this free-for-all of humanity, mangoes and poultry; and there is nothing I can do to stop it happening . . .

I am snapped out of my stupor by one of the jolly students who gently rocks my shoulder, sparing me from the bony-fingered granny. He politely and eloquently informs me that my big fat hairy Glaswegian arse is parked on the wrong seat, a seat that does in fact belong to his friend, another jolly young student type. I am all out of ideas, so I simply submit to fate and show him my ticket. He takes one look and to him, everything became clear. WL, he told me stands for Wait Listed. Wait Listed? All I can see now in my mind's eye is a granny chicken with big insolent eyes, eating a mango. I exclaim. Audibly. I ask him what that means, Wait Listed. He shrugs his shoulders non-commitally. I ask him if I would have to sit with the granny and the chicken and the mango girl. He looks worried. He kindly agrees to sort it out for me. He takes my ticket and digs out his mobile phone from deep within his pocket. Now, remember when I listed all that information they print on the ticket? Well, just above the space where they print your grandmother's maiden name, the colour of your first pet and your inside leg measurement, there is an official-looking number. He texts this official-looking number to some train conductor somewhere in cyberspace. Within seconds the phone beeps back the information that I have seat 22 in carriage A1. A1: the very first carriage on the train. And here I am in the very last carriage. I thank him, I pick up my case, my bananas and myself and head towards the front of the train.

Now here's a little detail you may want to carry with you if you ever find yourself at the furthest available point on a train from your designated seat. Unlike the trains in the UK, Indian train carriages are not interconnected: at least not always. (Needless to say they are interconnected on all those journeys where you find yourself in the right seat, in the right carriage, at the right time.) But as I should have remembered from my early endeavours to try and find my seat, this train is made up of three distinct sets of carriages with no connection between each group of three. I have not fully taken the time to appreciate this little quirk of carriage non-connectivity until I have banged and battered myself down the three lengths of narrow gangway, apologising to the myriad of legs and elbows I collide with as I try to move elegantly through the moving train. After the third carriage I reach an impasse, an impasse of sky-blue painted Indian metal. How am I going to get to my seat? Quite simply: I have to wait until the train makes its next stop and then dash as far as I can along the platform before the train sets off again. An inexact science, I trust you'll agree.

I wait impatiently for the first stop. I decide, in the interests of pragmatism, to ditch the bananas: they will only slow me down. I reckon I could cover the length of three carriages in about five minutes (five minutes would seem to be the minimum stopping time of Indian trains at stations). If I manage to achieve three carriages per stop, then it shouldn't take more than ten or eleven stops to reach the final carriage. Piece of cake. I limber up as the train seems to be slowing down into a station stop.

I alight the train and run like some Madras Moses, parting the sea of brown humanity before me. It seems I am the only one heading to the front of the train. The clock is ticking, my heart is pounding. I manage to pass six carriages and find myself running alongside third class again. I'm sure I see the dead-eyed granny and the mango-eating girl as they are egged on by the mutant chicken. I avert my gaze and keep sprinting. Miraculously the train stays stationary for just enough time to enable me to make my way out of the balmy, sweaty evening into the cool, calm and air-conditioned ambience of first class and the expectant emptiness of seat 22, carriage A1. I feel like I have arrived home. And not a stray chicken in sight.

I buy a hot sweet coffee for 5 rupees from the boy who walks up and down the carriage shouting 'coffee' (actually he shouts 'coppee', but I know what he means). In seat 22, carriage A1 I find myself ensconced with a fat, prehistoric man in a white linen shirt, white linen trousers and a white linen jacket. I fully expect his wife to be constructed from white linen. She merely looks long-suffering and tired as he continues the marathon phone call he has been engaged in since I joined the carriage, by now more than an hour or so ago. He continues grunting down the phone.

One would correctly think that the travails of my hunt for the mysteriously wait-listed seat and the nervous tension of the granny, the mango girl and the human-sized chicken might have exhausted me completely. My previous experience from Trivandrum to Chennai has taught me that the higher bunks seem to offer a more enhanced sense of movement of the journey. This can hamper sleep, so wherever possible one should opt for a lower bunk. My much sought-after and sprinted-for seat 22 in carriage A1 is a higher bunk. I decide to move before

I get too settled: the carriage is wholly under-subscribed and there is an abundance of free lower bunks to be had.

As I collect myself and my things they don't seem too fussed that I am leaving the compartment, although for a moment I swear I can see in her eye the desire to shout, 'Please, don't go, don't leave me with him . . . ' The fat prehistoric linen man continues his fat prehistoric phone call.

But my move to the lower bunk is to no avail. As I settle into my new seat, sleep is still a stranger. As I lie rocking on the train, I feel like the only man in the whole world that is awake. My mind drifts inevitably to my next location, the next instalment of my journey. Could there be two more contrasting locations than a sleeper train from Chennai and a coffee shop in Delhi? But it is because of a chance meeting in that coffee shop that I now find myself on this sleeper train. My Mysore meandering was motivated some months back by destiny and cold coffee. Destiny and cold coffee delivered Jeremy Patriciana to me. And now destiny and hot, sweet coffee are delivering me back to him.

My wife is obsessed with three things: India, yoga and really good coffee. After yoga in London she hunts down a really good coffee. When she comes to India she hunts down really good coffee. If she were ever to come to India for yoga, rest assured coffee-hunting would very much be on the agenda. Her research in the more well-heeled neighbourhoods of Bombay have led her to conclude that the single most reliable and delicious brand of cappuccino in India can be purchased from the chain known as Cafe Coffee All Day. Since her specifications in such matters extend to the number of shots, heat component and general froth factor, I defer to her superior wisdom. So whenever I find myself submerged in the subcontinent without her I always endeavour to find a Cafe Coffee All Day and raise an extra-hot double-shot frothy cappuccino in her name.

I was in Delhi early in 2007, in the middle of a short work trip that involved copious travel, and found myself rather discombobulated in a mid-range hotel on a Sunday. I had to remind myself that I was in Delhi and that it was in fact a weekend. I decided to step out of my room into the faded colonial glory that is Connaught Place. Because it was Sunday, it was busy; very busy. Families laughing, lovers quarrelling, dogs barking; then dogs laughing, families quarrelling and lovers barking. Such is the temporal nature of life.

I happened upon a buzzing Cafe Coffee All Day and knew what I must do: drink a coffee for my wife. The place was jumping; a TV blaring noisy and average American MTV. It was mostly full of spoilt brat Delhi kids drinking overpriced coffee and swearing loudly in Americanised English. A few tourists inhabited the air-conditioned sanctuary. I took a table for two. The place filled up so that the sole remaining seat was opposite me. In walked this exceedingly chilled-out guy with long hair and shades; he asked if he could join me. We got chatting and I discovered that Jeremy, a Filipino American, was a devotee of the art of yoga. So devoted was he that he quit life in California as a paediatric cancer nurse and had set up a small yoga school in a place called Mysore. This was too serendipitous, too much of a coincidence. I had always wanted to visit Mysore; my father-in-law studied medicine there in the late fifties and it sounded like a part of India untouched by modernity, still traditional in many ways. It seemed to me that places like Mysore had managed to slip under the burgeoning tourist radar of India. Obviously Goa, Bombay and the like were well-known and well-travelled destinations, but I had thought very few westerners would venture to Mysore.

I was totally wrong. Jeremy told me that Mysore was a hotbed for yogic activity; there were white faces everywhere and numerous yoga centres and hippy hang-outs, including his own.

He seemed such an incongruous person to visit on my adventure through India, a Filipino American former paediatric cancer nurse who is now running a yoga school in the city my father-in-law studied medicine at. Incongruous though he may be, Jeremy also epitomises a contemporary take on that sixties and seventies adventure to India I've mentioned before; foreigners who came to India for self-discovery through yoga, spirituality and a pursuit of inner peace. Now it's the spiritual component to the globalisation of India.

If Jeremy is on a quest to find himself he can aid me on *my* quest to find *my*self. How different is Jeremy's experience of India from mine when you actually shake it down? He is a western child of an immigrant who has arrived in India to pursue his truth. Isn't that exactly what I am, albeit an immigrant, one generation removed from India itself? If I can work out what he, as an American Filipino, is learning from India then perhaps I can apply that to my own experience. Cooking for Jeremy should be interesting; yogis are very funny about what they eat, although he has assured me that they are omnivores at his school. And most of the yoga practitioners I know all look like they could do with a decent meal. I intend to provide that, based around the delights of Lancashire and its hotpot. And maybe I will be able to touch my toes for the first time in a decade.

Here I am the next morning with yet another hot sweet coffee watching the beautiful golden light of Karnataka in the morning. There is a curious thing about the light in India. For some reason film never seems able to capture the sun's resplendent haze as dawn breaks beautifully over the subcontinent. Beautifully lit coconut groves, shimmering with texture and contrast to the naked eye become just a bunch of coconut trees when committed to film. Or perhaps I am viewing India through my own personal rose-tinted filter?

The train chugs and rocks and creaks onward to an ever nearer Mysore. Not long now, not long. The train slowly wakens, the coffee vendors and the light combine to stir even the deepest of sleepers.

As I said, Mysore is a place I have always wanted to visit and I have heard many different stories about the place. Mysore is famous for two things: the production of sandalwood soap, the fragrance of which is unparalleled in the world of beauty products; and possibly the most beautiful Maharajah's palace in all of India. The palace was completed nearly a hundred years ago and is said to be illuminated by no less than 5,000 lights – that's when they are all working. The city was politically and culturally prominent in the fifteenth century when it was ruled by the Wadiyar kings on and off until Independence in 1947. They were great patrons of the arts and culture. But to my mind the single most appealing fact about Mysore is its unusually small population for an Indian city. It is said to be less than a million people.

And the unusually uncrowded Mysore is lovely; at least the Mysore I am seeing. Jeremy emailed me his address and through the gift of text messaging has sent me directions that I somehow have managed to convey to the rickshaw wallah. We leave the smart train station heading off to the nearby suburb of Gokalam. As we travel down leafy wide streets canopied by over-arching trees splattered with brilliant red blossom, I enjoy the gentle calm to this cool beautiful morning. The sky is big and has a welcoming tranquillity about it. The morning breeze augurs well for a temperate day ahead. I shan't miss the oppressive heat of Kovalam and Mamallapuram.

Cooking for Jeremy gives me a unique chance to pull together a variety of elements from new India. The yogic tradition that stretches back to my own childhood is an obvious and delightful coincidence; the fact that foreigners are still coming to India four decades on in a desire to engage with eastern mysticism is fascinating to me. Combine this with the status of Mysore as an ancient Indian city, steeped in culture and tradition, and, finally, with my father-in-law's links with the place, it gives me an overall sense of warmth.

I arrive at what my rickshaw driver assures me is Gokalam. I am tired but pleasantly surprised by the prettiness of Mysore. Jeremy meets me outside the small Ganesh shrine in his street, an easy landmark for rickshaw drivers and beggars. At this point I realise that Jeremy is only one conversation better acquainted to me than those numerous rickshaw drivers and beggars. I barely know the man, yet have entrusted myself to him for the next few days. I'm sure I don't let my panic show. The centre occupies the second and third floor of Durga Mansions in a picturesque suburb of Mysore. The kitchen, where I will later be cooking, and the bedrooms are on the second floor and the yoga room and training area are up on the third with Jeremy's and Suresh's rooms.

Jeremy takes me up to the third floor immediately and offers to show me a few loosening moves. My timing is far from perfect since Jeremy has a meditation class with Suresh, his guru, and so we have limited time. I'm hardly complaining. I have just arrived and haven't yet visited the toilet. There is a very real chance that this body-bending behaviour may well cause me some 'natural' embarrassment. I am bent and pulled and pushed and breathed and I try hard to look like I know what I am doing whilst hoping against hope that my rectal gas will remain rectal. This yoga lark is bloody hard work. There seems a beautifully visual irony as the brown-skinned Indian man (me) struggles to follow the yogic shapes of the loose-limbed yellow-skinned Filipino American man (Jeremy). Whilst at the time all my efforts were focused on remaining upright and non-flatulent, with hindsight perhaps that moment said as much about modern India as my journey of self-discovery. Maybe.

Suddenly the enigmatic Suresh appears, as if out of the ether, noiselessly joining us. He also has long hair tied back. He has dark, brooding eyes and an honest, open face. When he smiles he shows kindness. He seems like a lovely bloke. And he has a Mexican bandit moustache. So that's the tableau: a slightly overweight, hairy Sikh bloke, a good-looking, buff Filipino American and a Svengali-looking Indian dude with a great moustache. All we need now is a buxom girl trying to learn yoga whose clothes keep falling off and we have the makings of a really bad porn movie.

Suresh intimates that it is time for their meditation class. Jeremy has been learning from Suresh for almost eighteen months. His training should be complete in another two and a half years. They kindly let me sit in on the meditation.

We enter the yoga room. A Bhudda sits contently in the corner, an iPod sits contently in its iDock. This juxtaposition should have given the game away immediately. Suresh and Jeremy sit down in a very strategic way, tucking certain parts of their left legs in and under certain other parts of their right legs. I soon realise that nothing yogis do is ever anything other than completely thought through. They plan to meditate for seventy-five minutes. Seventy-five minutes. I have never done anything that involves sitting still in one place for seventy-five minutes. And sitting in one place while watching two other blokes breathing and sitting still in one place, is not about to become the first way I spend seventy-five minutes sitting still. Thankfully Jeremy says that I can leave whenever I get bored. But what is the patience protocol in the world of meditation? Twenty minutes? Half an hour? I know I can't sit on the hard concrete floor for an hour and a quarter, not with what my arse has been through on the trip thus far. I resolve that it would be rude to leave any sooner than thirty-five minutes in, and that I should wait for an arbitrary number somewhere between thirty-five and forty, so as I don't seem too keen to exit.

They unfurl the curtains and a gloom descends on the already gloomy evening. A small candle is lit before a deity, offering the only real light in the room. The yogic two sit cross-legged, right foot on left thigh, left foot under right thigh. Impressive, and they haven't even started the breathing bit. Suresh takes his mobile out and sets the alarm for the end of the session. I love the collision of worlds; the meditative wonder of yoga and the harsh electronic alarm of a Sony Ericksson mobile phone. In many ways, all that is India is contained in this very room: the spiritual heritage that Suresh, a Karnatakan villager, represents; the contemporary fascination that the 'civilised' west has with the subcontinent, epitomised by Jeremy's presence; and me: the bastard child of east and west, the chronicler of the contemporary.

Suresh starts a gentle chant, a monotone that is strangely hypnotic. This continues for ten minutes or so. It is both calming and reassuring. Then, in a ritual complex in its simplicity, they each inhale gradually through a single nostril, seizing more air with each nasal inhalation. The third inhalation is the final. They then hold their breaths, and with open hands resting on knees, they count. They then exhale through the other nostril, in three controlled bursts. They repeat the same for the other nostril. It's slightly mesmeric, the sounds of air passing through the nose, the very deliberate movement of the hand to the opposite nostril to block it. Every so often, no doubt in a pattern clearer to the more well-trained eye, they perform a series of alternate nasal clearances, by which I mean the most definite clearing of nasal cavities. Then the process begins all over again. I am enchanted for nearly three quarters of an hour. The dull city sounds ever more distant with every inhalation, its random, unstructured noise falling into sharp relief against the tranquillity of hypnotic human breath. It's truly beautiful. But I really need to break wind, so I leave . . .

I wander about the rooms, generally trying to get a sense of the place. There are all the usual curios and accoutrements to spirituality lying around: Ganesh statues, Hanuman wall hangings, incense sticks, a pack of playing cards and some poker chips. A pack of playing cards and some poker chips? Surely some mistake. As I shuffle the cards and riffle the chips, Jeremy, fresh from his breathing and breath-holding, appears from around the corner.

'Do you play?' he asks.

'I found them lying over there, by the incense.'

I wonder why I sound so guilty. Of course I play cards. I don't know any Indian kid that doesn't play cards. All the best card games I ever learnt I learnt in India and played with my cousins. Back home in Glasgow some of the most fun nights were when my mum and dad had invited friends round. The smoked-glass topped coffee table was pushed to one side and they all sat cross-legged on the floor, a white sheet beneath them, whiskies by the men, tea by the ladies and they all gambled the night way. They played three-card brag, or Flash as they called it. I remember vividly one evening begging my dad

106

to let me play; I was only thirteen but he succumbed, especially after the insistence of Dr Jugal.

'Let the boy play. He will be sorely beaten, and then he will learn not to ask to play with the adults.' Jugal smiled a sinister smile, pretending to the rest of the room that he was joking.

As I collected up the twenty-eight pounds of my winnings some time later that same evening, Jugal was no longer smiling.

'Do you play?' asks Jeremy, again.

'Yeah. Poker.' I reply. 'Hold Em.'

His face breaks into a smile. 'Great,' he exclaims. 'I love Hold Em. No one to play with here. Shuffle up and deal.'

So I do.

I would never have thought a spiritually obsessed yogi like Jeremy would be a card player, let alone a poker player. It just doesn't seem right. I love the game and play often; but not like him. He wants to travel the world and play in tournaments. He reckons he's got what it takes to be a winner. I don't tell him that I have played in Vegas and everyone thinks they have got what it takes to be a winner. I'm not sure he wants to hear that. Jeremy reckons that through his yoga he is somehow enabled to look deep into the soul of his opponents and tell what hand they have, or whether they are bluffing or trapping. I'm not sure he can, and after I relieve him of his first one hundred rupees, I think my instincts may be right. He insists we play another hundred-rupee game. I'm not sure I want to alienate my host: I can't say no, yet I don't want to take more rupees off him.

Subtly I bring up the subject of money. How does he make a living here? He tells me that he charges each student board and lodging for their stay at the school. He already has savings from the States and those are more than enough to live off.

The money from students he intends to use to buy his way into poker tournaments. He is planning a trip to Barcelona in a few months. This is very strange. I never expected to be playing poker in India, least of all with a yoga freak. I take his next hundred rupees off him and suggest I start planning for dinner. I can tell he is awaiting the next opportunity to win his money back. I will let him try, but after I have cooked; at least then if he throws me out I will have achieved my goal.

This cooking adventure has disaster written all over it. When I'd checked with him, Jeremy had said it would be fine to cook meat. After I've lightened his wallet of 200 fine Indian rupees, I ask him where I can source my ingredients. I have planned it all out: Lancashire hotpot. Mutton (you rarely get lamb in India), potatoes, carrots, onions – all readily available. A big, bubbling pot of tender meat and buttery soft vegetables that warm the very soul, much like yoga itself. I could easily concoct a stock in the afternoon with some roasted bones and herbs. It was all going to be a very beautiful food-type thing.

Then the bombshell drops.

'We can't have meat,' he says, rather sheepishly.

'No meat. OK.' I try and look hopeful. Lancashire hotpot with chicken might work.

'And no chicken,' he continues, as if he had read my mind, a feat he never once managed to achieve during poker. It's going from bad to worse.

'Let me just check. No meat and no chicken?' I ask.

'No meat, no chicken,' he confirms.

'Why?' I implore.

'The cook is funny about meat and chicken in the kitchen. She'd rather you cooked vegetarian.'

'I can't really cook vegetarian.'

Jeremy is lovely and couldn't have been more apologetic. I try hard not to panic. Remember, I love vegetables. I adore them. I am not to be mistaken for my elder brother, Raj. Vegetables are great whenever they are accompanied by meat or chicken. However a meal containing *only* vegetables is like a broken pencil; utterly pointless. What is the focus of a plate of food if there is no symphony of flesh in the centre? British food is all about meat and two veg, not veg and two veg (which would be three veg, if the rules of simple arithmetic were to be followed). I would even be prepared to allow fish or shellfish to take pride of place in the centre of a platter. But nut roast? Or cauliflower bake? Or aubergine surprise? No. Thank you, but no. They are not complete and fulfilling meals. It is with this food-based philosophy in mind that I have never really perfected or indeed bothered my overweight Glaswegian arse when it comes to the cooking of vegetarian food. Life is too short. (Although my doctor suggests it would be considerably longer if I entertained the notion of a vegetarian diet from time to time.)

I'm humped, as we say back home on the Byres Road. Failure had to come at some point; I'm sanguine enough about that. But so early, when it all looked so promising? And to cap it all I feel dirty; deep-down dirty. Twenty-four hours ago I was charging up and down the platform at Chennai station looking for a non-existent train seat; I spent a sleepless night on that selfsame train; followed by the better part of a day bending my unsupple body and watching men breathe. I feel in need of some commune with warm, cleansing water. Surely every yogi would approve of such a desire? I excuse myself and head for a bath.

In Britain there is only one type of bath. You fill the tub with water and take a bath. Uncontroversially straightforward. In our family we call this a 'fish bath', so named by my Aunty

Pavittar, my dad's younger sister. I assume, though have never had it verified by Pavittar, that a fish bath is so called because it is the sort of bath a fish might enjoy, allowing them to swim in the open waters of a full tub. But this form of bathing, whilst wholly uncontroversial to the British psyche, is a complete anathema to the Indian way of being. A shower they could understand. But a fish bath? Indians do not understand how cleanliness is achieved by lolling around for hours in a pool of your own dirt. We advocate a different approach to the art of bathing; this we call the 'bucket bath'. Let me explain.

Bucket baths are great. Great and very Indian. As opposed to a fish bath which is also great, but very unIndian. Our house, like every Indian house in Britain and probably across the world, was geared up to the bucket-bath scenario, a washing technique I still love to this day. A bucket (known in Punjabi as a 'balti'*) would be placed in the bath and subsequently filled with water. The said water would then be manipulated, by crafty use of a small jug, over the bather's body. A pause would occur in the water-pouring process while soap was administered to the body. The water manipulation step would continue until all soap had been washed away. Finally, and this was the *coup de grâce*, the remaining water in the bucket that could not successfully be manipulated into the jug was poured over the bather in a single motion. The very essence of refreshment. It was both beautiful and simple.

As we grew up and became more experienced in the way of the bucket bath, new, subtle variations would be introduced. Simultaneous soaping and water-pouring. Left-handed water-

---

*Originally a *balti* would have been a steel bucket but colloquially came to mean any bucket or indeed large water-carrying receptacle. We never had a bucket per se for our bucket baths. Ours was an orange rectangular 'bucket' that not only assisted our bath-time but also when we were poorly and running the risk of vomiting; it was placed by our bedsides as a catch-all, so to speak. So for me, the word 'balti', when applied to curry, offers a certain incongruity, shall we say.

pouring, solo hair-washing (bearing in mind we were a houseful of long-haired woman and men) and latterly, shamed as I am to admit it, masturbating and water-pouring. Try it; it's great. Whatever way you look at it, the bucket bath is a triumph of humanity over dirtiness. As I wander down the stairs and back to my room, I stop for a moment on the terrace and enjoy the twinkling view over the scattered and uncluttered city. Within the crazy, mixed-up cosmopolitan influences of Jeremy and Suresh and the Americanisation of yoga and the rest of it, I am, somewhere deep down inside, very much at ease with my place here in Mysore. I feel very Indian. I still feel Indian when I notice that the bucket for my bucket bath resides in a tiny bathroom. I would struggle to swing a kitten in it, let alone a cat. I let the water run; it's cold. I start to get undressed. I suddenly realise that I need a bath so badly that even I find my own smell offensive. I'm impressively malodorous. I check the water. If anything it's getting colder and colder. I could cry.

I ask little of life, really. A nice meal now and again, a well cut suit, the music of Van Morrison and hot water for a bucket bath. With the shower or bath scenario the crucial difference with cold water is that you are able to completely immerse your body in the cold experience, shocking it instantly into acceptance. With the bucket bath it's an altogether more gradual experience. The warm and dry part of your body wonders why you are pouring cold water on the other parts of your body. This makes the recently made cold parts of your body feel colder still. While this is kicking off, civil war breaks out as the as yet unmolested parts of your body get wise to the imminent coldness. It's confusing and bloody hard work.

I don't want a cold bath. I really don't. But I have to. I can't wait until Bangalore.

I emerge from my non-specific wet-soaking none the wiser as to my cooking challenge. And to compound an already fairly compounded situation Jeremy, in his sweet, mild-mannered and measured way points out other limitations to my meal. Anna, a surly Spaniard from Lanzarote who does not like spicy food. Suresh's twenty-one day fast which may permit him to only eat a mouthful, out of politeness no doubt. And then there's the lovely old Karnatakan cooking and cleaning lady who Jeremy has never once seen eating for the entire year he's been here. Great.

So let's sum up the position: I have no ingredients to cook, no idea what I am going to cook and should I somehow, by divine karmic contact, devise the most complete plate of British-European food ever created by a Scotsman in India, I have only Jeremy to eat it.

I must look like panic personified because Jeremy offers to help me regroup by taking me on the back of his motorbike to the shops to see what would inspire me. I haven't been on a motorbike since I was a kid. And that story doesn't have a happy ending . . .

We were in Ferozepure, at my grandfather's house. I was about twelve at the time. Our trip was coming to an end and we had to take the bus from Ferozepure back to Delhi before jetting off back to Scotland. You may have noticed from your time in airports/railway stations/bus depots that Indian families like nothing better than descending, mob-handed with their kith and kin when it comes to despatching someone on a journey. Often eighteen or twenty cousins, uncles, aunts and neighbours' children will accompany two travellers to 'see them off' at the station. It was the cause of much embarrassment to us as kids, but it is something I have come to love. Even if it does make for the lengthiest of goodbyes and the occasional missed flight.

Anyway, in the best traditions, my family had picked up some cousins and the neighbours' kids to see us to the coach station. So tight were we for space my Channi Chachaji, my dad's handsome, enigmatic, slightly deranged brother to whom I am very close, had decided that I would get to the station with him, riding pillion on his bike. Channi is a renegade. You need to know this. He can charm all the birds out of all the trees; he has an indefinable joy for life, a childlike energy and an utter lack of linear time-keeping. This meant that some time after the rest of the family had left for the coach station, my young uncle and I were still drinking tea in the house. It was delicious tea but I had to be on that coach; if we missed that coach, we missed our flight; and if we missed our flight . . .

So finally Channi got his act together. He realised the time and panicked. We bolted downstairs and onto the Norton motorcycle and soon we are cutting our way through people, bullocks, carts, people on bullocks, bullocks pulling carts; lots of bullocks. You get the picture. Channi knows no fear; he's an ex-captain from the Indian army and has seen active service. He was hardly going to be frightened by pedestrians, bovines and walls. I had no idea where we were going and how long it would take. My knuckles were white, which given my skin colouring was a fairly strong indication of the fear I was experiencing.

All I remember is that we accelerated, swerved left and then right. My uncle swore quite vehemently. The next thing I knew I was flying through the air and landing on a vegetable cart, narrowly missing the tomatoes but definitely damaging some early season marrows. It transpired that Channi had braked hard to avoid a leper on a bike. Since I was a child and thanks to something Newton explained, I was unable to offer any force to resist the braking and consequently flew marrow-ward. Channi picked me up, slapped the vegetable vendor, an innocent in the situation, and wiped the marrow from my shirt. He looked me in the eye and told me I was never to mention this incident to my father. I promised not to. I got the coach and the secret remained safe with me for nearly three decades. Until now. Sorry, Channi Chachaji.

What a sight we must look, me in my full-length pink kurta riding pillion to a long-haired hippy-type and we are off to buy the groceries together. It's very sweet that Jeremy is so keen to help me in my quest. I am however wondering about his relationship with India. You see, I have a dual identity when it comes to India. I feel free to be critical of the country, but will also jump to its defence should I hear anyone else speak against her. And I'm not sure Jeremy likes India terribly much. It suits him to be here. India is a Hindu country and Hindus are famous for their laid-back attitude and general sense of welcome. That's probably why the Moghuls were able to invade, and then the British. Hindu India indulges people like Jeremy; it lets them come and suck what they can out of the country before leaving. Perhaps I'm being harsh, but I am definitely getting the impression that the single most important thing in Jeremy's life is Jeremy. He may be taking me shopping but he has expressed no interest in my journey thus far. He hasn't really asked anything of where I have been or where I am going. He hasn't even asked the logic of my cooking escapades. Interesting. I mull this over as we roar off towards the shops. I try very hard not to get my pink kurta caught in the mechanism of the bike.

It seems as though the fates have further conspired against me. Both the markets are shut, inexplicably on a Friday. I am running out of options. What am I going to cook? My mind is a blank canvas that has been white-washed further still, just in case the residue of a past idea should remain somewhere hidden in its fibre. I am utterly at a loss.

Then I see a vegetable stall man pushing his barrow of produce. It is laden with aubergines. Tens of beautiful aubergines. Maybe even a hundred of the spherically purple delights. Perhaps this is the divine karmic contact I have been waiting for?

India is a massive country. Actually it ought not to be a country, the way the USSR was never a country. Disparate peoples seem somehow to be held together by the few things they share rather than the myriad of things that separate them. One of the things I believe that Indians share is the way they feel about their vegetables. I already have experience of northern Indian towns and cities, and so far in the south and the east of India the same vegephilia seems to be present. The Indian housewife sends her maid out to purchase vegetables from the legion of men with carts that line every street of the country. These carts are flat-topped on large wheels; the sort of cart that has existed since shortly after the wheel was discovered. Atop these carts sit an array of beautifully presented vegetables. And while the range of produce may be limited on each cart, the supply seems plentiful. Tomatoes, lovingly cleaned and pyramidically placed, reaching skyward; Indian onions, intensely purple in the low afternoon sun; perfectly round cabbages placed neatly in rows. I cannot stress how wonderful these arrangements look, these temples of colour every few yards down a busy street. It says a great deal for the pride of the vendors, the way they display their wares. And what makes the experience even more intense for me is that I know that if I were to journey back, some hours after the moon has chased the sun out of the sky, these selfsame vendors would be asleep on their carts, now empty of vegetables. They live where they work. For me that is a poetry of sorts.

We make for the nearest vegetable stall. There is an abundance of aubergines in front of me. Baby aubergines, perfect for stuffing with spices before being fried with potatoes. Large, rotund aubergines, best for slicing and coating in a gram of flour batter before being deep fried and turned into pakoras. White aubergines, a vegetable I have absolutely no food-based knowledge of whatsoever. I am surrounded by almost every variety and type of aubergine. It is as if I have died and gone to aubergine heaven where the aubergine angels are singing. I announce to Jeremy that I have settled on my evening repast. It isn't complicated, it isn't fancy; there would be no seviching of anything nor the rustling up of a buerre blanc. But it was attainable and would allow me to make for Bangalore with my head held not high, but certainly above the mid-mast position. My plan is simple. Make a babaganoush with these skinny aubergines; babaganoush is a smoked aubergine dip, much beloved in the Middle East and the Mediterranean. Lemon juice, garlic and parsley conspire to create a smoky spiky herby dip. My mother-in-law makes an Indian version that is a brilliant accompaniment to lamb curry and inspired me to serve my rendition with roast lamb. It's well worth a try.

There is a knock on my door. We are back at Jeremy's yoga school and I have been dozing. The knocking on my door continues, softly but definitely. As the door is so close to my bed I answer, still in the process of opening my eyes and dressed only in a lunghi (a sarong-like wrap-around Indian skirt; my preferred choice of evening wear and very masculine). Suresh stands in front of me, looking enigmatically content, his kind eyes twinkling unremittingly at me. He is accompanied by a woman and two young girls. I stand there, turban-less and topless with no glasses on, as Suresh introduces the ladies to me. I patiently wait for his unfolding explanation. It transpires that word got round that some Britisher was coming to cook. This woman owns a small restaurant in Mysore proper and she is keen to see how the Britisher would cook. The last thing I was expecting was an audience. The silver lining to this cloud is the addition of another three mouths to be fed; hopefully.

I start prepping in the kitchen. It's not a massive space but more than big enough for my aubergine delights. There's a three-ring burner. I turn the two bigger burners on and place the long aubergines directly onto the flame. There are muttered Kannada phrases between mother and daughters. The cooking lady looks on from behind; I can't read her face to gain any sort of approval rating. I'm still slightly annoyed by her vetoing of meat and chicken and her unwitting destruction of my plan to concoct a Lancashire hotpot. The aubergine skins start to blister and burn. Large aubergines take as long as twenty minutes because not only does the skin need to burn to impart that deliciously smoky aroma, the interior flesh needs to cook. These skinny little articles should be done in minutes. I start chopping an onion and put a pan of water on to blanch and skin the tomatoes.

I fry the other aubergines, having salted and sliced them. It's an old Indian trick to draw the bitter water out of aubergines, courgettes and cucumber. Top them and sprinkle some salt on the flat surface; put the top back on again and rub it down on the salt. Leave them to rest, top and salt intact for a few minutes. The flavour change is unbelievable; it also means that when it comes to frying there is less water in the aubergines and so a crispness can be achieved.

As I'm slicing and salting, four pairs of intense brown eyes are fixed on me. The occasional mumbled whisper or girlish laugh is the only sound to break the silence. I realise that it is very rare for these women to see a man in the kitchen, let alone cooking in one. I ask the mother. She agrees. Few Indian men like to cook. A lot of Indian men like to eat. She and I laugh as she explains the joke to her daughters and the old cook.

I muster up half a dozen plates of pan-fried baby aubergine and paneer with a chilli babaganoush dressing served on a rich tomato and garlic sauce. I have to say that my ability to overcome adversity in the face of a vegetarian meal is laudable. And as much as pan-fried aubergine with a chilli babaganoush dressing is yet another not-very-British meal, it is nonetheless a meal. I stand in the crowded kitchen watching them eat, unsure at first but eventually accepting the flavours into their mouths. I realise that the food isn't terrible. Anna, the surly-looking Spanish yoga student, spits a mouthful of the aubergine out.

'It is too spicy!' she screams as she flees the kitchen. I can tell from the complete and utter lack of reaction from the others that they have become used to this sort of behaviour from her.

'How is it, Jeremy?' I ask a little nervously, wishing that he had proffered an immediate opinion rather than wait for my probing.

He ponders a moment and chews. 'It's not bad. But it would have been nice if you had cooked some meat like you said you were going to.'

I nearly fall off my feet at this point. I can't believe his gall. I want to blurt out all sorts of words and phrases and expletives in my defence. Of course it would have been nice if I had

My mum holds me in a moment of uncharacteristic stillness (on my part) outside the house in Wembley. Raj is held by the big fella. Now you see where I get my sense of style from.

Me, lodged between Raj and my dad. My only memory of sitting on the wall.

Don't I look great in red? My mum looking more like Eartha Kitt than Eartha Kitt did.

Little Sanj, or 'Sniff', as we called him, fooling around in Bishopbriggs. My dad in a rare moment of tactile affection. See how much better I look with a turban and beard?

The gun is in fact loaded – the joys of holidaying in the Punjab. A few hours later we were eating curried pigeon (none of which were successfully killed by me).

The gruesome threesome. Raj and I *always* had matching clothes, yet Sanj never allowed it to cause him deep psychological damage vis-à-vis exclusion issues.

Playstations? Jungle music? The Internet? Kids today have no idea how to have fun. See how Sanj is enjoying himself on Raj's shoulders with nothing more than a bad jumper and a light shade.

And it's not just my brothers that know how to party; look at that table heaving with food (as always, Raj, as the first-born, got the crown).

My impression of The Fonz from *Happy Days* in Glasgow. I loved that stripey green Kurta pyjama to the extent that I refused to let my mum wash it, lest it be away from me for an evening. I didn't smell very good in the early eighties.

My world famous owl impression. I really do look like an owl . . . Uncanny, no?

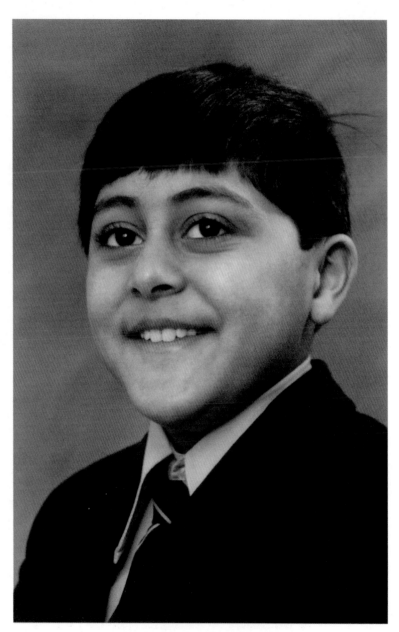

A great face (for radio).

The John Ogilvie Hall First XV. I played second row and I loved rugby. That's Aloke Sinha, standing second from the left. I'm between big Mick Donnelly and Andrew 'Baboo' McGlone. Some of my team members didn't end up in jail.

Meadowburn Primary School, Bishopbriggs, circa 1974. I'm trying my best to dominate the photograph. As you can see from the teacher's glasses, Reactolite technology was still very much in its early stages.

Billu Chachaji's wedding in Ferozepure. Raj is behind Billu. My dad is forcing Sanj to dance and I'm doing my impression of Posh Spice. This was a rare occurrence when all three of us were dressed identically. That's my cousin, Sonu, on the right. He's now a dentist. I have no idea who that man is standing over my father's shoulder but he frightens me.

cooked some meat. It would have been nicest for me, since I hate cooking vegetables. But rather than explode in an anti-yoga tirade of abuse, I have a moment of the most beautiful clarity. As I look at Jeremy, self-absorbed, self-obsessed Jeremy, I realise that this India, Jeremy's India, is no more than a façade. While on the face of it he has come to find something out about himself, it is actually just *all* about himself. He seems to have little love for or interest in the country. India merely suits him and this annoys me. Jeremy is just another colonist, like the waves of colonists who came to India and raped her of her resources. The only difference with Jeremy is that he is colonising the country's spirituality rather than her economy. Perhaps I am being a tad hypocritical. What am I doing here but furthering my own, selfish needs? Am I so very different from Jeremy? I think the crucial difference is that I am not a magical, mystical tourist who can choose to leave the country and break my links. My links are lines of heritage. Even in Mysore (a place none of my Punjabi forbears are ever likely to have visited), I feel an innate sense of India and Indianness.

It's been a bizarre journey already. Kovalam seems a lifetime away. It's certainly a lifetime since I had a hot bath. The tranquillity of Mamallapuram, the gentle acceptance of Nagamuthu and the relentless call of the Indian sea. And now this perplexing interlude with a poker-playing American Filipino yogi. When I was planning this journey in London I would never have imagined such a start; and it is only a start. I have two thirds of the journey ahead and I find myself with many more questions and significantly fewer answers.

After I bid Jeremy a safe return to his room upstairs, having happily taken even more rupees off him as payback for his insensitive comments about the lack of meat at dinner, I make to return to my room. But I have no intention of returning directly to my room. Checking that the coast is clear, I carefully sneak into the kitchen, the scene of my earlier Mediterranean triumph. The sink is deep with the detritus of dining; pots, plates, pans, the paraphernalia of perfection. I have one thing on my mind. Carefully, noiselessly I grab three of the pans from the sink. I quickly rinse them and fill them with water. I ignite all three burners on the three-ring burner. I watch lasciviously as the water slowly, painfully agitates itself to a simmer and, slower still, to a gentle, finally rolling boil. I take the pans, one by one, to my minuscule bathroom and fill the pallid, tired-looking bucket with the fresh, boiling, rejuvenating water. I place the pans back in the sink and return to my room.

I left Kovalam and its luxuries many days ago. I have not had a hot bath since then. And while all the cold waters of Arabia might touch my skin with the superficial promise of cleanliness, there is no replacement for the skin-tingling rebirth of a hot bath. And perhaps I haven't cleaned the pots out that thoroughly, but it seems only right that my body be marked with the slight aroma of aubergine, tomato and olive oil. And the aroma of victory.

CHIC ALORS! C'EST BANGALORE

ausage, bacon and eggs: the breakfast trinity. My life seems to be full of trinities. When I was young it was the holy one, so mysterious and enigmatic, and the subject of much discussion at my Jesuit School; As you know, I am one of a triumvirate of sons, lodged painfully between Raj and Sanjeev; and as a child I was obsessed with triangles. Properly obsessed. I was a freak of trigonometry, spending hours trying to construct the perfect equilateral triangle (for the uninitiated or those who had a social life during their teenage years, an equilateral triangle enjoys the aesthetic perfection of three equal sides and therefore three equal angles: 'tis a truly wondrous thing). I would sketch scalene after scalene triangle (a triangle where no sides, and therefore no angles are equal) and be repulsed by their ugliness, their gaucheness, their complete and utter lack of geometric charm. And then, as a special treat to myself, I would enter the room of the isosceles triangle, closing and locking the door behind me. For hours I would revel in the two equal sides, the two equal angles . . .

When it comes to food, sausage, eggs and bacon must be one of the finest trinities that exists. There are many others, of course. Avocado, tomato and basil; a *mirepoix*: the base of most soups and sauces comprising carrot, celery and leek; the base of a curry sauce: onion, garlic and ginger; bread, butter and jam. The list of trios is endless. But there's something about the breakfast trinity that elevates it to a higher plane. I believe passionately that a plate with eggs, bacon and sausage is breakfast. Mushrooms can come and go; potato scones are a more than welcome guest, but only ever a guest; toast is by no means a *sine qua non*; beans embellish but are not essential; and the tomato ... where else would we introduce grilled fruit onto a plate of porky food?

I have not always harboured such a deep and meaningful love affair with sausage, bacon and eggs. It is a relationship that started when I was seventeen years old, during the very excesses of the eighties. At that time, my cousin Aman, travel agent and single malt lover, had a brilliant new business proposal. This was in the days before cheap air travel. He set up a bus from Buchanan Street bus station that went all the way to Heathrow Airport. It was a beautiful idea. Glasgow wasn't an international flight hub in those days, so in order to travel home, Indians and Pakistanis had to schlep down to London one way or the other. Flights were expensive and there was no direct bus system. That's what made Aman's scheme so revolutionary. For a modest fare a family could, overnight, travel down and catch their plane. Bear in mind that these families, like mine, were returning home on money they had scrimped and saved over the years. I heard stories about fathers who worked three jobs to pull in extra money solely in order to take their families home. I know of mothers who ate a single meal a day in the hope of spreading the weekly shop that little bit further. The problem with my generation is that we think sacrifice is Cava rather than Veuve Cliquot.

In the best traditions of the extended family, Aman asked me to work the bus. I was just out of school, and had never travelled to London by myself. The excitement was overwhelming. My

124

job was to sell tickets to the handful who hadn't booked in Glasgow and to do the same at a stop on the way down, often Hamilton or Carlisle. To add to my onerous ticketing duties I would, upon arrival in London, take the tube into Belgravia and with scores of passports that Aman had given me, I would enable the processing of visa applications for Glasgow's Muslim community heading to Hajj. Hajj is the pilgrimage all Muslims are expected to make to Mecca, the birthplace of Islam. Almost all of the west of Scotland's Muslims were either Pakistani, Indian or British so they required the correct documentation to travel to Saudi Arabia; and since Glasgow was without a Saudi Arabian embassy a trip to London was required for this, too. From Bishopbriggs to Belgravia, via the services at Knutsford. Knutsford was my favourite part of the entire experience. As a representative of the travel company I, alongside the driver, was entitled to a free meal and hot beverage (excluding soft drinks) at the service station on our way down. Given that we were in Thatcher's Britain and the free market allowed the driver to exercise choice, the management at the service stations en route were wise to this and attempted to do all they could to lure drivers in; if the driver stopped for sustenance so did a coachful of hungry travellers. The only flaw in this plan was that Indian coach travellers are not big spenders, particularly not when the food offering centres around the concept of the all-day (and in this case all-night) breakfast. Pork-based meals are generally speaking not going to entice the hungry brown-skinned traveller, especially one with little money to spend.

I however had no such reservations and was all too happy to enjoy the twenty-four hour prandial offering they call breakfast. I was delighted by pork, beef and pork/beef based foods. To cap it all, it was free. Gratis. I am Scottish and Indian: I am twice as happy when I get stuff I don't have to pay for.

I think this was the point in my life when my love affair with the fried breakfast started. It was not the sort of meal we would have at home. Having said that, it has since become a staple in the Kohli household both north and south of the border.

All this thought of breakfast has inspired my culinary plan for Bangalore. Bangalore is the most modern of Indian cities, the cyber-desh if you will. It is the single city that most of the new westerner travellers interface with. For three decades Goa has had the sun-seeking hippies and the holiday-makers; since Independence in 1947, Delhi has enjoyed the comings and goings of the diplomats and politicians; but in the last decade or so, Bangalore has seen an almost exponential increase in westerners, linked to the world of computing and software. The city was recently voted as the best place to do business in the world; truly the face of modern India.

So perhaps, as a clever juxtaposition of modernity with the ancient, I should cook something classically old-fashioned to serve in this eastern altar to the future.

Toad in the hole.

It makes absolute sense. The humble breakfast sausage elevated to a higher place when combined with the finest Yorkshire pudding mix; surely one of the most quintessentially British of all dishes?

I can be almost 99 per cent sure that not even the most seasoned travelling eater in Bangalore will have tasted the delights of toad in the hole there. It is my opportunity to bring innovation through classicism.

But first I have to get there . . .

As you might have realised by now, my default when travelling in India is to take a train. The romance, the history, the physical sensation and the gradual exposure to Indian life, culture and quirks is so beautifully integrated within the train journey itself. There is also something magical about being so remote and unaware of the actual mechanism that makes the train move. I am of course aware that there is a locomotive at the front, but there is a certain enigma in not being constantly aware of the process of moving, of travelling. It's almost transcendental. There is none of this magic with a bus or a coach, a travelling experience that is all too apparent; and when travelling in India, often alarmingly so.

However, in India the train is surpassed by the bus for shorter journeys. Furthermore, and perhaps this is what makes me so very, very British, native Indians much prefer coach travel to the train. I feel compelled to experience their preferred mode of travel. Besides, it is only a very short journey from Mysore to Bangalore.

The 3 p.m. Volvo bus to Bangalore: 180 rupees and the promise of a speedy two-and-a-half hour journey to the capital of Karnataka. Mysore bus station is unsurprisingly full of buses, engines revving, creating clouds of exhaust fumes and hastening the dark skies of late afternoon. There are lime-green buses; red buses; orange buses; multi-coloured buses; there is every sort of bus imaginable and a few that even the most addled mind wouldn't have colour coordinated. In and amongst the vulgate of buses there is only one king of all Mysore buses: the white Volvo bus. White, sleek, gleaming, beautiful and Swedish; the white Volvo bus is the bus to be on if one is to be the envy of one's bus-travelling peers.

It really is the sort of vehicle to create bus envy in even the most disinterested of on-lookers. The seats have seat belts; the seat-belted seats are covered in freshly laundered white cotton; these freshly laundered, white cotton-covered, seat-belted seats recline; and having reclined on these freshly laundered white cotton-covered seats, safe and securely fastened in, one can sip from the complimentary small bottle of mineral water, whilst enjoying the movie that takes place on the in-bus entertainment system. To call this a bus is a disservice to the English language specifically, and to buses in general; this is a coach, a luxury coach no less. I begin to understand why Indians much prefer the coach to the train. The only aspect of the interior I would consider altering would be the mint-green curtains: mint green is so very last season.

I am sitting in the palatial grandeur of my white Volvo bus in the bedlam that is Mysore bus station. Even our driver is dressed better than the average driver. In his smart white uniform, replete with epaulettes and badges, his look is more akin to a naval commander than a humble bus driver. As our vehicle pulls away (it is clearly allowed a wider berth in the hierarchy of coaches and buses) the in-coach stereo starts playing a too-loud version of the title track of *2001: A Space Odyssey*. I would like to tell you that this is done with a sense of frivolous irony; but it isn't. I am in an irony-free zone. *2001: A Space Odyssey* is a film that deals with themes of human evolution and development, the rise of technology, artificial intelligence and the possibility of life beyond our own solar system. The music from the film has a pomposity, a grandeur and an elegance that reflects and enhances the intellectually challenging notions of the film itself. But it isn't the most suitable music for a bus journey between Mysore and Bangalore.

As the majestic film score rattles the windows, it feels as if the moon is to be our destination rather than Silicon Nagar, Bangalore. This pomp adds to the already existing circumstance; we truly are travelling in the king of coaches.

As soon as the music dies away, rather abruptly after such a grandiose start, it seems as if silence may be the order of the day. The journey thus far has had a light smattering of the bizarre about it: the music, the driver's nautically themed uniform and the mint-green curtains; not unusually weird, just a little strange. That is all about to change as the weirdness is cranked up to an entirely different level. The plasma screen at the front of the coach stutters into life. It's time for the movie.

The film showing on my journey is in an Indian language of which I have absolutely no understanding. The opening sequence has a rather overweight Sikh man in a kurta, the long cotton Indian shirt, loading a double-barrelled shotgun and chasing an assumed innocent through the streets of some anonymous Indian ghetto. As the only overweight Sikh man dressed in a kurta on the coach, I feel a tad uncomfortable at this point. The shotgun-wielding Sikh is now driving a forklift truck in pursuit of his hapless quarry. Showing the multi-tasking skills of India's premier martial race, the fat, silver screen Sikh drives towards an industrial plant while simultaneously firing and reloading at the sprinting victim. Clearly the Sikh baddie couldn't hit a cow's arse with a banjo, since every shot is missing by quite some distance. I feel compelled to explain to the enraptured throng on the bus that most Sikhs are far superior marksmen to this Keystone Cop type; on reflection I decide that silence is the better option.

Signs on the back of vehicles on the road to Bangalore

On a truck: 'Black Smoke, Lungs Choke'
On a Maruti Car: 'Dad says No Rush'
On a taxi: 'God Give, Man Live'

In India there is a lot of talk about the state of the roads. The difference between travelling on a good road and a bad (and sometimes non-existent) road can be hours of journey time. India's biggest challenge over the next century is that of improving its infrastructure. There are hundreds of millions of highly educated graduates, hundreds of millions of manual workers, hundreds of millions of merchants; they all just need to be hooked up with decent roads, transport links, communications and the rest. Once India joins up its myriad of dots, it will be ready to take on the world.

Surprisingly, this highway is good and clean and straight. We bisect fields and coconut groves; palm trees and red-tiled bungalows appear sporadically and then melt away. We pass the odd sandalwood forest. The movie seems to be ending happily; the fat, shotgun-toting, kurta-wearing Sikh lies dying slowly in some field and goodness has been restored in the world. Our gleaming white Volvo coach now labours its way treacle-like, through the suburbs of Bangalore. Our vicinity to the city is evident in a number of ways. The sky has darkened with the clouds of industry; our pace has suddenly diminished to a constant crawl; and tiny shops start dotting the side on the road, increasing in frequency and product offering.

The industrious nature of the Indian psyche is something to behold. It is exemplified best perhaps in the tiny little shacks offering every imaginable service from mobile phone repair to document lamination to tyre repair. Everyone everywhere is trying to make a living, predominantly an honest, hard-worked living. If there is a single quality about India I most admire it is the industry of the place. Growing up with the negative images of poverty, famine and the like I was never aware of quite how hard Indians worked. That my hard-working, industrious parents were Indian, the hard-working industrious community in Glasgow that they belonged to were Indian, and my hard-working and industrious wider family were all Indian, was proof lost on me.

Scenes like this always seem to put life in the affluent west into some sort of context. These tiny little businesses exist cheek by jowl with massive urban redevelopment projects. There couldn't be a more pronounced sense of the past meeting the future at the crossroads of the present. I see a cartload of sweet perfumed orange mangoes in the shadow of a sky-blocking shopping development, aptly named the Big Bazaar. I wonder how long the mango vendor will survive. The entire Bangalore skyline is punctuated by cranes. There is building work on every side. Ever since the arrival of the global multinational fifteen years ago, Bangalore hasn't stopped growing and developing. Once, what set Bangalore, the garden city of lakes and a cooling breeze, apart from almost all the other Indian cities was its mellow, well-planned urban calm. People from all over India would flock to enjoy the well-designated city space, stroll by the lakes, play in the gardens and shade under the abundance of trees. It was a city full of light and shade, both literally and metaphorically. Now the shade has gone and the incandescent light of international redevelopment shines on Bangalore, perhaps a little too brightly. The once-famous city lakes have been filled in with concrete and built over with more apartments, feeding the seemingly insatiable hunger of the chic young city dwellers; the verdant urban gardens have been razed and developed into yet another shopping centre. The trees and lakes ensured a unique microclimate in Bangalore. With their systematic disappearance the once temperate and mild city is now gradually becoming a breeze-free conurbation with leaden, pollution-filled skies.

I have been coming to Bangalore on and off for the better part of a decade and I have seen the city slowly morph from an oasis of calm into a vibrant and thriving metropolis. On my last visit, some four years ago, I remember thinking that enough had changed, there had been enough development. I felt that the city had reached the correct size and should grow no more. Even on this short journey through the suburbs and into the city I realise that the city has grown massively since I last made that observation. Four years ago I was already starting to worry that if Bangalore wasn't careful, it might well lose the very charm and beauty that attracted all comers. My current impression confirms that charm and beauty has been lost.

The coach station in Bangalore is mayhem, proper mayhem; it's the place trainee mayhem is sent to study and learn the true nature of mayhem before it returns to its own state and visits its newly acquired knowledge upon the locals there. Bangalore, as well as being the capital of Karnataka, is the transport hub for the entire south Indian area. Trains are sent trundling off in every direction; buses and coaches tear a path to and fro; planes block the sun on domestic and international flight paths. Bangalore is a busy place. And of all the available modes of transport the bus and coach are the favoured amongst the hoi polloi. The trains tend to be for the more genteel, even with their scary third-class carriages; and their service is less frequent than the eight-wheeled option. The bus is the Everyman of the Indian road.

Stepping off the bus I enter the massive station looking for my designated meeting point. Within minutes I feel as though I have seen or heard every possible destination in India. If they aren't hauling signs up on front of their buses, they are shouting their destinations repeatedly, at breakneck speed as if competing with fellow drivers. They shout like they drive: noisily, aggressively and selfishly.

It feels as if the entire world and its mother-in-law sits and waits, or ups and boards, or yawns and sleeps, or sips and eats, or alights and arrives.

I feel excited and nervous about Bangalore. This is the first destination on my quest that is familiar to me; I have spent time in Bangalore with my wife's family. It is also the first destination where I will be cooking for someone I know, someone I know well. Bharat Shetty is my wife's cousin and I have known him for the better part of two decades. Bharat Shetty is a bon viveur. He likes to smoke, he likes to drink and he likes to party. But most of all he likes to eat. Bharat is also a stranger to tact and diplomacy, a quality in him that I have always enjoyed. One knows exactly where one stands with Bharat. But while I have enjoyed his candour thus far, I'm not altogether looking forward to his candour when applied in relation to my food.

How old he is, I'm not sure, but I reckon he must be at least in his mid-fifties by now. He used to travel often to London and Europe on business and we would invariably end up dining out at some fancy restaurant or other. In those days I had next to no money, no real career to speak of, no prospects of a career, two kids and an overdraft. I would always feel very nervous about having to pay, for fear of the card being declined or the machine exploding with fatigue at my continual impertinence in asking for cash that simply didn't exist.

I can remember one time when Bharat and his then new wife Anjani came to visit. They wanted to eat Chinese food. We suggested the Royal China, regarded by many as London's finest Chinese restaurant. We opted for the Bayswater branch; the dark almost conspiratorial vibe of the place always reminds me of that restaurant in *Scarface* when Tony Montana gets drunk and starts referring to himself as the 'bad guy'. I feared that this evening I would be the 'bad guy'. We sat and we ate; wave after wave of food came and I spent the whole meal wondering how the hell I was going to pay. By the time the chilli squid in black bean sauce had come, I resigned myself to the ignominy of the credit card 'decline'. I enjoyed not a single mouthful, thinking through all the times Bharat had looked after me in Bangalore; my hand never once went into my pocket. The bill eventually came, too early. As my hand reached out for it Bharat snatched it away.

'Hey, you silly bugger,' Bharat barked lovingly at me. 'You are not paying,' he rebuked as he took out his bulging wallet. 'Silly bugger . . . '

He always chastised me in the way only an older Indian relative can, irritated that I would even consider such an affront. My relief was palpable.

It is Bharat who has come to meet me at the predesignated meeting point, under the broken clock. Up ahead I can see a clock that looks broken as I batter my way through the human traffic, head down and insensitive to the needs of others. India makes you like that, and in the time I have been here, I realise that my well-mannered polite Britishness is a millstone around my neck. It dissolves daily in the war of attrition you must wage to buy a coffee, cross the street, board a train. For a nation that can be so polite and so helpful, the people of India can also be terribly rude. But rudeness is in the eye of the beholder and I decide not to behold anything but my end goal, which is to meet Bharat Shetty. I bump frail old ladies out of my way, accelerate in front of a nursing mother, cut across a wheel-chaired grandfather. And as I make for the exit the cries of the small child I kicked out of my way start to subside, and I see the welcoming face of Mr Bharat Shetty.

'Where are your bags, man? Bags?' he asks, looking no doubt for more than my single wheely case.

'All here,' I say patting my beloved travelling companion.

'What the hell!' He really does speak like that.

Bharat takes me to his apartment and it's damn good to be home. And what a home! The seventh-floor apartment is smack bang in the middle of India's most vibrant and growing city, the very epicentre of Bangalore. There are few tall buildings in the centre of the city, so the top of this one with six storeys below affords an unbroken view of the urban landscape. Wherever you look there is new development, new building. The traffic below is chaotically Indian. The street is one way and as dusk descends legion upon legion of white lights descend the hill past the apartment morphing into red-lighted smears as they melt away into the Bangalore night; the flow from white to red seems constant.

'How was the journey, man?' Bharat asks.

'Fine,' I reply rather unconvincingly.

I look out of the window and admire the view again.

'Finest city in India, according to CNN, man. Finest city in India. Glenfiddich or Glenmorangie?' he asks.

There's no place like home.

Driving around Bangalore, it feels like the perfect place for me to understand my colonial past and my modern future. We often forget that as an independent country, India is but six decades old; it is still very much coming to terms with itself politically and socially. Many argue that Indian civilisation has existed for millennia, and that my theory about the nation being so young is vacuous and historically naive. But Indians never ruled themselves democratically prior to 1947. The British governed like any good colonial power, dividing and ruling, crow-barring open the already existing fault lines of religious, geographical and cultural differences that were rife across this massive subcontinent. These fault lines defined the different monarchies and territories prior to the British invasion. As much as India has the most ancient of world civilisations, philosophies and religions, as a unified, democratic force it is but a toddler. I am fascinated to understand what it means to be Indian because being 'Indian' is only really a recent phenomenon. It is much easier to talk about being Punjabi or Scottish or British, identities that have endured for hundreds of years. But being Indian is a less established a concept. And Bangalore, with its new wave of western business travellers, is new India. The people of this city are being asked new questions by the incomers from Germany, Holland and the US. What will these economic migrants make of Bangalore? What will they make of India itself?

'Do you want to see the city or shall we grab a drink?' Bharat loves a drink, but I want to see the city.

'Show me the city,' I answer. 'According to CNN it's the finest city in India, no?'

He smiles. 'Cheeky bugger!'

Cubbin Park, named after the eponymous lord, is a beautiful memento of the British, sitting as it does so near to the new Karnataka's State government building, which is itself a wonder of Indian architecture. Hordes gather to view this edifice which is across the boulevard from the High Court of Bangalore. Rounding a corner I see a statue of Queen Victoria. I am reminded of the images in the post-Glasnost Soviet Union of the populus tearing down statues of Lenin and Stalin, often with their bare and bloodied hands. But not here, not in India. There is still a great affection for the Brits in some quarters. Certain philosophers and thinkers believe that it is this fondness for the British that intellectually and politically holds India back, the notion that things would have still been better under the Raj. I do think that some Indians are prone to a slight inferiority complex about Britain in particular and the west in general. There is a belief that the west is best. I am fairly certain that this attitude pervaded my own upbringing to some extent. I'm not sure where it came from since my parents have never felt that way, but I do recall faceless drunk 'uncles' (not my real uncles) bad-mouthing India in a way that I can only describe as ungrateful. I distinctly remember thinking that it was bad enough that the local white folk were less than complimentary about India; they didn't need the support of Indians themselves. And this inferiority complex still exists today amongst a certain constituency of non-resident Indians as we are known. Perhaps as globalisation takes hold and the free market solidifies in India, as it seems to be doing, these archaic notions will dissolve and disappear. Perhaps.

'Do you like cakes, man? Cakes?'

'Yeah,' I reply. I don't have the sweetest of tooths, but I have a real penchant for pastries and cakes.

'I'm going to open some cake shops in Bangalore.'

'Really?' I can't hide my surprise. India really is changing.

'When did you think that one up?' I ask.

'Been planning it for years. Years, man. It's coming together. Got the sites scouted. Now I need some staff. I might have to bring a chef in from Dubai.' He pauses and seems to drift off in thought for a moment. 'Man, they make great bloody cakes in Dubai. Great cakes.'

'What will you be selling in these cake shops?' No sooner have I asked this question than I realise how stupid it is.

'Pastries, you buffoon. Cakes and pastries. Croissants, cakes and pastries.'

'Of course. Sorry.'

'But nice ones,' he adds. 'European ones, like you find in London.'

We drive past another statue of Queen Victoria, Empress of India. This must be the third or fourth monument to the lady I have seen today. I have to say, Victoria looks great, orb in hand, serene as ever. It's no wonder they named the sponge after her.

'You should open five shops and call the chain Victoria's Punj,' I say, 'punj' being the Punjabi word for five.

He looks blankly at me.

'Victoria sponge. Victoria's Punj?'

His blank look remains resolute. I don't think he knows what a Victoria sponge is.

I love a Victoria sponge. The simplicity of the light sponge, the sweet sharpness of the raspberry jam (it *has* to be raspberry) and the lusciously rich double cream all combining in the mouth to form the loveliest of cake-based experiences. And it was exactly this sensory experience that led to possibly the darkest and most troublesome food experience of my childhood; an experience I will never forget, nor ever will be allowed to.

It was the summer of 1980; June. The sun was high in the sky, the holidays extending in front of us like vistas of hope, the untouchable horizon being August and the inevitable return to school. For Hardeep the eleven year old even tomorrow seemed deep in the future. There were bikes to ride, hills to climb, buildings to jump off, dogs to annoy, football to play and adventures to be had. And that would all happen well before tomorrow ever arrived. There was nowhere better to grow up than Bishopbriggs. Chief amongst the reasons for the idyllic and halcyon nature of my childhood was the presence of my cousins, Sandy and Sanjay, in the same north Glasgow suburb. I have a little contextualising to offer.

My dad was the eldest of nine children. Two died in their childhood, leaving seven in total. Chronologically it goes like this:

1. My dad: known to his friends as P.D. but to all his siblings as 'Virji', elder brother.
2. Pavittar: great cook, maker of sweet and sour chicken but very, very slow at everything, particularly anecdotes.
3. Mangal: the chilled-out hippy of the family.
4. Minder: brilliant cook, exceptional; and a waistline to match. Her date and walnut cake is one of the finest baked delights I have ever had the pleasure to eat. Her youngest son became a chef.
5. Billu: the six-foot-five farmer and all round good guy.
6. Channi: the hot-headed, handsome devil that could charm birds out of trees and could also make the best pickled goat I have ever tasted.
7. Pinki: the youngest of the family, sixteen years junior to my father; still called 'baby' by my late grandmother, even when Pinki was in her fifties.*

Sandy and Sanjay were Pavittar's kids. Not only did I grow up with my aunt's experimental cooking, I also had my cousins nearby. As you know, I was one of three brothers. Chronologically we were: Sandy, Raj, Sanjay, me and Sanjeev.

*It always strikes me as the most complete of ironies that almost every brown-skinned Indian family has a boy or a girl called Pinki.

We had a five-a-side football team all ready to go. We grew up as five brothers rather than two different families. I always wanted to go to Sandy and Sanjay's house because it always seemed so much more fun than my own. Sandy was my big brother figure. Raj, my own elder brother, and I didn't have the closest of relationships. I'm sure I was a right royal pain in the arse and he wasn't as nice to me as he could have been. It's not easy being the eldest boy child in an Indian household and I think the pressure on Raj from my father inevitably affected Raj's relationship with me; that and the fact he would:

a) never go in goal

b) never come back and defend

c) always goal poach (goal-poaching is a technical manoeuvre of football made illegal by the creation of the offside rule. It basically means you hang around the opposition goal and wait for the ball to come into the general vicinity and then try and score, claiming the glory without having done any of the donkey work or performing any of the responsibilities incumbent in the team ethos. In England it is also known as goal-hanging)

d) always bowl extra-fast bouncing deliveries to me when we played cricket on bumpy grass (as if he WANTED to hurt me)

If Sandy was my true elder brother, then Sanjay and I indulged in our own sibling rivalry. We fought like cats and dogs. In fact cats and dogs would be asked to try and separate us when we were fighting, so vicious were we with each other. One Christmas we toppled headlong, fists flailing, legs locking, into the Christmas tree while an Elvis movie played on TV. When we were younger I used my extra height and weight to torture him; as his superior genetic imprint – and his many sessions at the lesser known but violent martial art of Budokan – kicked in, his revenge was sweet.

In between this change of administration came the summer of 1980. Sanjay and I had achieved a physical parity; we downed weapons and agreed an unspoken truce. We pursued the third way for that summer and reaped the rewards of peace. We played together happily, we climbed trees together happily, we jumped off garages together happily, we swam together happily, we ran together happily, we explored together happily and we stole that Victoria sponge together happily. We stole a Victoria sponge. Together. Happily.

We made a pact, the sort of pact that ought to have been sworn in blood. I was soon to learn the error of my ways in not insisting that our thumbs be cut and our already genetically mingled blood be further mingled. If I had at least sought that level of legal leverage, then my future might have been safer.

The cake had been stolen from the cupboard in our kitchen. We had in our possession Mr Kipling's exceedingly good cake. Obviously at the time we had no idea whatsoever of the profound colonial history of this cake, its echo of the sixty-four-year reign of the woman who had presided over a globe that was nearly a third pink. No. We just really liked the creamy, jammy filling sandwiched between the lightest and most delicious of sponges. We stole ourselves and our sponge to the eaves of the loft. Behind closed doors we devoured the cake, I perhaps having slightly more than half. When I say 'devoured' I am not using that word in some fancy rhetorical way; we actually devoured the cake, as if we had never before seen cake and this was our first meal in weeks. The cake was barely out of the wrapper before it was heading, through the gift of peristalsis, stomach-ward. In the afterglow of the cake rush we colluded never to speak of this to anyone. No one would miss a Mr Kipling's cake from the cupboard. After all, it was only a cake.

It was only a cake. It was only a cake. What a fool I was to think it was only a cake. It was the *only* cake. The only cake in the cupboard. The only cake in the house. Its disappearance would never go unnoticed. The cake had been purchased to be eaten by the entire family after dinner that evening. A nice chicken curry followed by a bit of cake. Suburban Glasgow/Indian bliss if ever there was. But, Mrs Hubbard-like, the cupboard was bare. You have to remember that when I was growing up our house was run on a tight budget. There was never any slack. We didn't have cupboards overflowing with eight different kinds of balsamic vinegar or a range of different olives. We had what we had and we ate what we had. There was never any waste. Never. So when a cake went missing, it became an international incident. Hands were wrung, rooms were searched and questions asked.

I was interrogated by my parents. Remembering my verbal pact with Sanjay – which foolishly hadn't been confirmed by blood – I refused to buckle under the pressure. They asked me about the cake and all I would give them was my name, my rank and declare that under the Geneva Convention of Human Rights, I was a prisoner of war. They weren't having it. They knew, somehow, that I had snaffled the Victoria sponge, and they were going to break me. But I held fast; there was something greater than truth at stake here: honour. The honour of cousins, the sort of honour that binds and ties and fetters two souls together in brotherly love for a lifetime.

Unfortunately what I didn't know was that Sanjay had fessed up to the plot as soon as he was asked by his mum. She didn't even interrogate him, question him or gently beat him.

She asked; he answered. Pavittar had the full story, and she had told my parents. They already knew what had happened, they just wanted me to admit it. But out of my misplaced sense of allegiance to my yellow-bellied turncoat cousin who had folded like a cheap folding thing, I would not sell him down the river.

In hindsight I knew I had done wrong and should have confessed. What still narks me, if I am honest after all these years, is the fact that I never got any respect for my albeit misplaced sense of honour. Sanjay and I never spoke of the incident again but I know from that day on our invisible links of brotherliness were cut for ever. Things between us would never be the same again. Ever.

Sanjay and Victoria sponge feel very distant right now. I have to face up to the challenge of Bangalore. I had a very clear and canny plan in London. I decided that I should cook at a call centre in the call centre capital of the world. The reasons seemed to be overwhelming. Where better to try and explore the coming together of Britain and India than in the very place where India speaks to Britain, in impeccable English, while helping broadband customers reroute their router; or aiding customers to cancel their direct debit to their local gym; or do anything that needs a well-trained and able voice on the other end of the phone, on the other side of the world? Lest we forget that Bangalore has had such a proud and pronounced colonial history within British India, a British India that's been so very crucial to my family and my very existence. To add a further layer of interest, Bangalore has changed so much since

I was last here, and so rapidly that I am almost a complete stranger in a city I thought I knew. Welcome to the future of India, the future of the world.

My canny plan to cook in a call centre manages, however, to fall on deaf ears. The multinationals that have arrived in India are exactly that: multinationals. They are not actually very Indian. They are, however, very multinational. They have all the protocols and policies of any multinational. They just happen to be populated by Indians and run locally by Indians. Generally speaking in India, if you need to get something, anything done, you just need some influence, as it is euphemistically known. Some call it corruption. I prefer the word influence. Someone, somewhere knows someone else, somewhere else who can get things done. That is the grease that oils the cogs of India. Bharat is one of those 'someones'. He knows everyone who needs to be known. At least he used to. Globalisation seems to have changed the rules; it's not enough to know someone. There are marketing managers and public relations executives in offices in San Francisco and Geneva. Bharat doesn't know them and they certainly have no idea what a man of influence he is. India, it would seem, is changing. Corruption has been corrupted.

What I am trying to say is that I am unable to convince any of the call centres to let me in to cook. They simply don't get what I am trying to do. Frankly it would have been easier for me to go into a call centre in Hartlepool and rustle up a lamb curry. I therefore have to refocus my endeavours. Refocusing my endeavours is not an easy exercise. I had rather blithely reckoned on Bharat gaining me access to a call centre. I am at a loss to come up with a substitute scenario that has the collision of the east with the west combined with telephony. I try to make contact with a couple of the firms of international management consultants that have recently relocated to Bangalore from Wisconsin. They suggest that I write to the Corporate Interface Services Team in Wisconsin to seek pre-clearance before the Indian Corporate Interface Services Team would consider my application. That seems like a long, drawn-out process requiring time that I do not have. Perhaps I have to embrace failure. But it seems so early in my journey to be considering placing my tail between my legs. There has to be an angle that I'm missing. And then it strikes me, with the excitement of that moment when a call centre has had your call on hold for thirty-seven minutes and you are finally connected to a human being. If I can't explore modern global India, then perhaps I should explore ancient colonial India. Genius.

There is a famous old place in Bangalore called the Bangalore Club. Let not the simplicity of the name fool you. This is colonial elegance at its very finest. It is said that this club is the finest example of how the Raj lived and endured India. It is luxury personified. A massive main building with high-vaulted ceilings. Huge windows and open doorways facilitate a cooling breeze through the many rooms, nooks and crannies. The perfectly manicured lawns, the dazzlingly white picket fences. The two-mile journey from Bharat's apartment to the club seems more like a sixty-year journey into the past. Were it not for the distinct lack of white faces, it might as well be the days of the Raj. The old white colonialists have been replaced by the new brown colonialists of Bangalore's upwardly mobile middle and upper classes. I am checking in for a couple of days; seems foolish not to.

It feels like the sweetest of ironies to reintroduce a bit of Britain into the club. Nothing could be more reminiscent of the Raj than BC, as it has affectionately become known. And walking in the grounds I feel transported back to the nineteenth century, fully expecting some Major Sahib wallah to march over to me with pith helmet and cane to start a sentence of rebuke with the words: 'Look here . . .'

There are two dining spaces in the club. The curtly named 'Dining Room' is indeed a magnificent room within which to dine. Near the entrance gate (as if to separate it off for not being in keeping with the ethos of BC), and no doubt a sop to the younger, post-Independent generation of Indians, is a room altogether funkier, groovier, more contemporary. Tiger Bay feels very much out of kilter with the manicured lawns and dress code sensibility of the main building. While the main space boasts the anachronistically titled 'Men's Bar', Tiger Bay has a massive plasma screen for showing sporting events (BC was, after all, founded on sport.) There is a banging sound system, a seductively dark bar and a chocolatier no more than a stone's throw from a man who would refuse you entrance and indeed rescind you membership should you deign to appear in Indian garb: no collar, no admittance; closed shoes only, no sandals. Rules that exist from when white men ruled. Ironic that the Indians of today have kept the rules laid down by their colonial masters. How modern is modern India?

In the main vestibule of the club is a glass-topped display cabinet within which sits an open ledger. The displayed page reads as follows:

Minutes of the proceedings of the subcommittee held on
Thursday 1st June 1899 at 7 p.m.
Present:
Colonel J.I. McGann
Lt. Colonel Baulders
Major Mackenzie Kennan
Major Clark Kennedy
The Bangalore United Service Club, Members Dues Sub
Committee approve the following irrecoverable sum to be
written off:
Lt. W.L.S. Churchill.................................... rupees 13.11

It would appear that the late Sir Winston Churchill still owes
the Bangalore Club some money.

'Tod in the hole?' Bharat is shouting down the phone at me.

'No,' I say calmly. 'Toad. In the hole.'

'Toad? You guys don't eat frogs. That's the French. Disgusting,
man . . . '

'No, Bharat. It's just a name. It's sausages and batter.'

There is a crackly pause.

'Frogs' legs sound nicer than sausage and batter, man.' And
he means it.

'Trust me,' I plead. 'Come at seven o'clock. OK?'

'OK,' he replies in his default tone, namely surly.

'Are you bringing anyone. How many should I cook for?' It
seems like a relevant question.

'Sausage and batter, man. Who can I bring?' And with that he is gone.

True to his word, Bharat shows up on his lonesome. Together we enter the kitchen at the Tiger Bay. I am more than a little nervous and feeling considerably guilty about being in one of the Bangalore Club's kitchens at what must be peak cooking time; in the UK I would never venture into a commercial kitchen between 7 p.m. and 9 p.m. But this is India and people eat late. Very late.

As I walk in I am greeted by half a dozen apathetic-looking chefs, each skinnier than the last and all bedecked in the finest chef's whites and matching tall hats. It's as though someone has ordered 'cliché chefs' from an agency that provides stereotypical chefs.

There's only one thing worse than a hectic restaurant kitchen and that is a quiet restaurant kitchen. The perceived upside of a quiet kitchen – the fact that there is no pressure and no frantic chefs working around me – pales into insignificance when compared to the hefty downside, namely that there is lots of pressure from the dozen eyes belonging to the non-frantic chefs who have nothing better to do than stand around and watch me.

'Hello,' I mumble, almost inaudibly.

I make up for my half-hearted hello with a semi shouted, 'Namasté,' which causes one of the chefs to start.

I was really hoping that the kitchen would be busy and that I would be allowed to find a quiet corner to cook my toad in the hole, before disappearing to my room and drinking myself into a stupor with a bottle of some single malt or other. That is clearly not going to happen.

Bharat introduces me to the head chef. 'This is my cousin's husband. He's from England.'

'Scotland,' I feel compelled to correct him.

'Whatever. He is going to cook some food here. Help him. OK?' Bharat gives one of his intense brown-eyed stares.

His intense brown-eyed stares are replicated by the six chefs as they watched me mix flour, eggs and salt. Quite how entertaining is the preparation of a Yorkshire pudding batter is a moot point, but watch they do, seemingly transfixed. (Although I have since realised that the difference between an Indian look of transfixion registers very closely to the look of mind-numbing boredom.) I feel compelled to show my limited knife skills to their most well attuned, whilst being fully aware of the potential credibility-losing embarrassment of a 'blood' incident.

Sausages are not impossible to get hold of in Bangalore, but neither are they very easy to find. There are a handful of specialist delicatessens in the city and they do stock limited numbers of items like sausages, bacon and artichoke hearts. But these shops are not easy to track down.

'I have heard of a shop that sells all this kind of stuff, man. Sausages and all that fancy stuff.'

I knew Bharat would know.

'Where is it?' I asked hopefully.

'Don't know. I have heard of it. Never been there. Anjani will know.'

At this point Bharat called Anjani and Anjani too had heard of such a shop but didn't know where it was.

'Geetie will know,' said Anjani.

And in a couple of minutes Geetie was on the other end of a mobile phone. She too had heard of such a place but she didn't know where it was, either. I am not sure how many people were implicated in this sausage-finding project but I decided that it would be far easier to forgo the sausage and work out an acceptable substitute.

That is why I have decided to use some strips of mutton. Ordinarily I would specify the exact cut of meat and wax lyrical about their provenance, perhaps even throwing in the name of the farmer and the type of anorak he enjoys wearing. I'm afraid I can offer no such details about these rather wan pieces of defrosted meat that lay hopelessly in front of me. I know meat is by its very nature lifeless, but these rather apologetic-looking cuts of sheep appear to have never enjoyed anything much of life; not so much as a gentle carefree gambol. But such sentimentality has no place in this kitchen. I feel the on-looking eyes and am compelled to look like I know what I am doing.

Bharat pops back into the kitchen accompanied by a handsome young man who looks dressed for a night's clubbing. This it transpires is the owner of the restaurant, Tommy. I'm guessing he has an Indian name like Chetan or Rohit or Rahul. But he calls himself Tommy.

'Hey, Tommy, this is my cousin's husband from England . . .'

'Scotland,' I correct Bharat without even looking up from my semi-frozen meat.

'Listen, man,' Bharat says to me, 'no one knows where Scotland is.'

'Hello, Tommy. I'm Hardeep from England.'

We shake hands.

'Are you staying for dinner?' I ask, I thought politely.

Tommy looks shifty. He looks at Bharat. He looks back at me. 'I have to go to my aunt's house for dinner. Save me a little . . .'

With that he is gone.

'Tommy doesn't like English food . . .' Bharat says, tactfully.

There will be no English food if I don't get on. Bharat slopes off no doubt in search of some single malt. I'm on my own; surrounded by chefs. I require flour for the batter mix. There are of course four types of flour on the shelf and I don't know the Hindi word for 'plain'. I have to guess. I beat the eggs and the salt and add the sifted flour. Gradually I drip in a mixture of milk and water to bring the eggs and flour together.

It's very strange being back in a commercial kitchen, my first foray since Arzooman and Kovalam. I suppose what is most daunting is the expectation level of those around me. Cooking at home allows for homely food, but this is a professional kitchen, filled with – unoccupied – professional chefs who have taken to exchanging whispered words, which are followed by knowing nods. I am absolutely sure that I am doing something very, very wrong. Could it be that I have chosen self-raising flour rather than plain? And if I have, why aren't they telling me?

I return my attention to my batter. Yorkshire pudding batter never looks like it's going to be any good; that's the joy of the process. This beige sludge becomes a delicious crispy yet soft meal.

Under normal circumstances I would have placed a baking tray in the oven smeared in lard or dripping or duck fat. I would set the oven to its highest and allow the fat to smoke. I would then toss in my browned sausages and decant my batter mix, replacing the entire ensemble back into the oven for a little over half an hour. But this is India; there is no concept of animal fat in cooking. I am forced to choose between ghee, clarified butter and a dodgy-looking olive oil. None are anywhere near ideal. I decide to blend them and cross my fingers. I heat the oil and ghee mixture on the hob and fry off my mutton steaks. Maybe they are neck fillets, given how they seem to be browning. I pour over the batter mix and place it all in a hot oven.

Have you ever, while cooking, waited to see if the flour you have chosen is the right type? Neither have I. Thirty-five minutes should fly by when surrounded by the cacophony and bustle of a working restaurant kitchen. But it is possibly the slowest thirty-five minutes of my cooking life. I imagine my Yorkshires cooking into hard little bullets of batter, ruined by gram flour. I have similar nightmares about monster puddings that spill out of their casings and slowly fill the entire oven with their burgeoning weight. I try to ascertain from one of the sous chefs whether the flour I chose had indeed been plain. I hold the flour dispenser in my hand as I question him.

'Is this plain flour?'

'Yes, sir. This is flour,' he replies, rather meekly.

'Yes but,' I continue, 'is it plain flour?'

'It is flour, sir. It is flour.' He looks at me as if I require hospitalisation.

'What is the Hindi for plain flour?' I ask rhetorically.

'It is flour, sir. Flour.' He is beginning to irritate me.

I watch and wait. I wait and watch. (What I should have done is simply open the oven and had a look. I have no idea why that most basic of thoughts never occurred to me.) I would find out in the next twenty minutes whether my choice of flour has been correct. In the meanwhile I have other food to prepare.

Many argue that toad in the hole's essential ingredient is the gravy. I would not agree but would happily concede that it is a far poorer dish dry than when swimming in the dark, meaty juices of a strong gravy. But again, this is India. I can perhaps cobble together a red onion and red wine sauce, but it would have none of the deep flavour of a *jus* or a gravy. And it is at this point I have a slight crisis in trying to work out how a *jus* differs from a gravy, and which I should attempt to make. I pull myself together and decide that I am to make the world's first ever gravy *jus*. I chop some onions.

I fry off half moons of red onion. I am astonished that a restaurant as good as this seems to be has no fresh herbs to speak of. I search high and low and ask the man who appears to be the head chef. He nods sagely, before leading me to a small cupboard where he shows me a bunch of dried mint, a small amount of thyme and a teaspoonful of dried oregano. None of them look particularly fresh. That is the extent of their herb offering. I forgo the herb component to the gravy *jus*. I add a good glass of the house red which is unremarkable in the extreme. I let this all bubble and reduce and then thicken the whole thing in the French style with a mixture of butter and plain flour (hopefully it is plain flour). I don't think the chefs have ever witnessed anything like this and confusion chases fear across their faces. The gravy is ready and will sit bubbling away for another ten minutes.

I should have chosen someone less forthright and honest than Bharat Shetty to come and eat with me, but I had limited options. Given the uncertainty of the type of flour used in my batter I could be inviting a great deal more abuse upon myself than I would have readily expected. Bharat's head pops round the door.

'Hey, man. What's happening? I'm starving.'

'Hey. Nearly done. Just taking the toad out of the oven.'

I am nervous. I was hoping that I could secretly remove the toad and if it had been a complete disaster I could have manufactured an 'accident', letting the dish tumble towards the hard floor, shattering into a million pieces. No one would ever have known about the flour error. But now Bharat is standing there, watching, waiting, hoping.

'I'm hungry, man. Let's do it.'

I steel myself. I haven't opened the oven for thirty-five minutes. It could now be full of mutant toad in the hole. The oven door is opened . . .

Hallelujah! It must have been plain flour. I must look like a Nobel Prize winner as I lift the toad in the hole out of the oven and onto the counter.

'Amazing,' I say, completely to myself.

Bharat looks underwhelmed.

I serve the toad, which doesn't look too shabby, and pour over the onion sauce type gravy *jus* thing. Everything is correctly seasoned and I can honestly say that given the circumstances I couldn't have done any better. It tastes even more delicious since I wasn't altogether sure there would be anything edible to eat. I'm sure I see Tommy the owner lurking somewhere in the shadows; his aunt must have cancelled. Suffice to say Bharat tastes and nods.

'Well?' I ask hopefully.

'They do very good king prawns here, man,' he says as he pushes the full plate of toad in the hole and onion gravy *jus* to one side. He has had a solitary mouthful. 'Big king prawns in coconut and chilli. Hey, waiter!' Bharat proceeds to order the aforementioned king prawns, leaving my hard-fought toad in the hole uneaten and forgotten.

As the waiter takes our order and removes Bharat's barely eaten plate of British food, I think about the meal I had originally planned to cook, the call centre adventure. I am sure that would have had a happier ending. What have I learnt from feeding Bharat? Nothing, if I am to be honest. I really wish that I had the chance to feed the new young Indians instead of this, tired and well-travelled, but lovely, Indian. You win some, you lose some. And this feels like a loss.

Later that evening, back at Bharat's place, I stood on the terrace, watching the city below. I felt strangely confused. I should have felt much more at home in Bangalore; Bharat and I have been friends for many years, the city was hardly new to me. But much as I knew India was changing, the rapidity of the change was difficult to comprehend. And that change was an international, global change. The very nature of the country was being altered by outside influence. I had hoped that I would come to Bangalore and somehow understand how the two sides of my life met; Bangalore seemed the perfect place to learn about this. That is what the call centre would have given me. Instead I ended up relying on Bharat who is himself part of old India, the country's past rather than its future. Perhaps the twenty-something graduates who spend all their lives talking to the rest of the English-speaking world would have embraced my toad in the hole in a more international manner, without feeling the need to order king prawns in a coconut chilli sauce. If I thought I was going to find anything of myself with Bharat, then I was sadly deluded.

I was left with an overwhelming sense of sadness. I felt as if I had taken a backward step. Mani and the tranquillity of Mamallapuram, the myriad of searching questions and the sound of the sea were not only a different India, but in truth a different country. It was almost as if the entire journey was an attempt for me to fight my Britishness, hide my own self. Mani saw me as an outsider and would have happily accepted me as such. Perhaps the problem was mine. Why did I feel the need to apologise for being British when in India, and apologise for being Indian when in Britain?

Bangalore left me wondering whether the east and the west could truly combine in a symbiotically balanced state; that and mourning the fact that my toad in the hole was such an unappreciated failure.

WHEN THE GOAN GETS TOUGH, THE TOUGH GET GOAN

There's a hierarchy you need to understand about Punjabis. It's sort of a modern-day caste system that imposes status. The theory is this: the further you have emigrated from that small village of your birth in deepest darkest Punjab, the better you have become as a person. Those Punjabis who wandered off to Delhi look down on the agrarian Punjabis who stayed at home and tilled the land and milked the cows; the Delhi Punjabis are in turn looked down upon by the Bombay and Bangalore Punjabis, and so on.

The East African Punjabis believe themselves to be God's chosen people; those in Kenya, Uganda and Tanzania look down not only on all Punjabis but on all peoples. This dynamic is all too immediate in my own family since my father is a Punjab Punjabi and my mother is from Nairobi. Some time before the Second World War my maternal grandfather was posted to Kenya by the British to work on the railways as a guard. He had four children: Malkit; Surinder, the lone son; my mother, Kuldip; and Jassi, the youngest. It was after Malkit Massi was born that my grandfather was told of the impending move to Nairobi, where his remaining three children were to be born. Since my grandfather's brother had not been blessed with children it was decided that Malkit, then no more than four, should be left with her paternal uncle to be brought up as their child. My grandfather and grandmother left the Punjab and their first born for a new life in Kenya. Malkit stayed in India until she was eighteen when my grandfather went to bring her back. The family was complete again, all six of them, but only for a few years until my grandmother's untimely passing. Malkit, a veritable stranger to her siblings, ended up as the matriarch, her teenage years cut short by the necessity of family. That is the story of my mother's childhood.

We talk about incredible journeys; this book is an immense journey. But it's only when I look back on the lives of my parents that I realise the true extent of 'journey'. I might travel for days in trains across thousands of Indian miles, but how can that compare to the personal journey of my mother? Born during the Second World War in a colonial outpost, she found herself at the age of twenty, married and in Delhi, only to move to London two years later and finally settle in windswept Glasgow. That is a journey. From the shacks of Nairobi to a palatial terraced house just off the Great Western Road. Raj, Sanj and I can barely contemplate the changes our parents have witnessed during their nomadic continent–crossing existence. And they are still reasonable, kind and loving people. I wonder if I would maintain such poise and equanimity.

My parents learnt about themselves, about their lives through the journeys they were compelled to make in an attempt to give their children a better life. I feel a little self-indulgent at this point in my journey when I reflect on how it is something I have chosen to undertake rather than been forced to make. What can I really learn by gallivanting around India? There is no economic imperative to what I am doing. I am not seeking a better life for my family. I am simply indulging the desire of a westerner, since that is what I am. I am a westerner, travelling India in search of myself.

Two overnight train journeys totalling about thirty-seven hours of travel over less than half a week have begun to take their toll on my poise and clarity of thought. I have caught a cold and like any man I find myself on the very precipice of death itself; at any moment I could tumble over leaving life behind me, coughing and spluttering with a blocked nose all the way into the ravine below. Bangalore to Goa looked like being another overnight escapade, another journey full of incident and accident, in a Volvo bus. I couldn't face it, I'm afraid. Another *2001: Space Odyssey* moment and another burly Sikh movie star with a shotgun and a forklift truck? No. I have stayed in Bangalore an extra night and opted for the early afternoon Jet Airways flight to Goa. As opposed to the nine-hour bus ride I would have a sixty-minute flight followed by a similar car journey. I should be at Carmona beach by early evening and eating a pork-based Portuguese-inspired curry by no later than eight o'clock.

Bangalore airport's departure lounge was once a surprisingly small affair. That is no longer the case, and the cosmopolitan nature of the passing travellers reflects the changing nature of the city. There is a genuine buzzy excitement here. On the way to the airport, Bharat, who kindly offered to drive me, told me that, like Madras and Bombay and Calcutta, Bangalore is in the throes of reverting to its original Kanada name of Bangaluru. Irony of ironies, as the city becomes more international, more global, more part of the economic colonialisation of India, it is simultaneously unknotting itself from its direct colonial past, filling the void with a newfound sense of optimism. The next time I land in this city, it will be into Bangaluru International Airport.

I've always thought that an airport is a snapshot of a city in terms of its aspirations and dreams; it is often the first and last impression a visitor has of a city and a country. And nowhere is this more pronounced than in India where airports are being thrown up and renovated with alarming speed and regularity. The airport at Bangalore was merely a domestic terminal a decade and a half ago. Now it has morphed into an ever-increasing gateway of international business opportunity.

I wander about the departure gate, my stomach getting the better of me, as usual. I'm peckish, unnecessarily so considering how much I have consumed in the last few days. This is yet more astonishing considering the fact that I have a cold and should really not have the slightest pang of hunger. Clearly I have hidden depths of greed that can overcome even the worst of medical conditions.

I wander over to the food kiosk and survey my options. The gleamingly clean glass-topped counters call out to me. There are snacks from every gamut of the Indian inter-meal offering: the pakora, the samosa, the spiced sandwich, the bhaji, the puff, the idli, the dosa. I survey every option, secretly wanting them all but knowing that even my belly would fail to accommodate that. But my eyes are especially taken by a snack known as an aloo boondi. Does snacking get any better than this? Imagine spiced, mashed potato enhanced with freshly chopped chillies and coriander; these balls of delight are then enveloped in a gram-flour batter and deep fried. A homage to the carbohydrate. These delights invariably find themselves served with a punchy, tangy tamarind chutney or even a mint sauce. Delicious. As I gaze longingly at the boondi through the glass I realise that I must have them; I simply must. I feel a cosmic sense of oneness with them, a deep sensation of déjà vu. Perhaps I was predestined to nibble on this snack? Perhaps it was written in some other place that this potato morsel and I would come together as one at this place, at this time. I feel as if I was simply meant to be here. I am overcome with an inexplicable familiarity with this sight. I have been here before, witnessed this before. But where?

Then I remember: the image of the rat in the airport food kiosk thrust before me by the bearded pastor on the train to Madras. It was this airport, this very kiosk, maybe even these very boondi.

Unbelievable.

Unsurprisingly the edge from my hunger has been removed quick-smart.

No sooner has our plane taken off than the pilot is preparing us for landing. The briefest of flights. The bluest of skies. The whitest of clouds. Perhaps Goa will be the destination of superlatives? Certainly the airport isn't; it is surprisingly small and compact for a city that sees so much passenger traffic. Taxis and touts wait outside in the baking heat, sensing fresh, cotton-clad blood. But this is late July, low season, and there are only a handful of westerners ripe for fleecing, and they too seem slightly more savvy than most. The look of collective disappointment is one well worth watching. There's nothing quite like a tout scorned.

I opt for the non air-conditioned cab which will save me the princely sum of 300 rupees. For 650 rupees I can open the window and stick my head out. I will have the wind in my beard and the sun on my face. Or the sun in my beard and the wind on my face. Either way, my face and beard and the wind and the sun will be involved.

The road to Carmona is good. We pass through lush, verdant forests and bisect tiny villages, some no more than a handful of shacks. Every now and again an expansive colonial-style bungalow appears, its gaily painted exterior of pink, purple, orange or blue failing to hide the otherwise faded grandeur. Since it is both low season and election time a lot of the shops are shuttered, some of the tinier hamlets completely bereft of activity. As the journey unfolds, deeper into Goa, my single initial impression is how strong Christianity is in this part of India. On the sun visors of cars, on the bonnets of cars, on shop hoardings, Christianity is everywhere. We pass St Jude's garage where three moustachioed men grapple with a motorbike. Roadside crosses mark the route and every now and again appears a caged shrine and a handful of believers paying their respects. This couldn't be less like any India I have known.

And it couldn't be less like the India I just left. Bangalore is a city that keeps thriving and blossoming and growing with a youthful exuberance, a jewel in the crown of the modern subcontinent. Nothing could be more of a contrast than Goa. It is a beach paradise, a quirky and unique place within India. For many years it was the country's best kept secret. Now that the secret is out I wonder for how much longer Goa can maintain that mystical, enigmatic state of being.

I should explain that there are two Goas: the tourist Goa and the real Goa. I have been to the tourist Goa before, to the north, and frankly it felt more like the Costa Del Goa rather than the magical, mysterious paradise of India. That Goa I found upsettingly un-Indian. It might have been Magaluf, Dubai or anywhere but India. I have never been to South Goa, the place Indians go on holiday. Perhaps that Goa, Indian Goa, holds the last vestiges of mystical enigma. When I was drawing up my itinerary Dad was in two minds about whether Goa would be meaningful. He felt that Goa was the Indian equivalent to a Scottish shortbread tin; it's not that he doesn't like shortbread, he just doesn't feel that a man in a kilt on a tartan backdrop is particularly typical of the experience of Scotland. Similarly he wasn't altogether sure what I would garner from Goa. He felt the collision of tourism and the ever-rampant free market had tainted every Goan nook and cranny. And why not? India should not be any different to any other nation when it comes to crass, flesh-displaying drunkards who use the strength of their exchange rate to re-colonialise poorer countries.

This was one reason I was keen to come to South Goa: I thought that in trying to understand my own duality, in attempting to come to terms with my own sense of 'home', as someone quintessentially British, I should come to the place where so many of my fellow Brits come as they search for answers. I'm not sure whether I will find any answers here but I am certainly hoping to leave with another set of questions.

There is a second reason: I am very keen to try pork vindaloo. I am even hungrier for it now, having been thwarted in Cochin. Growing up it was impossible to find pork cooked in an Indian style. This was in part because most Indian restaurants in the UK were run by Muslims, a religion for which the pig is regarded as too unclean to eat. We Sikhs think nothing of tucking into all things porcine and luckily my parents have always been fond of that which is widely regarded as the 'king of meats'. Pork was cooked and enjoyed at home. But that was Punjabi-style pork, delicious but not the best way to prepare pig meat. When I reached my late teens and started to explore and read about food myself, I learnt from a lady on TV called Madhur Jaffrey that there was a Goan way of preparing pork. Pork vindaloo crashed into my consciousness and ever since I've had the avowed intent of searching out this dish and devouring it. The last time I was in Goa for a couple of days and the pork was hard to find. The word vindaloo itself has been hijacked by the Indian restaurant scene. I wish to reclaim it again for the Goans. A modest task, I think you'll agree.

୧ড়ৄ

Ten examples of Christian influence on daily Goan Life on the journey to Carmona

Jesus Video Cassette Library

Santa Maria Holiday Cottages

Amchi Jesus Bus

Holy Trinity Cold Storage

Infant Jesus General Store

Immaculate Conception Snack Shop and Cyber Cafe

Jesus of the Cross Plywood Stores

Sisters of the Cross Guesthouse

Father Sebastian Audio Visual and Lamination Services

୧ড়ৄ

Orlando Mascarenhas is my car mechanic. He lives out in Heston, west London and what he doesn't know about the internal combustion engine is not worth knowing. I can remember hearing his name as long ago as I can remember being able to hear, full stop. Orlando isn't a common name for Indians. It was a rather glamorous name in a family full of Malkits, Satinders and Rajs. (Why does every Indian family have at least four boys called Raj? It is of course an irony that the Raj that most people know and remember is a load of white people in pith helmets and jodhpurs; for me it's any family gathering invariably involving a samosa.)

Orlando was spoken about like some latter-day Merlin who would conjure a car into working order through some dark art of automotive repair. I rediscovered him in the spring of 2007 when my wife's car needed what appeared worryingly to be thousands of pounds' worth of work. The curse of the speed bump on the German suspension system. I brought the Passat to Orlando and three hundred quid later it was right as rain. I then took my car for a service and we got talking.

It transpired that Orlando was Goan. I never knew this about him. But I should have guessed from his name, which is Goan Christian, to be exact. As I worked out how many hundreds of pounds he had saved me on my wife's car, Orlando told me that I was lucky to catch him – he was on his way to Goa. Orlando travels to Goa three or four times a year. From mid-November until mid-January he goes to enjoy the cooler winter sun, the more temperate climate; his family join him as soon as school breaks. He returns in May or June with the kids for half-term and again in the autumn break. And come summertime he's back on a plane and Goa-bound. He may take an extra trip when the fancy possesses him.

As I stood in Orlando's modest house in Heston everything about him and his life started to fall into place. He wasn't living in the small two-up, two-down; he was existing there. Goa was where Orlando came to life. Even just talking about it his body became energised, his hands started describing the sea and the sand and his eyes twinkled. If this was how animated he became about the place in the oil-soaked drizzle of west London, I wanted to experience him in situ, in the midst of his sun-kissed paradise. He seemed the perfect person to visit on my journey.

'When are you going?' I asked.

'Tuesday.'

'Don't fancy going again in a couple of months, do you?' I was half joking.

'Hold on . . .' He wandered off and shouted his son's name upstairs. 'Carlos! Carlos! When are your holidays?'

I remember thinking at the time how strange that there were Indian people with names like Orlando and now Carlos. Orlando returned, smiling. But then Orlando was always smiling.

'We will be there. Kids' half term.'

'Can I come and cook for you?'

Orlando looked a little confused. 'You can cook for me here in London . . .'

I explained my quest, my journey, my attempt at self-discovery. 'I really want to come to Goa.'

'Then please be my guest.'

Orlando is East African, like my mother. His father had worked with my maternal uncle and my maternal grandfather on the railways that the British seemed to construct wherever they colonised. Orlando came to the UK in 1975 with a view to studying science, but life so very often impacts on aspiration and he found himself working at British Airways by day and spannering the odd car by night. Such was his reputation for automotive alchemy that the night job started paying more than the day job. His plan was clear: he would work all the hours the cosmos sent and he would rebuild his father's house in Goa. This he did all the way through the 1980s, flying to and fro to supervise works. Then in 1993 he decided to buy his own place in Goa. Back then no one knew or was particularly interested in Goa apart from the soap-dodging, lank-haired hippies.

Orlando greets me warmly in front of his house. This is his home in Goa, a two-storey villa in a gated community abutting the beach at Carmona. It could not be more different from his life in Heston. Perhaps it's the contrast with the slate, rain-laden skies of west London, the chill in the air, the general sense of greyness of the capital of England that suddenly makes Carmona seem not just the other side of the world but an altogether different galaxy. Orlando's villa is beautiful. Bougainvillea stretches upwards and around the powder-pink exterior. Inside it is cool and airy with four good-sized bedrooms and two terraces. I stand on the back terrace looking out to the Arabian Sea and I wonder why Orlando ever leaves. I ask him. The answer is obvious.

'Gotta work, man. Gotta make the money . . .'

The house is part of a wider resort. There are maybe another seventy or so villas and there's a pool and a badminton court; but this is Indian Goa, not Costa del Goa. These holiday homes are owned almost exclusively by Goans or Indians who spend a few weeks or months of the year here. A handful of retired Indians live here year round, for whom the sun and the pace of life are simply perfect. Low season it may be, but for me the heat is almost intolerable.

Goa is a unique part of India for many reasons. In the last ten years or so it has developed from hippy hang out into India's most visited tourist location. Paradise is becoming more easily attainable with numerous five-star hotels and leisure complexes being developed on the coastline. Orlando tells me that in the old days fresh fish was much easier and cheaper to get hold of; now all the best stuff is sold on to the restaurants. He remembers when he was a child his family would give freshly caught fish to western travellers and ask them to cook it; then they would all sit together and enjoy the meal. But that was then.

'Do you feel Indian?' I ask, almost at the end of my first cold beer in days.

Orlando reaches for another before answering. 'I'm Goan, man. I never call myself Indian. I'm Goan.' His reply is a little fiercer than I think he intended it to be. He sips his beer before looking at me again with his kind eyes. 'We're different, us Goans. Different, man.'

That there is a marked dichotomy between the Goan sense of identity and the Indian isn't altogether surprising. Until December 1961 Goa was still Portuguese. It was only after armed conflict that the Indian army forcibly reclaimed the state. Goa had been a colony for almost 500 years, one of the world's oldest recognised colonies. The Portuguese influence is still evident: Orlando Mascarenhas is evidence enough, surely! Orlando remembers his parents speaking Portuguese and he himself remembers understanding the language.

Orlando is keen to take me out and about, proud to show me his Goa.

'We never cook at home, man. We get food in for lunch and then go out and eat in the evenings. My friends run a few good places.'

'I want to try pork. Is that OK?' I ask tentatively. There's still something very strange about asking for pork in India.

'Should be fine. We'll go to the Traveller's.' I like Orlando's confidence.

We drive out to a place called the Traveller's Tavern some fifteen minutes away. I notice that although the sun set some hours ago the heat has hung around. It's not warm; it's hot. When we arrive I feel rather alarmed at the state of the place. To say the Traveller's is a shack would be unfair on shacks. A four-foot-high brick wall traces the outline of the space; every few feet a wooden post rises up, upon which rests a thatched roof. It's basic in the extreme. One only wonders about the kitchen which remains unseen and unheard in a separate hut at the back. They say one should judge the quality of an establishment's food by the quality of its toilets: if that were the case at the Traveller's I would have been leaving there sharpish. But this is India, albeit Goan India. My mind and my bowels are open to new experiences.

This place is run by an old friend of Orlando's, and there's another guy hovering around the bar; he seems to have one leg longer than the other and a moustache that wouldn't look out of place on the set of a low-budget spaghetti western. Orlando thinks it a good idea that we have a little pre-prandial stiffener. I would kill for a vodka tonic but that would appear not to be on offer. Instead the local spirit arrives at the table. A clear spirit, cashew fenny is made from the fruit of the cashew tree. Each fruit bears only a single pair of cashew nuts (hence the expense of the nut). The nut is attached to a fruit, and this fruit, in time old tradition, is fermented and turned into alcohol.

'Have some, man. It's the local speciality.' Orlando is not the sort of guy you want to disappoint. Neither are the owner of the bar and his friend. They stand watching as I grasp the glass in my hand.

I am compelled to have a taste. I decide to down it in one; I am from Glasgow after all.

It's harsh.

'Lovely,' I say, forcing a smile where a smile ought never to belong.

It's like lighter fuel. Or grappa. I just don't get grappa. And I'm not loving cashew fenny either. I'm hopeful that the lining on my throat will eventually grow back. I have never understood why people drink alcohol that doesn't taste nice.

I let Orlando order the food. The pork-free food. I can't believe I have come all this way and they've run out of pork. The owner explains.

'The pork we have to order in the morning. It's low season so we don't get so much. The pork we ordered was all sold by lunchtime.'

'Get some for tomorrow night, OK?' Orlando looks sternly at the owner, who demurs.

Orlando asks what I like to eat.

'Food,' I reply, cheekily. 'Anything and everything.'

Twenty minutes later the table is heaving with dishes. It all looks amazing. There is fresh mackerel cooked with a rechard masala. The gutted fish are filled with the spicy red sauce and fried. King fish curry in a thin, soupy sauce; very oniony and sweet. Then we are sent a plate of spicy sausages – chipolata-sized pork sausages wrapped in beef intestines and then deep fried; they are rich and fatty. These sausages are the only pork in the restaurant since they are cured and can keep for days. Finally a plate of masala beef tongue which is much tastier than it sounds. It is cooked in a coconut, vinegar and chilli sauce and is best accompanied by the Portuguese bread.

A few hours later, having successfully avoided any further adventures with the cashew fenny, we drive home in the dark. The complex rich flavours of the spicy, vinegary masalas and the fatty sausages warm me from the inside, colliding occasionally and uncomfortably with the harsh paint-thinning taste of the cashew fenny. And while the Goan food warms my insides, my outside is being toasted by the temperature which seems somehow unaware of the fact that it is approaching midnight, refusing to get any cooler than the low thirties. The windows open, the wind in my beard, I look forward to the air-conditioned comfort of my friend's home. That is something about Orlando that I really admire. Systematically, piece by piece, he re-designed his little corner of paradise within India's little corner of paradise. While he lives modestly in Heston, he lives like royalty in Goa.

We arrive back and I yearn for bed. Orlando yearns for more cashew fenny. It would be impolite to refuse. Again. We decant drinks and turn on all the fans and AC units.

'It's going to be a hot night.' Orlando wipes a bead or two of sweat from his brow.

We down our drinks and I make for bed. I am cooking tomorrow and I need to have more than my usual number of wits about me. I lie in bed, enjoying the cooling breeze of the conditioned air, the hum of the machine like a lullaby.

I am moments away from the sweetest of sleeps when suddenly the world seems to grind to a silent halt. The AC falls quiet. The night lights fail; there is darkness everywhere. I hear noises in the hallway and the unmistakeable light of a torch, flitting under the door. Orlando is up and one of the kids, Carlos, is moaning. I stagger out of my room to find out what's going on. It transpires that the generator has failed. Being a mechanic, Orlando feels he can fix everything, but even his resolve is insufficient in the pitch dark of a Goan night. He apologises profusely.

'No problem,' I say nonchalantly. 'I like the heat.'

I am plainly quite stupid. The temperature feels even hotter at one in the morning than it has done all day long. The air is still and oppressive. Have you ever tried to sleep in a breeze-less thirty-six degrees? It's impossible. Even my sweat is sweating. I doze lightly rather than enter the full body embrace of sleep. By four in the morning I feel almost hallucinatory.

Orlando has arranged for a taxi to come and collect me in the morning and take me to shop for food. The driver's name is Rosewell; he knows his way around the markets. Orlando rarely visits the Margao market. He has no need to. He never cooks when he is here. They simply go out and eat.

'Are you sure you want to cook, man? We can bring food in or go out and eat.'

Orlando hasn't quite grasped the point of my journey.

'I am here to find myself. To try and discover who I am and how I fit in to all this.' I make a non-specific hand gesture out of the window.

'OK. But why cooking?' He looks genuinely quizzical. His kind eyes search for an answer.

'Because I believe in food. I think food is the way to people's hearts and souls. Understand someone's food and you understand them.' I feel enthused by my eloquence, robust in my rhetoric.

'OK, man.' Orlando is less than convinced.

Rosewell comes with his Ambassador to take me shopping. It is a twenty-minute drive from Orlando's place to Margao. The Goa I'm seeing on this trip is very different to the Goa I have seen before. Since the moment I landed I have seen the real Goa, with real people, living real lives. I have seen but one westerner in the day or so I have spent here.

Goa is a conundrum, a contradiction. There are miles of the most beautiful beaches, homes to the hedonists, the winter sun-seekers. Yet drive inland, as I am now, and there are still vestiges of the commercial history of the principality. Large municipal buildings, shabby now with the passing of time, which were once administrative offices of the Portuguese authorities; warehouses that look as if they belong in Lisbon or Porto rather than by the Arabian Sea. Goa was one of the most important trade hubs of the Portuguese empire. Churches and

Christianity seem to be ubiquitous and this doesn't feel like any sort of India I have witnessed before.

This Portuguese and Christian influence brings a rather unique culinary proposition. Given that a quarter of India is Muslim, not only is it hard to find pork in an Indian restaurant in the UK, it is very difficult to find pork anywhere in India, too. This is compounded by the fact that Hindus are not particularly fond of pig meat either. The state of Goa is the honourable exception. With its overwhelmingly Christian population and fierce sense of independence, pork is the staple dish wherever you venture. A local delicacy is stuffed piglet which roasts for five hours while the men fish in the backwaters for snapper and crab. By the time they return the piglet is cooked.

So there appears to be only one thing for me to cook in Goa. I love pork. And my favoured cut of pork has to be belly. The crispy crackling hiding the tender fatty flesh, deep with flavour. I shall cook roast pork belly, mash and peas, all to be served with home-made apple sauce. What could be more British?

MMC New Market does exactly what it says on the tin: it's a market that's quite new. After a challenging ten minutes or so finding parking in what seems a veritable vehicle free-for-all, Rosewell turns the engine off, taps the steering wheel and smiles that enigmatic Indian smile (the Goans may not think of themselves as Indians, but when it comes to enigmatic smiling, boundaries seem to disappear). It is earlier in the morning than I hoped after a night of little sleep, much sweating and borderline hallucinogenic dreaming. But early morning is the only time to procure pig in Goa. They are freshly slaughtered as the sun settles into the sky and then disappear into the homes and kitchens of Goan locals. This place is as real as Goa gets, no white faces. You might think that I blended into my surroundings perfectly, but no. The locals could be staring at me for one of two reasons:

1. I am the most devilishly handsome man they have ever laid eyes on. The women all find me highly desirable and the men all wish to be my best friend.
2. I look like an outsider and do not fit into contemporary Margao life.

I think both you and I, reader, know which is more likely. My lilac turban and clashing pink kurta top might seem to be quintessentially of the subcontinent, but I now realise it is clearly more sub-fashion. I am dressed the way white people dress when they wish to make a statement about how they are embracing India. Indians don't really dress in the way I do. That much has become painfully apparent. I stick out like two sore thumbs.

The market itself is unremarkable, brisk and businesslike. There are four roads, forming a square and it is within this area that the market functions. Each road has an entrance. I walk in through gate four; this is where the pork is to be found. It is rather ramshackle, a place that has grown organically through use rather than a business that was planned and structured. As many stalls are empty as are being used. There is a smattering of vegetables, some clothing and a few cheap plastic toys, no doubt imported from China. This is not a tourist market. I turn a corner away from the street and suddenly my world has changed: all I can see is pig and pig entrail. But before you see it, you smell it. I'll let you work out for yourself the smell of freshly slaughtered pig. Unlike a character from a Coppola movie, I'm not so fond of the smell of new pig in the morning, and I've never in all my life seen so much freshly killed animal.

It's still warm to the touch. It seems that every part of the pig is available for purchase, including the oink. Offal is tied in bundles and hung over the portioned legs. The belly remains uncut and looks too like the animal for me to feel wholly comfortable about purchasing it. But purchase I must.

On closer examination the belly is very fatty, too fatty. More than half the joy of pork belly is in the exact science that melds fat and meat so that after cooking it becomes crispy and earthy all in one mouthful. I fear this belly may be too crispy and not earthy enough, but it would appear to be too late. I have no option. I take three pieces of pork belly, which causes no small degree of consternation to the vendor who only seems set up to sell one kilo or two, nothing in between. Since he only has the 1kg and 2kg weight to balance his scale, he forces me to buy a fourth piece, the equivalent of an entire piglet belly costing me a king's ransom of £2.20. The pig is wrapped in what I hope is yesterday's newspaper. I fear the ink from the page may transfer its story onto the pork.

I now wander the market looking for potatoes for the mash, peas and apples. Apple sauce and pork are like Astaire and Rogers, Gilbert and Sullivan, Morecambe and Wise; some things are simply meant to be together. It's a strange sort of market, a blend of food and fancy goods. Now you probably take for granted the phrase 'fancy goods'. Fancy goods however are the most troubling sorts of goods for me. Their very description is oxymoronic and deceitful. These goods are bad and they're anything but fancy. Rovi, my beloved cousin, is an expert on fancy goods. He has travelled the world sourcing fancy goods; buying fancy goods; selling fancy goods. He is the king of fancy goods. Quite how to define fancy goods is a challenge. They are curios or trinkets, made in bulk and more often than not plastic or acrylic or otherwise manmade.

There isn't a good that's fancy that Rovi hasn't an opinion on. Even Rovi would survey these fancy goods and question the platonic essence of their fanciness and their goodness. A small multi-coloured, plastic monkey with a ball attached to its hand by an elastic string? Not fancy and not terribly good.

I leave the market potatoless, pea-free and without apples. Panic sets in. What is the point of roast pork belly without mash and apple sauce? Rosewell, through the gift of broken English combined with my irreparable Hindi, tells me there are some roadside stalls where we can purchase vegetables and fruit. We extricate the Ambassador from the mayhem of ice delivery, which seems to be turning into a full-blown musical outside the market, and escape, the pork warm against my leg (there's a phrase I never thought I'd find myself writing).

Now, you would think it would be relatively unchallenging to purchase potatoes in a country that does more things with potatoes than the National Association of Potato-growers on International 'Do something different with a potato' Day. You would think. Or perhaps this is my ignorance of pan-Indian vegetables. Given my Punjabi ancestry, I assume all of India is the same when it comes to food availability. The Punjab is rich in agricultural resources. There's nothing the Punjabis can't grow. Potatoes are a staple of the north Indian diet. Potatoes with everything. That would appear not to be the case in Goa.

Four stalls later I am still bereft of carbohydrate. The good news is that I've managed to purchase some peas; at least I think they're peas. If projected at high velocity, one can imagine these green spheres becoming military missiles of mass destruction, perforating any person who would dare to come into its path. They're bloody hard. Nonetheless, they are, technically, peas. I have also acquired apples. Fifty rupees for four apples; it is not much cheaper than British prices. This is explained as we drive away. Rosewell tells me these are imported apples. Even India thinks other people's apples are better than theirs. I return to Orlando's tattie-free.

'Don't worry, man,' Orlando says. 'We got some sweet potatoes somewhere.'

But sweet potatoes are nothing like potatoes at all. In fact, I've often wondered why grocers and supermarkets are not prosecuted under the trade descriptions act for wilfully misleading us into thinking that a sweet potato is a potato that's a bit sweet. With the pork belly being too fatty, what I really need is the floury mouth-filling comfort of a real potato. Don't get me wrong, I love a sweet potato like the next man. There is nothing finer to accompany Caribbean goat curry than a deep fried sweet potato. Roasted in the oven with thyme and honey, sweet potato can be a significant launch pad to any sort of main course experience. Even mashed with chilli, garlic and spring onion (a sort of Caribbean champ), it is a meal in itself. But it simply won't work with my over-fat piglet pork belly.

In the late-morning light of Orlando's first-floor kitchen, my suspicions about the fat to flesh ratio of the belly are confirmed. Not only is it too fat, the skin still has nipples on it. Thankfully, the nipples make the hair seem more palatable, unlikely though that seems. I've clearly been sold a pup. Before I spiral downward into a porcine nightmare, Rosewell returns, a bag of potatoes in his hand. Never before have I felt the desire to kiss a man full on the lips. Rosewell knows he has done a good thing and I ask him to stay for lunch. Unfortunately he can't, such is the life of a freelance cab driver in Goa. At least I have potato now to assuage my issues with the pork.

I decide the best course of action is to trim the belly as much as I can. The problem with fatty belly cuts is that fat is by its very nature slippery, and grabbing hold of the fat before gently divorcing it from the flesh is trickier than one might think. Thankfully some of the fat allows itself to be removed but in amongst the nipples and hair, there seem to be mud marks on the belly; the sort of mud that even Ariel at sixty degrees would struggle to shift.

In amongst shearing nipples, slicing fat and removing hair I find myself thinking of Keith in Waitrose. I never have to do this to the pork belly he sells me. But then Keith and Waitrose on Finchley Road feel like a million miles and many lifetimes away from here. Short of an oven to roast the belly, I have to rely on an old north Italian method. They are renowned for twice cooking their pork belly. First they poach the pig slowly in milk, then roast it to a crisp finish. I will poach and then fry, keeping my fingers crossed for the selfsame crispy finish.

Orlando's kitchen is not a cooking kitchen, it's a kitchen to be looked at; he can't remember the last time they didn't eat out. The de-haired, de-nippled, de-fatted and de-mudded pork fills Orlando's biggest glass pan. I can see, through the smoked glassware, the defiant pork, insolent in its milky bath, willing this recipe to fail. If I'm to be honest, I can't say I'm feeling so confident myself. As the milk starts to warm, I peel and chop the apples. I chop half the apples very finely with the hope that these will break down and dissolve more readily, forming the sauce around the larger chunks of apple; it's my intention to give Orlando and the kids a two-textured apple sauce. The apples sit in a large pan with a dash of water and more than enough sugar to help the process on its way, bearing in mind Indian sugar for some reason seems to be significantly less sweet that Tate & Lyle. My pork and apple sit hob by hob, side by side and I watch and sweat. Inspiration takes hold of me. I add a healthy slug of cashew fenny into the apples. When in Goa . . . I peel the potatoes and the trinity of pans in front of me suggest a meal may well be served. As to the quality of the repast . . .

I can't help but wonder about Orlando's wife stuck in London miles away from her family and then I realise the parallels with my own family. My mother was stuck in that Sinclair Drive shop while my father showed his sons his India. Are Orlando and his family any different?

The milk comes to the boil and I turn it down to simmer. The apples look about as saucy as they're going to get, which doesn't look nearly saucy enough. When you read the ingredients on the side of Bramley apple sauce, you wonder how difficult it can be to make yourself. I suggest you try it and soon you will know the alchemy of apple sauce. I hope that having turned out the apple sauce and refrigerated it, the sugary syrup will thicken, and it might just work. The pork has been simmering now for twenty minutes. I know I keep banging on about the fat content, but you have to understand, the very composition of this Goan pork has rendered my every calculation meaningless. I'm not sure whether I should boil fattier pork for less time or more time; I'm not even sure whether I'm meant to boil it at all. Too late because I have. I turn off the heat and allow my piggy friend to sit in its milk bath for a little longer. There's one thing I'm sure of; I'd rather have overcooked pork than undercooked pork. I am also acutely aware that this evening we are to return to Travellers for that elusive pork vindaloo. My pork offering had better be good.

I kill the fifteen minute wait by phoning my brother-in-law Unni in Bombay. His wife, Anu, is my wife's cousin; they're very close. Unni is a commercials director who has started making movies in the new vibrant, modern India. His love of European cinema and my love of modern India seem to be a happy intersection in our lives. He holidays annually in Goa.

'What are you doing?' he asks me.

I explain to Unni where I'm staying.

'We are buying a place there. There, in that complex.' Unni is incredulous. That makes two of us.

Now I am aware of the dimensions of the globe, the circumference, the radius, the surface area of the planet. No matter how one looks at it, this world is many things but small. It transpires that the house he has made an offer on is four houses away from Orlando's. You travel halfway round the world but coincidence is never far away.

I bring the robust peas to the boil in heavily salted water. I don't know what it is about these peas but they really scare me. My fear is well placed. I have never in all my life witnessed peas emit so much green to the water they boil in. Now, when I say green, let me explain. At the start of the cooking process, the peas were green (correct) and the water was clear (correct). By the end of the cooking process, the peas are less green (not right) and the water is radioactively green (very, very wrong). I am really not sure whether I should serve these peas, but on balance I'm serving the peas and not the radioactive water, so I feel a little more comfortable about their presence on the plate.

It's time to bring everything together. A frying pan with oil is heated on the hob. I dry the milk-soaked pork belly in the vain hope that the oil, like some biblical miracle, will manage to crisp up the skin. It's never going to happen. I place as many pieces of pork belly into the hot oil as will fit and genuinely pray. I'm not quite sure who I'm meant to be praying to, given my own personal confusion towards the supreme being and the fact that I happen to be in the most Christian place I have ever been to (including the Vatican). Nevertheless, I find myself almost audibly uttering the words, 'Please God, make them crispy.' I distract myself by mashing the now boiled potatoes, embellishing them with luscious Indian butter and a little milk. I retrieve the apple sauce from the fridge. Now I'm muttering, 'Please God, make it saucy.' Clearly, if there is a God, she or he is otherwise occupied since my apple sugar and fenny mix is sticky rather than saucy. I'm hopeful that Orlando and the kids will have very limited experience of proper apple sauce.

We eat. Carlos, being Carlos, feels it is too hot for mash and rightly deems the pork belly too fatty. Having said that, I can't ever remember seeing him eat anything. He would have been very happy with a bowl full of Coke. Charlene likes the fat when it is crispy and loves the mash. Orlando leaves nothing, but then again, Orlando is a lovely man, so I wouldn't let that be any sort of reflection on the quality of the meal.

The meal over, the afternoon heat descends and with bellies full, a kip is required. So we sleep, with the promise of a drive down to the beach for sunset.

It takes no more than twenty minutes to drive to the beach, chasing the sunset full of pork for the second time in one day. A few hundred people gather at Colva to watch the sky darken, to eat ice cream and to paddle through the ebbing, incoming waters. I would have thought that coming to Goa, the very epicentre of the traveller's journey of self-discovery, might have offered me a few more answers. But I am feeling that I am leaving with yet another clutch of questions. The last thing I expected to find on this quest was an Indian duality like my

British duality. Orlando is a proud Goan, but does not regard himself as Indian. Is Orlando any different from me? He is, in so far as I am engaged with my dual heritage, my Britishness and my Indian past. For Orlando, life in that regard is very simple.

Perhaps that is why Goa doesn't really feel like India. This is an alien land, a mini-nation of fiercely proud and independent people that bears very little relation to India herself. I am almost halfway through my journey and I seem to have seen a hundred different Indias and a hundred different Hardeeps on the way.

Perhaps my dad was right. Maybe I should not have bothered with Goa. And maybe cooking British food for Indians is futile. The journey is beginning to feel futile. I am not at all sure what I am learning.

The waves crash and the sky is incarnadine, the multi-coloured bodies slowly become monochrome as the glorious gloom of night descends. Suddenly, for a moment, my whole journey becomes clear in fading twilight. I have travelled halfway around the world to find myself. But I now realise that I cannot truly do so until I lose myself in the experience of India.

All the while I have been travelling, from Kovalam through Mamallapuram, Mysore and Bangalore I have been trying to relate everything to what I already know, as if I were some sort of scientist. Standing on this beach, feeling the sand between my toes and the grains of time slipping silently through my fingers I begin to understand. The darkness brings light.

Then I hear in the distance an all too familiar sound. A broad Lancashire accent.

'Have we missed the sunset? Bloody hell. My feet are bloody throbbing . . . ' A fat, sunburnt tourist is waddling towards the beach, wholly unaware of her own volume and blissfully unaware of her terrible dress sense.

'My bloody feet . . . '

And in an instant, clarity, like the sun, has vanished.

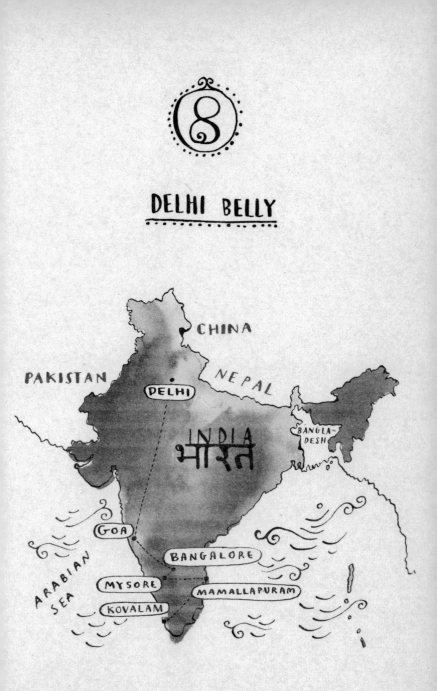

DELHI BELLY

CHINA

PAKISTAN

NEPAL

PELHI

INDIA
भारत

BANGLA-
DESH

GOA

BANGALORE

ARABIAN
SEA

MYSORE

MAMALLAPURAM

KOVALAM

Hi, Dad.'

'How's it going? Where are you now?' He was clearly happy to hear from me.

'Left Goa this morning. I'm in Bombay now and heading for Delhi,' I said. The bus from Goa had been remarkably unremarkable. It had been the single journey I was dreading the most. Yet I have arrived in Bombay rested and relaxed. It promises to be a smooth onward journey all the way up to the north. But promises can easily be broken.

'You flying?' my dad asked.

'No, Dad. Train. Change at Bombay.'

'Are you not stopping in Bombay, son? If you are you have to meet Joggi Saini.'

'No, Dad. I'm not stopping here. Can't do everything. I'm going straight up to Delhi. I've done Banglore. How many cities can I see?'

'OK.'

'Dad, quick question. When you left India, did you know who you were, or were you trying to find yourself?' No sooner had I asked the question than I knew the answer.

'I never understood this finding yourself nonsense. Maybe it's a cultural or generational difference. I always knew who I was. Finding myself was never a luxury I could afford.'

'OK. Sorry, Dad.'

'Now, have you told Manore Uncle you are coming to Delhi? I spoke to him yesterday and they are expecting you. Rovi will look after you.'

'I'll call them today. Everything else OK, Dad?'

'Yes. Fine. How's the cooking?' he asked.

'You know . . . ' I allowed my answer to tail off in a non-committal sort of a way.

'Son?'

'Yes, Dad?'

'When you come back . . . ' He paused.

'Yes?' I prompted.

'There are some documents to sign. Call me from Delhi.'

I hung up.

I've been to Delhi many times. When I was a boy, Delhi was the gateway to north India. To get to Ferozepure we had to fly into the capital. Delhi was also the last Indian city my dad lived in. His wanderlust was nascent even when he was a young man. The vista of Ferozepure was never going to be enough to satisfy him, much as he loved the place of his birth. He was bound to seek his fortune elsewhere. My father as a man in his mid-twenties left his physical and spiritual home for a short placement in New Delhi; he planned to be there just for a few years. That was more than forty years ago.

He ended up never returning home. Home. This echoes with my own life. I too left Glasgow – my home – at the tender age of twenty-two. My plan was to leave for three months. That was in 1992 and I have never returned there to live.

Delhi to me is a strong and shining beacon from my childhood. I remember with astonishing vividness the fun that my dad always seemed to have whenever we were there. He would be relaxed and smiling, even though we were always in transit to another place. He knew the city intimately, despite the changes it had gone through since he'd lived there. He very much loved Delhi. We would venture out on a Vespa, hugging him tightly for dear life; such journeys were probably memorable for those very hugs, stolen from a loving but non-tactile father. Delhi felt like my dad's city and because I loved my dad, admired him, I too wanted Delhi to be my city; I wanted to be just like my dad.

The thought occurred to me as I prepared myself for the last few stops on my journey that my emotional energy was increasing. Maybe this entire journey I was undertaking was actually about me and my dad. Maybe, in launching myself on this quest of self-discovery, all I really wished for was my father's approval. After all, he sprang to life when I had suggested the possibility of such a madcap escapade. And although he expressed his reservations, as only he could, about my desire to share British food with the Indians, he was nonetheless supportive of my endeavours. Wouldn't it be the sweetest of ironies if I was going halfway around the world and enduring thousands of miles of travel around the Indian subcontinent in order that I might seek the approval and blessing of a 74-year-old man in the West End of Glasgow? Maybe this whole trip was about the big fella . . .

Twenty-one colours of turbans I have seen my dad wear

Lime Green
Sky Blue
Burnt Orange
Sunset Pink
Soft Peach
Mint Green
Chocolate Brown
Rose White
Midnight Blue
Deep Purple
Verdant Green
Shocking Pink
Electric Yellow
Dried Earth
Tonic Grey
Soft Heather
Strawberry Red
Unripe Satsuma
Military Khaki
Storm Grey
Lemon Curd

My father was a customs officer at New Delhi airport. He planned to spend only a short period there, enjoying the metropolitan buzz of city life while he surveyed his options. He ended up making a home for himself and living a bachelor lifestyle. His best friend, Manore Kapoor, had settled there with his wife, so my dad was as happy as he could possibly be.

Manore Uncle's wife, Kapoor Aunty as we affectionately call her, was a legend in the kitchen, even in the sixties. My dad had the best of both worlds: all the fun of bachelordom with great home-cooked food from his best friend's wife.

I think in many ways Delhi was the making of my father. He was a small-town boy with aspirations. Delhi gave him a flavour of a life less ordinary. It nurtured his aspirations. It was the start of a journey he has yet to complete. And how poignant for me that I am on an as yet incomplete journey and I find myself in New Delhi. As I arrive in the city I think back to the beach in Goa, to my moment of clarity when I realised that I would have to give myself to India rather than hope that India had anything to give me. As you know, I have visited India many times, for many reasons, but never have I travelled here seeking knowledge through the prism of myself. That is what is making this journey so significant and so daunting.

I feel I should be learning about myself, I should be acquiring new information about who I am and why I am here. The problem is that stepping off the plane in Kovalam all those weeks ago was an entirely different man. Now I'm in a city I have known for most of my life and I feel like I barely know who I am; this quest has changed me. I am sure of very little, except that the notion of Indianness for me is utterly meaningless. I am not Indian; not in the slightest. Did I feel Indian in Kovalam or Goa or Mysore? I felt Scottish, British and Punjabi. Here, almost in New Delhi, I feel Punjabi. I am a Punjabi Sikh Glaswegian who also feels some empathy with being British. That's how I feel today, on my way to New Delhi.

I have never arrived in Delhi before by train. There's a very good reason for that. The train journey from Bombay to Delhi is listed as lasting twenty-nine hours but they could pick any prime number and that would also be believable. The number bears no resemblance to the actual journey time. I find myself in carriage A at Bombay station. Now, I thought Madras station was swollen with humanity; Bombay station makes Madras look like Chipping Campden mid-morning on a wet Wednesday. It is as if all of India and their extended families from overseas have decided to descend upon the city at the same time. The concept of personal space is constantly being questioned. On the way from the taxi to the concourse, I am simultaneously touched in seven different places by six different people.

You would think it relatively straightforward to hop on a train between the two of the biggest Indian cities, but logic doesn't always apply to India. There are four trains leaving this station for Delhi in the next four hours. I'm not altogether sure which one I'm meant to be on. All I know is I'm in coach A of one of them. As I've become so accustomed to doing, I take a small census of opinion from those on the platform and then from those in the carriage of the most likely-looking train. It seems as if the Indian mail train that leaves Bombay at 16:43 is the train I'm destined to be on.

Destiny is a word with thousands of new connotations in India. Was I predestined to be on this train? If it's the wrong train and I was predestined to be on it, was I predestined to realise I was on the wrong train? Or, was I predestined to be on the wrong train and not realise I was on the wrong train and, so predestined to travel on the wrong train? But what of that predestiny, if it has placed me on the wrong train and not alerted me to this fact? Yet I still find myself arriving at the same city I would have arrived at had I been on the train I was predestined to be on. I'm not sure I understand any of this, either.

Coach A it is. I happily place myself in the hands of destiny. I am in many ways destiny's child; I'm a survivor. In a strange way, the length of this journey doesn't scare me. There's almost something biorhythmic about a journey of this length; something magical about the way one's body starts to move with the motion of the train, becoming one with the steel, the wood and the glass of the locomotive. There is comfort in the length of the journey, an inherent sense of preemptive accomplishment. There is the ebb, there is the flow, there are the peaks, there are the troughs, there is the ying, there is the yang. And then, there's the diarrhoea.

And what diarrhoea. In the world of needles, there are a multitude of sizes, shapes and styles. Jesus once spoke of the difficulty of a rich man gaining entry into the kingdom of heaven being on a par with the ease at which a camel could slip through the eye of a needle. Imagine, if you will, the smallest needle with the smallest eye. Fix that image clearly in your mind. It is easier to slip a camel through the eye of that needle than it is for me to stop shitting through it.

I didn't even get an hour or so's honeymoon period before the liquidity in my bowels made itself known. And when I say it made itself known, it was a bang rather than a whimper. No sooner had we left the station than I'd left my seat; and the contents of my guts left my body. (At least I thought it was the contents of my guts; I'm a big man but even I was astonished at the ability of the human body to produce liquid excrement with such regularity, such immediacy and with such pain. Such deep, deep pain.)

I thought the best thing to do upon evacuating my bowels for the fifth time was to seek some solace in slumber. It is amazing what happens to the human body when assailed by what we can euphemistically call 'internal difficulties'. There's a reason why you very, very rarely defecate in your sleep. Your body will not allow it. Therefore you endure the shallowest of sleeps, a sleep that is essentially not sleep at all, but rather what we in Scotland call a *dwam*; a zombie-like state that exists somewhere between a sense of full wakefulness and a vague feeling of sleeping. It's the worst of both worlds and extending that into a third dimension is the gurgling promise, nay threat, of a belly you thought you had emptied for the last time somehow filling itself up again with liquid drawn from the four corners of your already battered and bruised body. I think it is clear that I wasn't having the best of times.

Contradictory though it seems, although your body keeps spewing out more liquid than it could possibly have absorbed, you need to replace your fluids. I know this thanks to Rajiv Sinha.

Smoking cigarettes is absolutely the biggest crime in the Sikh religion. You can harm small animals, beat your children and embezzle funds from the *gurdwara* committee and still maintain some degree of respect within the community. If however you were to light a cigarette, not only would you be burning tobacco, you would also be setting light to any prayer, any hope or any chance of not being completely and utterly ostracised by the wider family of Sikhs. Smoking is forbidden within the scriptures of the religion; it is outlawed; it is forbidden. Sikhs hate smoking. I feel my point has been made.

When I was thirteen years old, I smoked. I was a rebellious and foolish teenager. (This will be the first time my parents will know about my smoking; I suspect my mother had her suspicions, but this is as confessional as it gets). I smoked, and I was wrong to smoke. I was a fat Sikh boy at a Catholic school; I had no friends and wanted to do all I could to ingratiate myself with anyone who would stop for a moment and allow me to be ingratiating. You have to understand that the eighties was all about the hair and as a kid with a turban I was always going to suffer. This is all about my childhood struggle for identity. I had no idea who I was when I was growing up in Glasgow. There were no role models for fat Sikh kids. No pop stars, footballers or actors that looked like me. All the people I could relate to were of an older generation; they weren't British-born Scots. I was clutching at straws in an attempt to work out who I was.

But that wasn't the sole reason for my dalliance with fags. I smoked because I thought it made me cool. It also meant I had things that people wanted, namely cigarettes. They would have to be nice to me if they wanted me to give them a cigarette and so I had instant friends. Smoking was my own private foolishness and I thought I was the only one who would suffer the consequences of my low-to-middle tar actions.

For some unknown reason, Rajiv Sinha took it upon himself to police my life. And his intervention led to my elder, stronger and draconian brother, Raj, laying into me. Raj managed to use the Sinha boy's information to lever all sorts of 'favours' out of me, an abuse of privilege he spun out for many years.

To this day, I honestly and sincerely have no idea why he did it. But whilst many in Glasgow will have forgotten the miners' strike, the assassination of Indira Gandhi and the second goal Holland scored against Scotland at the 1978 World Cup that put us out on goal difference, they will still remember Rajiv Sinha and his unwarranted sharing of information.

There is another point about the Sinhas that merits a digression. During our friendship Meatloaf released his debut album, the multi-platinum, rock-iconic *Bat Out of Hell*. No teenage Glaswegian boy's house was complete without a copy of the album, each boy having his favourite track. John-Paul Glenday played his audio cassette version so often, he actually managed to erase the entire recording. But the anthem that united us as an army of conceptual rock-album lovers was the title track itself. In the context of my life, the Judo-Christian notion of a mammal like a bat exiting the fire and brimstone of hell was secondary to the fact that Meatloaf sung: 'like a sinner [Sinha] before the gates of heaven, I'll come crawling on back to you'. Therefore, whilst others interpret the anthem as being about redemption and the concept of a life beyond the temporal, I just imagine Aloke Sinha, Rajiv's brother and my great friend, before the gates of heaven on a silver Black Phantom bike.

My enmity with Rajiv developed over the years. We would sneer at each other, but I'd yet to find a way of exacting the correct calibre of revenge upon his Bollywood-loving body. In the words of John Milton, 'They also serve, who only stand and wait.' I stood. I waited. I was served.

When Rajiv was sixteen he ended up in hospital in Glasgow, seriously dehydrated after a mild bout of diarrhoea turned into a form of dysentery based on the fact that he refused to drink any liquids, thinking the liquids were causing his diarrhoea. Fuckwit.

It wasn't even as if his system had been assailed by foreign bodies. He was at home in Bishopbriggs. From that day on, I've always been aware of the need to replace lost fluids during an unforgiving attack. And on this train on this journey at this time I suddenly feel perhaps my vehemence towards Rajiv has been somewhat misplaced all these years. I should never have wished ill upon him; perhaps he would never have had diarrhoea, perhaps he would never have ended up with a mild form of dysentery, perhaps we would still be friends today and perhaps I wouldn't be feeling moments from death. Perhaps.

I find myself between a rock and a hard place. For some reason there seems to be very little water for sale on the train, but there seem to be a lot of tea and coffee vendors. You may know the effect hot liquids like tea and coffee have on the bowel; the last thing my oversized Glaswegian Sikh bowels need is any further encouragement. That is my rock. My hard place is the fact that I can physically feel myself dehydrating; I have no choice. I drink a cup of tea or coffee, coffee or tea, from every vendor that passes by. By some fluke of Indian Railways bureaucracy, not only is my berth the bottom berth, thereby giving me easy access up and out without contorting my anal cavity in a way that may encourage rogue slippage, my seat is also almost adjacent to the toilet. From a prone position, I can be moaning, bent double on the western-style (!) toilet in less than eighteen seconds.

Most of the rest of the journey is a blur of tea, coffee and lavatory visits. I feel my body weight halve as night becomes morning, morning melds into afternoon and afternoon metamorphoses into the next evening. If I'm honest, I'm not altogether clear quite how I'm going to make it through the journey. But I do. I think we sometimes take for granted the resilience of our minds, the resilience of our bodies and the resilience of good quality Calvin Klein underwear. As the train pulls up in New Delhi station it is as if the entire experience has been a personal test visited upon my being; I start to feel better, almost instantly. Perhaps it's because I know Rovi is waiting for me and I know he is taking me home.

Rovi meets me at the station. Who, you are wondering, is Rovi? Rovi is Wovi's brother. Rovi and Wovi. Wovi and Rovi, sons of Manore Kapoor, my dad's best friend from college.

Whenever we came to Delhi we stayed with the Kapoors. Our first visit to them was in 1979. I remember it vividly because my dad had taken us three out for a drive and when we came home we saw Rovi and Wovi going through our suitcases. It was highly amusing to catch them red-handed rifling through our belongings. Highly amusing for us, if not for them. They knew they had been rumbled; they knew they were alibi- and explanation-free. We stood and watched as they replaced everything silently and left the room.

That trip was also the time I got to sample one of the delights of north Indian cooking. I was about ten years old and had just woken from a jetlag-induced slumber; my father was sitting at the table with the Kapoors tucking into what looked and smelled like a sumptuous lunch.

'Come here, son.' My father beckoned me over. I remember at the time there being smiles exchanged but hadn't quite registered that they were at my expense.

'Try this.' He offered me a laden spoonful from a dish of curry that lay in front of him.

'What is it, Dad?' I was young; I was newly awake; I was hungry. I wasn't refusing to eat it. I just wanted some idea of what I was about to eat.

'*Kalaa* . . .' he said, his loving use of Punjabi encouraging me to eat.

'OK.' He was my dad. I trusted him.

I guided a spoonful of the diced white substance, smothered in a rich brown sauce into my mouth. It felt a little strange but not altogether disgusting. But I distinctly remember registering the experience of a brand new texture in my mouth.

They all started laughing. Clearly I was missing a crucial piece of this cuisinal jigsaw.

'Do you know what it is?' asked my father, fighting back the tears.

I shook my head.

'Goat's brain curry,' he said. 'It'll make you clever!' he continued.

'Goat's brain curry,' he repeated through tears of laughter.

I stood there chewing as they all laughed at the goat-brain-eating fat boy from Glasgow.

'Clever like a goat?' I asked, not previously aware that goats had been particularly celebrated in the animal kingdom for their searing wit and intelligence. This made them laugh even more. It was at this point in my life that I realised there was something of the accidental entertainer within me.

On the table beside the goat brain curry was a dish that I would walk over broken glass merely to inhale its aroma. It's another north Indian speciality and in all my life I have never found a better version of this dish than Rovi's mum's; in many ways it's worth the airfare to Delhi alone. We call it *bartha*; it might better be described to the non-Punjabi speaker as smoked aubergine curry. And it is truly, truly sublime. It is similar in preparation to babaganoush, the dish I prepared for Jeremy the yoga freak and his Svengali, Suresh, in Mysore. The aubergine is placed directly on the flame until the skin is charred black. The masala cooks simultaneously in a pot. Onions, cumin, chillies, tomatoes, turmeric and garlic sizzle away slowly until they form the spicy brown paste to which the de-skinned, mashed aubergine flesh is added and further cooked. Peas are often introduced to create a smoky, spicy, slightly sweet dish of perplexing deliciousness.

It had been my plan since I left London to ask Rovi's mum to make *bartha* for me; I hadn't tasted her *bartha* since that day in 1979 and had dreamt about it ever since.

I had asked Rovi to book me in to a wee, unassuming neighbourhood hotel. Delhi is full of them. As we pull up to the Crossroads Hotel I know that I'm in the right place. It's a sweet little place just off the main road, near the new Delhi Metro, a train system that seems to have revolutionised the city. The reception of Crossroads smells like any mid-rate Indian hotel should smell: of sandalwood and man sweat. The place is a homage to marble and velour and there seem to be flat screen plasma TVs everywhere, as well as shrines to various Hindu deities. Modern India in a nutshell. (Probably a betel nutshell.)

I check in thinking this will be the end of the night. I am wrong. It's late but Rovi wants to take me on a midnight tour of the old city, a place called Jama Masjid in the Muslim quarter of Old Delhi. I can't say that I am that keen to travel around, given my nightmare journey with diarrhoea. Decent public toilets are not something one can ever bank on anywhere in India, not even in the capital city. But Rovi is a difficult guy to say no to.

Soon we find ourselves travelling though the Old City. It was built in Moghul times, a walled fortress of a place. The city was accessed via a number of gates, gates which are now themselves fenced off and protected as items of architectural interest. The walls have long since fallen but the demarcation between the bright, shiny, broad boulevards of New Delhi and the dark, dank alleyways, nooks and crannies of Old Delhi couldn't be more apparent.

We pass the majestic Red Fort, the Moghul emperor's seat from which the Chandni Chowk stretches out, the main market street of the Old City. We drive through the crowded streets, peopled almost exclusively by men. Each area contains a different market. There is a book market, a textile market and a vegetable market outside which stand trucks overladen with cauliflowers. Rovi is keen to take me to a place called Paratha ki Gully, the alley of parathas. For the uninitiated a paratha is a delicious flaky bread indigenous to the north of India. It is made with flour and water and the dough is enriched with ghee or butter making the deliciously flaky bread a meal in itself. It can be served simply with yoghurt and pickles, or the paratha can be stuffed with any number of delicious fillings: potato, minced lamb, paneer, cauliflower, fenugreek, white radish, even egg. In the Punjab it is the staple breakfast dish, which probably explains why the life expectancy of Sikhs is lower than any other ethnic Indian grouping!

Paratha ki Gully is still vibrant after midnight. The alleyway itself is no wider than a couple of metres and there are stalls or shops lining the side of the road. This is a side of India kept only for the Indians. The businesses are closed but preparations are being made for the next day. A man absent-mindedly counts potatoes; two men sit cross-legged gossiping and laughing as they chop pumpkins; steel dishes clatter and clank as boys wash and clean them after another day's cooking; a couple of men eye us suspiciously as they eat their daal and chapatti dinner.

We wander further down, our alley meeting another alley. Rovi explains that these alleys spider their way into the heart of the Old City, twisting and turning, tributaries of life. Two small boys, no older than seven, are earnestly scraping the bottom of a *halwa* pan. *Halwa* is a dessert traditionally made in these parts of carrot, ghee and your body weight in sugar. The rim of the pan is wider than the boys are tall.

It is curious to consider how, as much as Indian food has been taken to the very heart of British life, it is only the savoury dishes that have actually succeeded there. Indians have a very sweet tooth and we are renowned for our love of sweetmeats and puddings, but these are joys yet to be fully appreciated by the western palate . . . and dentist.

ᱬᱬ

Seven Indian sweets that are delicious

Gulab Jaman: A dumpling made from dough that is the result of thickened condensed milk. Lest the thickened sweetened milk be too healthy, these balls of saccharine delight are then deep fried until they turn golden brown on the outside, maintaining a delicious spongy white texture within. For good measure the round roses (a literal translation of *gulab jaman*) are doused in sugar syrup. They are absolutely delicious hot or cold.

Ras Gula: This can be colloquially described as an Indian milk ball. Much as that is factually correct, it barely begins to tell the story of this sweet treat. These little beauties are the by-product of milk that has been split, much in the same way as paneer is made. The solid part of the split milk is kept and blended with cardamom before being rolled again into the ball shape. Meanwhile a pan of water is put onto boil and an excessive amount of sugar is added. The balls are then carefully added to the boiling syrup where they gently cook. The *ras gulas* are then left to cool and are served with a healthy spoonful of the cooled sugar syrup. Delicious, if a little cloyingly sweet.

Ras Malai: A variation on *ras gula*. *Ras malai* requires the split milk not to be crafted into a spherical offering. Rather the milk solids are more slab-like in their consistency and are drenched in milk that has been flavoured with pistachio nuts and/or almonds and/or cardamom. A personal favourite of mine. Less sweet than either *gulab jaman* or *ras gula*.

Jalebi: A deep-fried flour-based sweet. The *jalebi* looks a little like a pretzel and is definitively north Indian, with links with

Persian food history. They are normally a vibrant orange colour and very sweet. They too are served with a sugary syrup but in the Punjab they are often served with milk. They are sticky, sweet and lovely.

Barfi: Yet another condensed milk dessert. Rather than eaten after a meal, *barfi* is a snack enjoyed with tea. There are as many flavours of *barfi* as there are flavours at all. Almond, pistachio, saffron, rose water, even chocolate *barfi*. They are normally bite-sized and served in squares, parallelograms or occasionally rhombuses. These sweets go some way to explain the love Indians have for geometry.

Kulfi: Regarded as Indian ice cream, but in truth it is frozen milk. Unlike ice cream *kulfi* is not churned and therefore is dense and complex rather than aerated and light.

Falooda: This is dedicated to the colour pink and perhaps explains my own love of the colour. A rose-water-flavoured milk is enhanced with sweet vermicelli strands, basil seeds and ice cream. Like *jalebi*, *falooda* has strong links with Persia and was more than likely inspired by the Moghul invaders.

Rovi and I venture deeper into the dark city. It feels a little like Harry Potter's Diagon Alley; strange characters lurk in shadowy corners, unfamiliar noises can be heard behind every wall and there is the smell of soured milk (maybe that wasn't in J.K. Rowling's books . . .). We have left Paratha ki Gully far behind and are now wandering towards Chandni Chowk. There is a famous old restaurant that started here back in the early part of the last century. Karim's is regarded by Delhites as the best example of Moghul food anywhere to be found in India. We turn another corner and the road has become smoother and cleaner. We have found it. A placard outside tells me that Karim's was started in 1913 by Hafiz Karim Uddin. It was initially just a *tawa* off Kababian Street. A *tawa* is a flat steel skillet. It comes in a variety of sizes and has a multiplicity of uses in the north Indian house. Chapattis and parathas are cooked on it, small snacks are shallow fried on it, even chicken and lamb can be fried on it. The story suggests that the original Karims was an al fresco cooking experience nearly a century ago.

Rovi insists that we stop and have a small snack. My heart and my head would love to, but my stomach has other plans.

'Not a great idea,' I explain to Rovi, patting my distended belly.

'You're in Delhi, you have a bad belly. Delhi belly!' He laughs. I can't help joining in.

We wander back to the car, enjoying the scene in reverse. Outside one stall a dozen or so men sit on the ground, their hands stretched outward in supplication. Rovi explains that these wretched souls are waiting for someone to bestow a little charity on them. They are hoping that some rich individual might offer the stall holder the price of a meal on their behalf. Begging for food is more likely to meet with success than begging for money. At least the donor has some comfort in knowing that their contribution has been put to good use. I ask that price. Twenty rupees will feed a single man. About thirty pence. I feel physically sick. I think about how much I myself eat, and waste, the money I squander on half-eaten sandwiches and tepid cappuccinos. I leave enough money to feed twenty men but can't bear to watch.

Driving around the city at night the traffic is blissfully unaware of the late hour. Delhi is a daunting city, constantly changing. One moment your horizon is wide, filled with tree-lined boulevards and colonial architecture. A couple of left turns later you are in the midst of a medieval town, the imposing buildings blocking the moonlit sky. Urban India never sleeps, but Delhi seems to be urban India on espresso. It has the constant buzz of a city that is constant. Rovi tells me that I was lucky to miss Diwali last year; the traffic was unbearable. People left their cars and walked, carrying gifts for their families to celebrate Hindu New Year.

'It was madness. Unbelievable madness. It took four hours to travel a few kilometres. Everyone was in their car taking presents everywhere.'

Rovi tells me that as a result of India's newfound affluence, people have more money to spend. So when it comes to festivals like Diwali, the Hindu Festival of Light which is commonly regarded as their New Year, families decide to shower gifts on each other in a way that seems to embrace the free market more than the cleansing quality of light. This seems a far cry from the Delhi of my dad's day. Even when I first came to Delhi as a boy you couldn't get any products that weren't made in India. It's difficult to believe now but the only cola drinks you could buy were Indian-owned brands like Thums [sic] Up or Campa Cola. Now India is the bastard child of globalisation: there isn't anything you can't get here. It's midnight and we are stuck in a traffic jam.

'This is the other side of the economic boom,' Rovi mutters, as irritated as his lovely nature will allow him to get. Of all the consequences of a burgeoning economy very bad traffic is not one I would have ever thought of. Rovi never seems to tire of fetching and carrying and bringing and delivering; for him to complain about traffic things must be bad.

'Thank God for the metro.'

Delhi is India's only city to have a subway system and it has been a massive success. Hundreds of thousands of Indians travel to and fro on a daily basis. The sweeping streets of the suburbs are smoothly and efficiently linked to the stone-built edifices of the bureaucratic heart of India. Journey times have been slashed. The train stations and the trains themselves are clean and reliable; two words not readily associated with all things Indian. The mind boggles as to what the state of the roads would be if Delhi didn't have such an effectively elegant underground system. Delhi feels like another future for India, a future in which Bangalore is already playing a part. Between them it seems as if India will be more than capable of dealing with the unfolding century and the millennium ahead. But I am in Delhi to cook and hopefully also to find myself.

My plan is simple. It's a massive place; there is no way I can find a single group of people to cook for that is at all representative of the entire city. Unlike Bombay with its world-renowned association with the movie business, Delhi has everything. Everything and politics. I don't fancy cooking for politicians, so the next best thing might be to cook a small dinner party for a bunch of Delhi socialites. Delhi is full of old-money Indians; the city teems with the bolder and more beautiful children of the bold and beautiful and it would be fun to meet them. I have a contact from London, a lady with a great name: Lucky.

And what better to cook than soup? A lovely, traditional Scottish soup. Ever since I bottled it in Kovalam and failed to cook stovies, I have been rather remiss in preparing the food of Britain. What the Delhites need is cock-a-leekie soup. The soft, buttery leeks combining with those that still have some give all melded together in that lovely chicken broth. Everyone knows that any good soup is made better when allowed to sit for a few hours, preferably overnight. A lady called Clara taught me this.

When I was at university in Glasgow, there was only one place to go and eat, the Grosvenor Café. To say the Grosvenor was a café is like saying Jimi Hendrix was a man who played the guitar; it barely begins to tell the story. The Grosvenor was an institution, a sanctuary, a way of life. I grew up in the Grosvenor, I lived in the Grosvenor, I loved in the Grosvenor but mostly I ate in the Grosvenor. When my wife was my girlfriend, we spent afternoons drinking coffee and chatting. So frequent a visitor was I that in the days before mobile phones, people would phone me at the Grosvenor.

The Grosvenor was run by an Italian family. The patriarch Renato, his wife Liliana and his sister Clara. There was something called the Grosvenor five-pound challenge. So cheap was the food at the Grosvenor that we students reckoned it was impossible for even the hungriest of us to eat £5 worth of Grosvenor food. To put this into some sort of perspective, back in the eighties when the fashion was terrible and the hair was big, to spend £5 on food at the Grosvenor meant the consumption of an egg burger (a beef burger with an egg), a croissant filled with tuna mayonnaise, two fried egg rolls, apple pie and ice cream and a thing called a ben loars (I don't really know what a ben loars was but it was named after a small Scottish mountain, that's how big it was). If you managed to scoff that much carbohydrate, it would cost you eight pence over £5. (I'm not sure I've eaten that much food in a day, let alone a single sitting, not even during my Sadhya meal extravaganza in Kovalam.) Not meaning to be boastful, I did hold the record for my time at university when it came to the Grosvenor challenge. I bet you didn't realise you were reading the story of a man who achieved the high £3.80s early in the winter of 1988. I was a ben loars and an egg roll short of the status of legend.

I would walk by the Grosvenor three or four times a day between lectures and I remember distinctly one day the most entrancing of aromas emanating from the tiny kitchen. It could only be one thing: Clara's minestrone soup. Now, I know it was Glasgow and I know it was the 1980s, not perhaps a city or a time redolent of gastronomy, but the Scottish Italian community had been alive and kicking for decades at that point and we were very grateful to them for the food they brought. Chief amongst objects of gratitude was Clara's minestrone soup. It was bloody delicious. And it came with a roll and butter. I've eaten at multi-Michelin-starred restaurants, I've eaten with royalty and ambassadors, but there are few things finer than Clara's minestrone soup with a roll and butter.

Naturally, upon smelling the minestrone soup, I decided to miss the next lecture and have a bowl of this fine Italian broth. I ordered a bowl. I was salivating at the mere thought of the pasta, tomato and bean concoction. The waitress returned to my table to tell me that there was no minestrone soup. At the same time I saw a bowl of minestrone soup being delivered to the table next to me. Well, you can understand my confusion. I pointed to the adjoining table and told the waitress that their bowl of soup looked deceptively like minestrone. The waitress told me that Clara said I couldn't have a bowl of minestrone soup. I was hurt. Deeply, deeply hurt. Clara came over. 'What's wrong?' I asked. 'Do I not get any minestrone soup?'

'No,' she said, 'you can have the minestrone soup tomorrow, you can't have it today.'

'But you've given it to them,' I protested insolently.

She leaned in and I'll never forget what she said: 'They can have soup today, it was made today, but you, you are special, you can only have the soup tomorrow. It's better tomorrow.'

And do you know what? I *did* feel special. From that day on, I always had soup the day after it was made and it always tasted so much better.

Soup is a rural Scottish staple and I intend to cook it in the heart of an Indian metropolis. It is a beautiful juxtaposition. I should tell Lucky. I dial her number.

'Hi, Lucky. It's Hardeep here.'

'Hi!' Her voice crackles with life. 'How are you?'

'I'm good. Just got into town. I was hoping to come and cook for you guys tomorrow.' I am intentionally vague about who she might invite.

'What are you cooking? Something exciting, I hope. I'm a bit of a cook myself.'

I feel more than a little pressure.

'I have all of Gordon Ramsay's books, you know.'

Of course she does.

'So what will you be rustling up? I love all British food, apart from soup. I hate soup.'

'I'd never cook soup in India,' I say and then laugh just a little too hard. 'How do you feel about shepherd's pie?'

'I love shepherd's pie.' She sounds genuinely happy.

'Great!' I say, still trying to work out why I have bottled it. Again.

⟡

My father's words are yet again ringing in my ears.

'Son, if British food was all that good, then there would be no Indian restaurants in Britain . . .'

I'm feeling vulnerable right now. In Delhi, with all the memories of my childhood, of my dad, I can't help but feel more than a little foolish. Why am I cooking shepherd's pie for a bunch of cosmopolitan Indian glitterati who have no doubt eaten at the finest restaurants across a handful of continents? Why on earth would they want to eat my shepherd's pie?

I try to remind myself that this journey is not actually about the food. The food is a mechanism to unlock doors to people who might be able to shed some light on who I am. Why would a bunch of Indian socialites come out for an evening's Indian food? Where is the fun in that? The shepherd's pie is the quirky enticement, the edge to the evening. I can't imagine they have ever been invited out for meat pie before. There's probably a good reason why . . .

These socialites are my contemporaries. They are who I might have been had I been born in India and raised here. They are all better looking and eminently more successful than me but they should prove to be an invaluable touchstone to my own sense of self. How similar are these upper-middle class Indians to this middle-class me? I will endeavour to find out through the gift of shepherd's pie.

Where do you begin with shepherd's pie? It's all about the meat. For my money, there's only one type of meat for shepherd's pie and that's lamb. I've arranged to meet Lucky at INA market in the centre of New Delhi. This is widely regarded as the most upmarket of all the markets the city has to offer; it's where all the foreigners shop. And as soon as you enter you understand why. The place is a temple to imported goods and produce: tahini paste, pastas, pak choi, fresh herbs, even rocket; this is clearly a place designed for European cuisine and is wholly unIndian. Apart from the imported products, most of the market seems to offer seafood. I don't think I've ever seen such amazing king prawns in all my life, some as big as my hand (and I have substantial hands). Beautiful-looking catfish, delicious tilapia, sizeable sea bass, pomfret, lobster and squid. This couldn't be less like the market in Goa. The range of produce here is mind-boggling and perhaps more reflective of the fact that Delhi has long been the home to international politicians and business people. Whereas in Goa I struggled to find potatoes, in INA market I can get hold of two types of anchovy paste and a tin of artichoke hearts. Impressive.

As we walk through this undersea world I can see the meat section ahead. On a raised area two men sit, one with chickens dangling dead and upside down above his head. He plays nonchalantly with a knife as he awaits his next customer. I shall not be bothering him today. My attentions are with the other man who sits cross-legged surrounded by mutton. I manage to get a decent-looking leg of lamb, leaving two sorrier-looking specimens hanging in the otherwise bare room. A tray of offal lies lazily in front of the wooden chopping block.

The picture is a bit like the early work of David Lynch, with hanging carcasses and blood everywhere. Or perhaps that's more Peter Greenaway. I order two kilos of lamb leg and instruct the butcher to cut the lamb into cubes. He is accustomed to cutting lamb into cubes for Indian curries, but they are too big for my needs. But I decide against entering into a dialogue with him; in this instance, size really doesn't matter. (I know many of you will be expecting mince in shepherd's pie; I, however, am a firm believer of nugget-sized mouthfuls of lamb. The texture of minced lamb is less interesting than the variegated chunks of gravy-covered delight that, to my mind, makes the finest shepherd's pie.)

Now, I have bought meat in three continents on dozens of occasions. I have visited Tokyo butchers and witnessed their art and craft; the meat men of Peru displayed their skills to me, and Khalid at KRK on Woodlands Road in Glasgow is no stranger to me, but in all my travels in all my time I have never seen a man prepare meat the way the butcher at INA market prepares it. Never. He sits cross-legged with the knife lodged firmly between his big and second toe, the sharp edge pointing away from him. The blade is held strong, unmoving, as he pulls the mutton towards him. He is like the human version of a meat-cutting machine in a delicatessen, the sort that shaves slivers of parma ham. The blade does not move as he dextrously cubes my leg of lamb using his two free hands. There's something fundamentally wrong about a man cutting red meat using his feet.

Having purchased some carrots and potatoes and a bag of frozen peas (which seems utterly incongruous in India), Lucky and I head back to her apartment. Lucky's apartment is nothing short of breathtaking. She left London a year ago having lived and loved the city for the best part of a decade. After reading history and English at Oxford she joined the world of publishing. She misses London but what's to miss? She has a massive three-bedroom apartment with a terrace that itself is the size of a two-bedroom flat in Pimlico, and it is on this terrace we will dine this evening.

Fresh from the memory of the foot-chopping butcher, I wash the lamb more thoroughly than normal. (Although, he did have surprisingly clean feet, considering.) While the potatoes come to the boil in plenty of salted water, I concentrate on sorting the lamb out. Ordinarily when I'm cooking lamb curry there is nothing finer than marrowbone and cartilage mixed in with the meat. This adds another depth of flavour, another flesh experience to enjoy and devour. Perhaps the acceptability of bones in Indian food is linked to the way in which we eat.

We pick up food with our fingers, so we are more able to select flesh from bone. Perhaps that's why bones seem to work so readily in that form. However, a big bit of bone and marrow in a shepherd's pie would be an altogether different experience and not a terribly pleasant one. I therefore remove the bones, some cartilage but not all the fat; the fat gives great flavour to shepherd's pie. I then chop the pieces down further still and fry them in a little olive oil, having tossed them in some seasoned flour.

I'm well aware of the fact that pretty much any cuisine in the world will taste bland in comparison to Indian food. So, in the interests of self-preservation, I throw in a couple of green chillies. What did you expect? The lamb is sealed after which I add salt and pepper and a glass and a half of a 2003 Pinotage. (I am aware of how pretentious that just sounded.) Having reduced the liquor by half, I add two really good dashes of Worcester sauce, some diced red peppers and a good handful of chopped mint. Strictly speaking, peppers and mint don't belong in shepherd's pie, but if you break shepherd's pie down to its constituent parts, it's basically meat and potatoes with a bit of sauce. The glitterati of young Delhi society have been asked to come round for dinner. I can't just give them meat and potatoes and some sauce.

The lamb is turned out into a casserole dish and allowed to cool. This, my friends, is possibly the most crucial point in the preparation of shepherd's pie. Trust me. If you do not allow the lamb mixture to cool and dive straight in with your butter-soft mashed potato top, the mashed potato will sink into the hot lamb, thereby rendering the separation of parts useless. Who wants lamby potatoes on top of potatoey lamb? The interface between the lamb and the potatoes is what makes the shepherd's pie work, else we would just mix them altogether and put them in the oven, wouldn't we? Nothing is more crucial than this separation.

Actually, there is one thing that is more crucial than this separation; that might be having enough potatoes to actually cover the lamb.

So preoccupied was I with making sure the lamb was correctly salted, correctly sized and sufficiently spiced, I hadn't realised the paucity of potatoes I'd put on to boil. Embarrassingly it would appear I don't have nearly enough potatoes to create the pie-like crust that is the single component that elevates the pie of a shepherd into a higher realm of eating. It's at times like this I wish my mum were here. She would know exactly what to do. Somehow, using a hairpin, an old battery and a courgette, she would fashion a device that could puncture the space-time continuum and create instant mashed potato without a robot in sight. Instead, I face ignominy. It will be an incomplete mashed potato top. I check my watch; it's not too late to do a runner.

As I consider my options, the doorbell rings. It would appear I now only have the one option: dinner must be served.

With the top of my shepherd's pie looking like the later work of Pablo Picasso, I place it in the oven. In thirty minutes hopefully it won't look too much like a Jackson Pollock. I try to console myself with quality accoutrements. Boiled carrots in butter with pepper and mushrooms in a white wine and fresh coriander sauce, finished with butter; butter in everything. I now have time to kill. The guests have gathered on the beautiful candlelit terrace; the views over the city are sublime. We make the necessary small talk as vodka is sipped and beer is glugged. I can't begin to tell you how much I feel like I'm in the wrong place at the wrong time. I zone out of the conversation for a moment as the vodka works its magic and I spin thirty years back in my head to one of my earliest memories of Delhi at night . . .

If ever there was a story that epitomised my love and respect for my father, this is surely it; the story of Mr Muker. My dad's a very generous man and he always endeavours to visit family and extend gifts wherever possible. It transpired that in 1981 a cousin's cousin had found themselves in Delhi. We were visiting, too, so my father took it upon himself to visit this cousin's cousin, one Mr Muker. Of course, it would have been helpful if my father had had a phone number or an address or any details or clues about this Mr Muker. All my father knew was that Mr Muker worked for the government. In India, in the eighties, most people worked for the government; so this information barely narrowed our search. However, my father has never let a lack of information stand in the way of visiting family. He discovered a Mr Muker lived in an adjoining suburb to Manore Uncle. With presents under his arm (a dress for a five-year-old girl and a toy for a two-year-old boy) all six feet two inches of my father, sixteen stone of Manore Uncle and twelve-year-old me placed ourselves upon a 125 cc Bajaj scooter and took to the nocturnal streets of Delhi. We moved around the city like the wind; a slow, slightly lardy wind, and a not particularly comfortable wind, if the truth be told. But in less than an hour, we were knocking on the door of Mr Muker.

Now, there's something you need to know about Indian hospitality. In polite western society, you would never imagine pitching up at somebody's house at nine o'clock in the evening unannounced, uninvited, unexpected. The Indian way is the opposite: whoever turns up at your door, whenever they turn up at your door and whoever they may be with are to be welcomed, given a cup of tea at the least, (although whisky or rum would not be considered inappropriate) and would be fed

Indian sweetmeats if not offered a full-blown meal. This perhaps explains the eagerness with which the invading marauders of the British Empire were welcomed; I mean, if a nation is going to give you tea and sweetmeats, there's every chance they'll give you their mineral resources and man power, too.

We were ushered in by a rather surly servant. We sat in an empty drawing room, my father still clutching the presents excitedly. To say Mr Muker looked disgruntled would be an understatement. He looked really pissed off. Compared to his harridan of a wife, however, he was sweetness and light. Tea and sweetmeats came without beckoning and the conversation was a little stilted. In an attempt to break the ice, my father handed the presents over hoping to see a five-year-old girl and a two-year-old boy. The children of the house were somewhat older and of slightly different genders. There were two girls, one eight and one nine. The dress for the five-year-old girl may have stretched to fit the eight year old but the gift for a small boy would surely be lost on the elder daughter. However, it's the thought that counts, isn't it?

Obviously, Mr Muker required some context, some frame of reference for this unsolicited social scenario. My father started explaining who he was. The mention of the mutual cousin and the name Babbi fell on deaf ears. Mr Muker didn't have a cousin called Babbi. My dad asked whether Mr Muker worked for the Indian government. Not only did Mr Muker work for the Indian government, Mr Muker was the commissioner of traffic for New Delhi and surrounding areas; one of the most influential jobs in the whole of India's civil service. My dad expressed astonishment at how high Mr Muker had risen since leaving his home town of Faridkot only a few years ago. Mr Muker straightened his back, sat forward in his chair and said sternly that not only was he not from Faridkot, he had never *been* to Faridkot.

It soon transpired of course that we were in the wrong Mr Muker's house. Tea had been drunk and sweetmeats consumed, and most crucially gifts had been given. The wrong gifts to the wrong children. My father hoped that his laughter would be infectious. Never before had laughter been so uncontagious. We stood up, my father muttering apologies but saying how nice it was to have met Mr Muker anyway.

As we got to the door, my father said that at least now he would have no worries of troubles should he ever require the assistance of the commissioner of traffic for New Delhi. By the look on Mr Muker's face at that point, I reckoned the safest thing for my father to have done would have been never to have travelled in New Delhi again for fear of a personal vendetta against him.

We stepped over the threshold and the relief was almost palpable. As the door closed behind us, my father turned and asked Mr Muker if we could have the gifts back. Thankfully he duly obliged. After all, we still had to visit the real Mr Muker. I don't ever remember visiting the real Mr Muker. Perhaps we never did.

Tonight I feel like I felt all those years ago; an interloper bringing unsolicited gifts to the wrong people. They are just too polite to say anything. Yamina, who has studied social and political science at Cambridge, asks what's to be served for dinner.

'Shepherd's pie,' I blurt, hoping that the speed of my saying it will somehow disguise the nature of the dish.

'God, I hope it's better than the one we had at Cambridge.'

I was hoping that perhaps they'd had limited exposure to shepherd's pie. It's so much more difficult to be critical when you have no benchmark. It feels like it's going to be a long night.

Small talk becomes big talk and the evening degenerates into a heated debate about the political state of arts within India. I hope that people will drink themselves into a state of forgetfulness and there would be no need for me to serve dinner.

'I'm starving,' says Lucky, helpfully. I look at her and know I have to do the necessary.

As we eat the shepherd's pie there is talk of the resurgence of independent cinema in India and we continue vociferous exchanges about the westernisation of India. Lisa reaches down and takes a bottle of Tabasco out of her bag, placing it next to her empty plate.

'I always carry this with me. Everywhere. Even in fancy restaurants in Miami. This is the first time in ten years I haven't added Tabasco to a meal. I even forgot I had it with me . . .'

Yadesh, who has met Yamina at their time together at Cambridge, is not a fan of British food.

'I loved Britain, but really they have to sort out their food,' he says affectionately about the cuisine of my country of origin.

'I am British,' I say.

'You were born there. You are Indian really.' He tucks in to the next mouthful of food. 'They really do cook some bland English shit.'

It is clear from his implication that he isn't referring to my shepherd's pie as bland English shit.

'You don't mean my food, do you?' I tease playfully. 'Because my food would be described as bland Scottish shit.'

It is very strange, but at this very moment, as the laughter and the chat ring around my ears, I am overcome with a very simple and straightforward notion. As far as these Indians are concerned I'm not British; pure and simple. I have simply been born there. They have very little expectation of me in terms of understanding contemporary Indian life. They see me as the son of a man who was born in India. This is very confusing. I have spent the evening feeling very different to these people, to my Indian contemporaries. It is quite revealing for me to feel so very British, so very Scottish on the roof terrace of a third-floor apartment in a desirable neighbourhood in New Delhi, yet be regarded as completely Indian by these Indians. There is no point in arguing about it. This is their perception and I have to try and make some sense of it.

The next time I look up, all the plates are empty. But my heart feels full.

Later that evening I meet up with Rovi again. He takes me for a late-night kebab. This has become a bit of an institution between our families, a roadside kebab on every visit. We stand eating at the makeshift table enjoying the silence of men.

'Rovi,' I ask, mid-mouthful. 'Do you think of me as Indian or British?'

Rovi chews and ponders, ponders and chews.

'Hardeep,' he says sweetly, 'you are neither Indian nor British. You are just Hardeep.'

I think it's the best answer he could ever give.

VALLEY OF THE DALS

303 *things I counted in New Delhi Train Station*

A man in a wheelchair wearing a neck brace, in his pyjamas
and carrying a Zimmer frame.
A one-legged man carrying a newly boxed Tefal electric
steamer on his head.
A woman falling backwards out of a slowly moving train,
perhaps realising it was heading in the wrong destination. She
takes with her several fellow travellers who were more than
happy with their direction of travel.
Three hundred rats across ten metres of railway track (big fat
rats, as big as small cats, which is technically even bigger than
a kitten).

❧

From my Indian train experiences, I've learnt by now that there
seems to be some unwritten code, some unspoken convention
whereby at the appointed hour all the passengers in the
compartment stand up and start to prepare their beds for the
night. This is in no small part driven by the fact that if one person
is preparing their bunk it renders the rest of the compartment
useless to casual nut chewing and gossip. On the train from Delhi

225

to Jammu, I have luckily been booked on the lower bunk and unfurl my two white sheets and thick wool blanket.

Soon I am off to sleep, even before the carriage lights are extinguished. But it is a short-lived visit to the land they call nod, and after a couple of hours of blissful ignorance I am again in a state of wide-awake consciousness as the train rocks gently northward into the night.

Signs on the train from Delhi to Jammu

> HARASSING WOMEN PASSENGERS IS A PUNISHABLE OFFENCE

> Obscene remarks, teasing, touching, stares, gestures, songs and unwanted attention are all forms of sexual violence punishable by up to two years or a fine under section 354A, 509 and 294 of the Indian Penal Code.

> HELP THE RAILWAY SERVE YOU BETTER
> - Travel only with the proper ticket and show it to authorised personnel on demand
> - Secure your luggage with the rings/wire provided below the seats. Passengers themselves are responsible for security of their luggage
> - Please switch off fans and lights if not required
> - Please keep surroundings clean and do not spit in coach
> - Please do not use transistor or radio without earphone
> - Please secure doors and windows properly, particularly at night

PREVENT FIRE

Inside the compartment:

Do not throw lighted match stick

Do not carry explosives and dangerous goods

Do not carry inflammable articles like kerosene and petrol etc.

Do not light up a stove

Do not celebrate with fireworks

Help the Railways Reach You Safely

The interminable night eventually passes. I feel like the only man on the planet still awake. The train has started pulling into stations where a few passengers alight. The delay has caused an air of uncertainty in every quarter of every compartment in every carriage. There are no announcements and not all the signs in the stations are particularly clear. A young man, still half asleep, jumps from the third bunk, dervish-like collecting his belongings and simultaneously tucking in his shirt for fear that the train may depart with him still on it. I have no idea how late we are since I have no idea where we actually are; there's no point in asking the name of the station since it bears no relationship to any geography in my head. It's already past 8 a.m., so we are definitely late; it's simply a question of how late. I doze a little for the next couple of hours, and we eventually arrive in Jammu a little after ten.

Only five hours late. I console myself with the notion that it could have been worse.

Srinagar is a place I must visit on this journey for a number of reasons. I once spent an idyllic summer here on one of the trips my father brought me on. My dad's sister Harminder, or Minder as she is colloquially known, married Pritam Singh, a fiercely proud member of the Indian Army. Pritam rose to the heady rank of colonel, and in reaching such heights found himself and his family stationed in Srinagar. The summer of 1981 was spent with Pritam Singh and Minder Aunty and their three kids Sonu, Jonu and Monu. (Their real names are Jaspreet, Harpreet and Mandeep respectively. Quite how the nicknames of Sonu, Jonu and Monu were arrived at is a dark art of familial nomenclature of which I have no understanding.)

Srinagar is possibly the most disputed city of Partition, which in one sense puts it at the very heart of the nation of India. Soon after Partition tribal warlords from Pakistan, backed by the newly formed Pakistan Army, invaded the city and tried to claim it. Indian troops were flown in and eventually the invading hordes repelled. Since then, Srinagar has always been regarded as a cause celebre by the Indians, a city freed from aggressive Islam, the jewel in the new crown of India. The reality however belies such a reason for celebration. More than three quarters of the city's population wish to be Pakistani.

If I am searching for some sense of myself, for some sense of home, then Srinagar might be a place to begin to understand my confusion over the collision of my identity. Srinagar is a mirror to my soul when it comes to matters of duality. If I am trying to understand what part of me is Indian and what part British, is there anywhere better to understand that than in the disputed state of Jammu and Kashmir? This is a place where people have fought and died for their sense of self, and continue to fight for their right of political and cultural self-determination. Maybe I can learn a little of my Indianness here; and maybe that might help me grapple with my Britishness.

I don't know what I was expecting when I arrived in Jammu. My overriding memory as a child was of driving up through the mountains, listening to Queen's *Greatest Hits*, which had just been released. Thinking back now it seems hilarious that we thought Queen were so quintessentially British; little did we know that Freddie Mercury's real name was Farrokh Bulsara and he was in fact from a north Indian family. He assiduously kept his ethnicity, his identity, secret. Yet we should have known; all those tight white vests and the oversized moustache: others might have interpreted it differently, but to me he was so very obviously Indian! Freddie Mercury presented a version of himself to the world, a version that belied his heritage. I can't help wondering whether I am a little guilty of a similar crime.

My dad speaks with great fondness of the stunning natural beauty of the region; he has spent much time in and around Srinagar, walking the foothills of the Himalayas and trekking on religious pilgrimages. He's not actually at all religious: I think he just really likes travelling and walking. I am now here as much for him as for me. It's as far north in India as is safe to travel; by safe I mean war-zone safe. Politicians are geniuses at the art of euphemism – 'conflict', 'troubles', 'border disputes' – employing all sorts of language to cloak the reality that India and Pakistan are still at war with each other about the line of control. Things have improved discernibly of late, but nonetheless, the two countries have hundreds of thousands of troops lined up, facing each other. Every now and again it kicks off. It is sad that the stage for this quiet war happens to be one of the most beautiful places on this planet. But then, as Colonel Pritam Singh used to say, 'No one fights for anything ugly, do they?' He had a point. Not much of one. But he did have a point.

And this is the first thing that hits me in Jammu station. Wherever I turn, wherever I look, there are soldiers. The station itself seems to be run by the military. It is said that more than half the Indian Army is stationed in this state. It is also said that the generals refuse to countenance any deal for autonomy with Pakistan or with the people of Jammu and Kashmir since any such change would leave the Indian Army with very little to do, thereby eroding its power base within the political sphere. Such is the world of politics. It seems crazy to me, a Scot who has some sympathy for the ever more vocal voice of Scottish independence, that India forces the overwhelming majority of a state to be part of a country they have no desire to be part of. But what do I know? I still hope Scotland will march over the River Tweed and liberate Berwick from the English!

I have been instructed to find a Sumo to drive me to Srinagar. A Sumo is the brand name of a seven-seater Jeep much used in India and is exactly the sort of vehicle that can deal with the mountainous terrain ahead. I like the notion of being inside a Japanese wrestler. The Sumo system is quite simple. They charge 300 rupees per traveller for the journey; 2,100 for a full load. They then proceed to fill their Sumos with all-comers on a first come, first served basis, whether individuals, couples or entire families with luggage. To maximise space within, the luggage is placed on the roof rack, in best Indian tradition. Think of it as a tombola taxi – you may get lucky, you may not. I am feeling lucky; I am quite taken with the idea of making the journey with an assortment of Kashmiri strangers, overhearing conversations and sharing my own monosyllabic Hindi stories.

Wandering out of the station I ask a soldier where the Sumos are to be found. He points me down some stairs to the car park where there are indeed scores of them; but no drivers. I walk around looking like a lost tourist when I happen upon a small taxi office, fiendishly hidden behind a hut, underneath a weeping tree, as if intentionally to escape observation. In my best broken Hindi/bad Punjabi I find out that only a handful of Sumos are prepared to make the trip to Srinagar. Two have already left, the supervisor chappie tells me. I have paid the price for not sprinting headlong out of the station and making immediately for the Sumos. Obviously the few moments I lost asking the soldier where the Sumos were has proved costly. It's irritating but nothing can be done about it. I will need to wait for more passengers to make up the numbers. How many more? Six more. I am the only chump still looking for a ride to Srinagar.

I find the next Sumo allotted to leave and sit in the front seat, making myself comfortable. The driver places my small suitcase on top; it looks so lonely up there on its own. I sit and I wait. If a Kashmiri crow were to fly from Jammu to Srinagar, it is probably no more than a 200km journey, if that. But I have chosen to give over the next eight hours of my life to a journey that will take me round and round, up and down through mountains in ever-decreasing circles until I finally arrive in Srinagar. It will be an epic journey; I am quite keen for it to start.

But half an hour later my case is still the only case on the roof rack, and I am still the only passenger. The driver busies himself preparing the rickety old Sumo for the journey. He notices that my fulsome Punjabi Glaswegian arse is warming both the front passenger bench seats. He tells me that someone else will be sat next to me on the journey. I tell him not to worry since I am happy to pay for both; there's no way I could have another individual sat so close to me for that length of time: not without first having bought them dinner, or at least a cocktail. The driver tells me that he has to wait for passengers from more trains. Given the unreliability of service and the fact that I am keen to complete my journey up the side of a steep mountain on a narrow, badly built road peopled by maniacs driving in daylight, I consider my options. I will wait a little longer . . .

From the passenger seat of the Sumo I am but yards from the water supply. I have seen at least fifty men and boys fill buckets, wash rags, clean their faces and hands and feet, and generally ablute. Here is what I have seen:

1. An octogenarian holy man with his full white, ZZ Top-like beard, hiding most of his face and chest, bless the water supply, dressed top to toe in faded yellow robes and retro Adidas trainers on his feet.

2. A middle-aged man purchase seven shawls from a nearby vendor, paying for only six.

3. A small boy clean the ears of a much older man, using a twig, a tissue and a small bottle of palm oil.

These are all things I have seen. What I haven't seen is a single other passenger wanting to share my Sumo to Srinagar.

The one thing I have on my hands is time; time to think. It is difficult to believe that I am less than a week away from the end of my odyssey. Kovalam seems like a lifetime away, the coconut warmth of the south of India. I laugh to myself as I think about how strange and faintly ridiculous I must have seemed asking to cook British food in a five-star hotel.

Then the move to the simplicity of Mamallapuram; the ridiculous to the sublime. Something profound happened to me as I watched the Indian Ocean crash against the beach on

India's east coast. The time spent with Nagamuthu, son of Mani, made me realise that I am just a man; my search was as simple as it was complex. Mamallapuram started me thinking that I was not going to get answers, just some different questions. Mysore further fed the idea of a new set of questions and I continued to pose those questions to myself, all the way to the North.

I don't think I could have planned the gamut of experiences that my third location gave me. Mysore and Jeremy: the contemporary soul-seeker, who came to find his own solace in India, and ultimately turned out to be the modern-day colonialist. Jeremy seemed to give so very little to India but felt free to take. But how different was I? What was I giving back? I wondered.

It was another leap from the yogic idyll of Mysore to the burgeoning modernity of Bangalore. Maybe the fact that I felt so comfortable in the globally welcoming city of Bangalore says more about the city than me. There is a new India that will welcome and work for all-comers. The question is what is the sense of Indianness that resides in this new India? There I found myself asking myself the same sort of question about my own Indianness.

Goa: biscuit-tin India, the clichés and stereotypes, the home of the hippy, the place where people go to find themselves. What had I found? It was there that I learnt that I was very, very British.

Bombay was an adventure as much for the gastric part of me as the spiritual. Delhi was full of the memories of my dad, of his life and his times. There I realised that maybe this journey was all about me trying to please him as his son, to show that I am worthy. Maybe.

And here I am, sitting and waiting to travel to Srinagar. And why? Because my dad wanted me to visit the Kashmir Valley.

The more I think about this quest for self-discovery, the more I realise that it has all been about my dad. That is no bad thing. He's my dad. I am more than a little elated that this journey has become a homage to the most incredible man I have ever had the pleasure to know: Parduman Singh Kohli.

These thoughts rush through my head. I feel clarity and confusion in equal doses. And I am still waiting for fellow passengers to buy the remaining seats in my Sumo. Perhaps, like the answers to all the questions for which I am searching, these passengers will not arrive. It's been an hour. I decide to give up waiting. It looks like I will be buying all the seats. I offer the driver the 2,100 rupees that his supply and demand economics requires of me. He smiles; it is a charming smile, the smile of deep satisfaction, of money earned.

Had I known that it would be both his first and last smile of the day, perhaps I would have taken a moment or two longer to enjoy its rarity.

We start a series of gradual inclines, followed by less gradual declines, as we wend our way through the trees and mountains of the Kashmir Valley. The road has been hewn out of the side of a mountain, a tiny lip of connectivity through an otherwise untenable and untravellable landscape. It feels like we are spinning on the groove of the mountain, neither halfway up nor halfway down. Our progress is clear since whenever I look back I see the last few kilometres of road we have covered; this gives me both a sense of progress and a sense of hopelessness, given the time it has taken to make these meagre miles.

The driving is interesting to say the least. I have become accustomed to Indian driving, which is based firmly on the karmic cycle and a deeply held belief in God. This fatalistic approach to road safety, since it is almost universally shared, results in a system of traffic management that, despite its precariousness, does seem to work. It's never dull driving in India. But this journey brings another set of challenges to those of us from the 'mirror, signal, manoeuvre' school of lane discipline. This mountain road is barely wide enough to accommodate two opposing streams of traffic; that is when there is a road. For some of the journey there is no road at all; just rubble and the occasional stream. Despite its limitation the road carries a myriad of coaches, buses, trucks, cars, military vehicles and cows in both directions, each trying to overtake the other. Through a complex code of hand gestures, beeping horns and flashing headlights my driver overtakes in the face of oncoming juggernauts, swerving at the last moment as the blare of their horn cuts across and through us. At times we are but inches away from a metal on metal moment. All this two or three thousand feet above the valley on a badly made road with no protective barrier. I am never more than a metre from death. It feels like a video game, without the amazing graphics. Or an on/off switch.

My driver clearly knows how to pace an eight-hour conversation; he has chosen to take the 'enigmatic silence' approach for the first couple of hours, punctuated by the odd burp, spit or other venial bodily function. Some might mistake his singular lack of conversation for taciturnity, but I enjoy his willingness to allow our relationship to grow and unfold with time. And time is one thing we certainly have plenty of.

In the lower reaches of our ascent we pass numerous monkeys who gather by the side of the road. I'd forgotten about the monkeys. How could I?

My three cousins, Sonu, Jonu and Monu were roughly the same age as Raj, Sanj and me. Whilst I was regarded as the tricky troublemaker in my family, coincidentally so was Jonu. The extent of my tricky troublemaking was the infamous Victoria

Sponge Cake Theft incident that I have mentioned. That and some occasional rude language. Jonu's tricky troublemaking was in an altogether trickier and more troublemaking league. Jonu stole a monkey. I laugh when I think about it. On the way home from school as an eight-year-old, my cousin Jonu showed up at his house in Srinagar with a baby monkey under his arm.

As a parent this is clearly a challenging situation. A monkey has been stolen. Yet it is a baby monkey. It cannot simply be left to fend for itself. Quite how Jonu managed to extricate the monkey from its family group remains unclear to this day. My aunt, Minder, was at a loss. She felt obliged to allow the money to stay in the house. All seemed fine for a while. The baby monkey was cute and adorable and after a few hours even Minder found herself endeared to the newborn primate, feeding it milk from an old baby bottle. Everything was hunkydory.

Or it was, until the rest of the monkeys got wind of the fact that the baby was missing; it only took them a day and a half to notice. Somehow they managed to trace the baby monkey back to my aunt's house. They gathered in some sort of parliament of protest around the complex; bear in mind that my uncle, Colonel Pritam Singh, was one of the more senior Indian Army officers in the state. He had an armed guard who was also rather freaked out by what seemed like a Bollywood remake of *Planet of the Apes*. Then, all of a sudden, as if in a rehearsed manoeuvre, the monkeys started banging on the roof and the doors and the window, screeching and wailing in a cacophonous bid to save their child.

This may sound funny now, but one can imagine how alarming it must have been at the time. The baby monkey was as alarmed as Jonu and the family. It clung onto Jonu for dear life. There was no way it was letting go. Catch 22: how were my aunt and uncle going to return the baby monkey when the baby monkey seemed to want to do anything but be returned?

Day became night and the monkeys would not abate. After much deliberating and planning, Minder hit upon a genius idea. They fed the baby monkey paracetamol which made it drowsy and eventually made it sleep. They then placed the slumbering primate carefully in the porch, hurriedly retreating behind the wire screen. The baby monkey was snatched back and the screeching and wailing stopped almost instantly. The hordes of monkeys were gone in a moment, melting into the night.

Suffice to say that as we drive along I am content to only look at these monkeys that line the route.

❦

Signs on the road from Jammu to Srinagar

Speed is a knife that cuts Life
Slow Drive, Long Life
Speed Thrills but often Kills
Drive Like Hell, End up There
Speed is a Demon; Life is a Reason

❦

I'm looking forward to Srinagar. I have arranged to stay on a houseboat on Dal Lake. This was dad's idea. He and my mum, accompanied by Manore Uncle and his wife, spent a few days there a couple of years ago. They had a great time, by all accounts. I am meant to be staying on the same boat they stayed in. Before leaving Britain this detail seemed just that, a detail. Now, given my epiphany that my entire quest is actually about my dad, the fact that I will be on the selfsame houseboat he was on brings a whole new significance. I really am following in his footsteps.

I am left to work out what I will cook and who I will be cooking for when I get to Srinagar. There seem to be no obvious candidates to feed and no particular dish to cook. I'm running out of ideas having cooked some of my best dishes earlier on my journey. Perhaps I could cook for the Sumo drivers? I look at the face of my driver and quickly disabuse myself of that notion. But I realise that I do need to make some arrangement with Mr Chatty for lunch.

After a little negotiation, the strong silent driver and I have agreed that we should stop to eat halfway through our eight hour journey, which at this rate would be about two o'clock. I am hugely excited about stopping to eat. One of the strongest food memories of my entire life is from the first time I made this journey. It is a meal that has stayed with me for nearly three decades. And the irony is that I never actually tasted it! As a twelve year old I remember seeing locals tucking in to plates of rice, topped with curried kidney beans smothered with a ladleful of clarified butter or ghee. This dish is known as rajmah chawal. I can see it as vividly now as I did nearly thirty years ago; a small, basic concrete shack teetering on the edge of the road, a sheer drop of a few thousand feet below, serving plate after plate of rajmah chawal to lots of happy diners. We three boys were forbidden from partaking of the food since our tender, westernised stomachs would be sure to react badly to the local standards of hygiene. Instead we ate crisps. I suppose that is what made the event so memorable for me. Falling in love with the sight, the sound, the smell, the very story of this food; everything but the actual taste.

No doubt in the decades that have followed I have elevated that meal of rajmah chawal to an altogether more ethereal place in the panoply of great foods. Of course I have had many bowls of rajmah since, from my sister-in-law Surjit's (which, like all her cooking, is truly delicious), to that available at the famous Khyber restaurant in Bombay. Each has been tasty in its own way, but none has been close to the rajmah perfection of that roadside shack on the way to Srinagar.

So it is with boyhood excitement and intestinal trepidation that I count the minutes down to lunchtime. We arrive at a place called Peeda a little before two o'clock. I cast my eye and my mind over the place, trying to match it to my memory; perhaps the place has changed in the intervening decades; besides how reliable could the memory of a twelve-year-old boy be? But my memory is surprisingly intact; this could only be that selfsame place, teetering precariously a few thousand feet above oblivion. Now, I would like to say that my certainty is based on something romantic: the same, now considerably older, man serving the rajmah chawal who catches my eye and recognises me after nearly three decades; or perhaps I find the tree into which I had carved my initials, knowing somehow preternaturally that I would one day return and actually try the food. Neither of these are the case. The reality is that one of my abiding memories of the place is the fact that it had no toilets, and when I had to relieve myself as a boy my father sent me around the side where I pissed down into the valley a few thousand feet below. How often are you allowed to piss thousands of feet down a valley as a child, with parental blessing?

So here we are. A small smattering of concrete shacks with steel-shuttered fronts. Simple and functional and to the point. At the front a square concrete stove, wood-fired. Upon it sit four pans of varying sizes. The largest, nearly a metre in diameter, is half full of rajmah; the next largest is full of rice; the third pot has aloo gobi, cauliflower and potato, and the final smallest pot bubbles with clarified butter, ghee.

There are eight, maybe nine tables neatly laid out in the space and an assortment of different chairs and benches. It has the feeling of a place that has organically developed slowly through time into somewhere to eat. As if the stove-based aromas aren't enough, a handsome young man beckons potential customers in with his mantra-like chant of 'rajmah chawal, rajmah chawal, rajmah chawal . . . ' I need no beckoning. I am sitting down and have already ordered. Moments later a steel plate arrives: a bed of rice upon which lies a blanket of kidney beans and the cursory ladleful of ghee. A small dish of pickle and sliced onion accompanies the main event. It's not much to look at but it smells amazing. The complex richness of the ghee blending with the bold earthiness of the kidney beans and the virginal simplicity of the rice. I steel myself; by rights I shouldn't be here. This is not the sort of food a western traveller should eat. And that is what I am. This could be a massive intestinal mistake. My stomach thinks it's from Glasgow; it has grown up eating food in the west, food prepared to an altogether different level of hygiene. I have not familiarised myself with the bacteria of Indian street food and therefore haven't had the opportunity to build any resistance. I cannot vouch for the cleanliness of this place or indeed the provenance of the ingredients. I still have a four-hour, rough-road journey ahead of me without the guarantee of a toilet, and I am about to fill my stomach with potentially dodgy lentils and clarified butter. I have only just recovered from the bowel-thinning nightmare of the journey between Bombay and Delhi. The last thing I want is another bout of subcontinental diarrhoea. But I've waited twenty-seven years for this . . .

Was it worth the wait? Certainly it was the finest rajmah chawal I have ever had the privilege of eating. Words alone cannot do it justice; its simplicity, its richness. No doubt memories enhance flavour, but it was a deliciously satisfying plate of food. All that for twenty-five rupees, about thirty pence.

I get back into the Sumo and wait the long wait. A belly full of beans and the depth of my fatigue soon become apparent. My stomach seems to be holding up, but the rest of my body is flagging rather gloriously. I fear that I will fall asleep sitting upright and suffer whiplash as the driver swings left and then right, braking hard in the face of oncoming traffic. I now appreciate the price I have paid to take an empty car up the mountain. I ask the driver to pull over so I can get into the back and lie down to sleep, perchance to dream. How much more enjoyable this journey would be in a leather-seated, air-conditioned Range Rover . . . This would be the perfect terrain for its four-wheel drive engineering. Instead they clog up well-kept boulevards and smooth-surfaced roads of Hampstead, Kelvinside and Didsbury. I doze in the back; there seems to be some unwritten law of physics that the further back you are in an erratically-driven vehicle, the more the forces of acceleration and deceleration have an impact on you. My body is yet more battered and bruised; my right knee has been cut red raw with the constant banging against the unforgiving steel of the seat in front. After an hour of unsatisfactory napping, we stop for tea and I resume an upright position.

The sun seems to be setting for the millionth time, elevating the beautiful valley to another level of luminescent splendour, a splendour that lasts but a few moments, as it gives way all too quickly to a sudden and definite darkness. And with the darkness comes a chill, a chill that reminds me of home, of Glasgow and of soup. I can feel we are nearing our destination and a milestone confirms my hunch; 39km, 25 miles. I would normally expect to do that in twenty minutes up the M1, but here it's at least an hour's drive. Roadside fires light our path like beacons guiding us into the town.

And then, without fanfare or accolade, we arrive. Srinagar, nondescript and dark. The Sumo pulls into its depot and I am met by Rovi's in-laws who couldn't be happier to see me. They take me home, drown me in their generous hospitality and then take me to Dal Lake where they have booked me a houseboat for my stay. The darkness has got darker and the chill chillier. I wrap myself in my well-travelled and rather chic black pashmina (a man very comfortably in touch with his feminine side, I think you'll agree) and board the *shikara*, one of the legion of small boats that ferries folk around the lake. In fifteen minutes I am on my houseboat; within twenty I am in bed; half an hour or so after gliding across the lake I sleep the sleep of champions.

Twelve names of houseboats on Dal Lake

Cheerful Charley
Tehran
Prince of Vales [sic]
New Lucifer
Texas
Neil Armstrong

Mughal Palace

New Good Luck

Bostan [sic]

Kings Rose

Kookaburra

Helen of Troy

I wake up refreshed. Ten hours of blissful sleep. But it is cold, properly cold. Scottish cold. I have never been this cold in India before; never. It must be just below freezing at seven in the morning. Three quilts and I still feel the chill. I gather myself and remind myself that I am hale and hearty and have endured sub-arctic temperatures during my working life as I leap, gazelle-like from bed.* My plan of action is simple: I will take a trip around the lake and see what potential cooking opportunities there might be. I bathe in surprisingly hot water and add an extra layer or two of clothes. I then set about having a wee explore of my surroundings. The boat consists of two palatial double bedrooms, a dining room, a reasonably sized galley kitchen and a lounge that would not be out of place in one of the better appointed Hyndland tenements, the massive sandstone Victorian apartments Glasgow is so famed for. Sizewise *Merry Dawn* can only be described as capacious and well proportioned.

---

*This is a book; I am writing it; you know and I know that my leap from bed was more of an uncoordinated stagger and shuffle, and if I resembled any of God's creatures I was surely more elephantine that gazelle-like. But if I cannot be allowed a modicum of literary licence to portray myself as fleet of foot and elegant in my own prose then what hope is there for me?

The houseboat's interior design on the other hand is an altogether different matter. Might I describe it as quaint? Actually that is unfair on the word quaint. Put it this way: if the National Association of the Lovers of All Things Quaint wanted to enjoy a week's break in the Kashmir Valley, they would book this houseboat, and even they would comment on its quaintness. The rooms are full of brocaded 1930s style furniture; there are curios and trinkets and bits and pieces everywhere. A faded flag of Canada sits on the bureau; a tapestry showing a prince fighting a tiger; nine pots of plastic flowers in the lounge alone; a black and white photograph of Brigadier Bourke, a military man I have never heard of; a woven basket in the shape of a duck; and a cuddly sky-blue toy dog. The ceilings are beautifully ornate; hand-carved wood in every room. Undoubtedly *Merry Dawn* is charming; but most of all it is mine, at least for the next couple of days.

It feels very strange to be on a houseboat in Srinagar. It is as if I am not in India any more. Dorothy-like, I feel I am somewhere over the rainbow. This is very different from my childhood recollections of Srinagar and jars with what I was expecting. As far as I can remember, I have never spent a night sleeping on water. Yet here I am. And the fact that I don't feel like I am in India makes me feel even more self-conscious about my cooking quest. Having just left Delhi, a place brimming with childhood memories, and heading for my final destination, my home at the house of my grandfather, Srinagar feels very alien. It also feels very lonely, very quiet.

Every stage of this quest has seen me fighting my way through crowds. Whether I was in Madras train station, taking the coach to Bangalore or walking through the streets of Bombay, I have never had much time alone. My time for reflection seems always to have taken place in the company of Indians. And this is the way I like my life. I like to be with people. While I may be among them I don't always feel part of them. There is a comfort about being alone in a crowd. I am slightly fearful of the solitude of Srinagar, the solitude at this stage of my journey, the penultimate stop before having to find some definitive answers. The last thing I need is three days pondering whether the whole trip has been a complete and utter waste of time and that when I return my life, my sense of self will remain exactly as it was before I left. Perhaps I should have planned that my second from last stop be in a town with lots of nightclubs? Instead I am alone, on a massive houseboat on Dal Lake.

I feel that I should take in a tour of my surroundings, begin to appreciate the much-spoken of beauty of the Kashmir Valley. I venture out onto the pontoon at the front. As part of my hire agreement I have a *shikara* on standby all day and it was duly waiting for me.

A *shikara* is a boat unique, I think, to this part of the world. It is an elongated banana-shaped shard of wood, flat bottomed, almost too simple to be water worthy. Yet with seemingly effortless aplomb these boats glide the lake's tranquil surface. Regular *shikara*s are no more than a basic wooden structure; the drivers sit either on the very front or the very back in a buoyancy-defying position as they methodically break the water with their heart-shaped paddles. A romantic touch the heart-shaped paddle. My *shikara* is the deluxe version, with a canopy and a cushioned seating area, resplendent in red velour.

The sun has been coaxed out from behind the mountains and the Kashmir Valley looks beautiful this clear crisp morning. As we push off from the mini jetty, I look back at my houseboat, *Merry Dawn*. It is the first chance I have had to properly appraise it since arriving under the canopy of darkness the night before.

Merry Dawn is perhaps forty metres long and nearly five metres wide and is one of scores of similarly sized houseboats that stretch across the lake.

The lake beneath, the sky above and the comforting monotony of the *shikara* man's paddle on water; he guides us across the lake's polished surface with the minimum of fuss. We pass water lily and lotus fields as women harvest the crop. We pass floating vegetable plots, growing everything from carrots to spinach to white radish. We paddle through a small floating market, shops on stilts selling anything and everything. It is an effortless journey, made more effortless still by the warming rays of the Kashmiri sun.

As we round the final bend heading back to *Merry Dawn* I see a most peculiar sight. Smack bang in the middle of the lake, standing proudly and independently on its own is a small convenience shop/boat. Milkshakes, confectionery, cigarettes, cold drinks are all on display. This floating grocery outlet is astonishing. It is exactly like numerous other Indian style kiosks but on a boat. It even has a small gas-fired hob where the owner is frying some potato-based snacks. I ask my *shikara* man to pull up alongside. This place could be the answer to my dreams. Where better to cook in Srinagar than on a lake in the heart of the Kashmir Valley? And who better to cook for than the *shikara* drivers? There is a beautifully complete circularity to it. In my best broken Hindi I explain to the understandably sceptical owner, Khalil, that I would like to requisition his boat-shop-cum-snack bar for a couple of hours later today.*

It takes a little time and the offer of some money to compensate for loss of earnings but I think he gets the message.

---

*I obviously don't know the Hindi word for requisition; I don't even know the word for boat shop.

I have a place to cook and a constituency to cook for. All I need work out now is what to cook? I instruct my *shikara* man to take me to the nearest market so I can best establish what to cook in my newly requisitioned kitchen. My boatman tells me that I have missed the *sabzi mundi*, the floating vegetable market, which operates early in the morning in the very heart of the lake from about six and is finished by eight. Luckily Kashmiris like their meat and fish so I don't feel compelled to offer much in the way of a vegetarian option. As we glide off to the roadside market instead, a thought occurs. I am currently on a lake; lakes often have fish in them; what could be more perfectly British, and indeed Scottish, than fish and chips? Since the majority of customers at Khalil's are *shikara* drivers, it feels right to serve the lake men some lake food. It has to be fish and chips.

The first meal I ever ate in Scotland was fish and chips. It was from the Philadelphia chippy in Kelvinbridge, wrapped in the *Sunday Post*.

In the Spring of 1973 we packed up our entire lives, my parents, my two brothers and I, and we stuffed it all into our mint-green Vauxhall. We drove the eight hours up the motorway and, bleary-eyed, we arrived in the street-lit darkness of Glasgow. Before we even went to my uncle's flat we feasted on fish and chips. I can still taste the salt and vinegar. There seems to be something poetic about the fact that the first meal I ever ate in my adopted country should be the meal I serve in this place, a place that wishes to be part of a different country.

I am indebted to my father for making the choice to move to Scotland, since I think being Scottish has improved my life immeasurably. I am funnier, wittier and better looking for it, and am far more likely to invent things and educate the world about the philosophy of economics. That is what it is to be Scottish.

My journey through India has brought me into contact with more markets than I would ever see in a year in Britain. And here I am, another destination on my quest, another market. This roadside market offers a couple of varieties of fish, mainly pomfret, a round flat fish, and a few Kashmiri trout which look similar to the British version. I go for the pomfret option; a delicious fish that isn't easy to get hold of back home. It seems churlish to pass up the opportunity to cook it today. In the Punjab it is cooked in a tandoor, the silver flesh cut and rubbed with spices. It is also filleted and curried. It is often found in Thai cooking, deep fried whole and served with a sweet and sour and chilli sauce. I intend to batter and deep fry it and served it with potatoes. Time is of the essence since night falls abruptly at around 6 p.m. and not much happens thereafter; in fact nothing at all happens after nightfall. This, in some part, is a result of previous military curfews. Although no such curfew is in operation now, people have fallen into the habit of staying in of an evening.

I have limited choices for my batter. In a perfect world I might have opted for a tempura-style coating, light and airy, the corn flour mixed with soda water to add an effervescence to the batter. Or perhaps a beer batter, malty and slightly sour. Neither is an option in Srinagar. The most interesting option would be gram flour, flour made from chick peas.

My mother was amazing. The drabbest store cupboard staples could be reinvented into a new and delicious snack. In the kitchen she rarely disappointed such was her resourcefulness. She worked this alchemy on the budget of a working-class immigrant. And how did she do this? With gram flour. Oh yes. Welcome to the world of the pakora.

Growing up there was one snack that was the staple of our household. Should we be hungry mid-afternoon: pakoras. Should we be visited by unannounced guests from Romford on the way to the Highlands: pakoras. Should my dad, gregarious party lover that he is, invite half a dozen work colleagues round for dinner: pakoras. Pakoras were the panacea to food emergencies in our house. Maybe that's why my mum got so very good at making them.

The recipe is beautiful in its simplicity. Gram flour is seasoned with salt, pepper and chilli powder. Water is then added to form a thick batter. Into this batter you can throw all manner of things. As carbohydrate-loving Punjabis, my mum opted for sliced potatoes. The raw flat discs cook in the steam created within the gram flour covering. This is something that people don't always appreciate about battering and deep frying food. Much as the outside is fried, the inner delight is actually steamed, protected from the harsh oil by the batter jacket. Once they were ready we would devour them with the essential accompaniment to the pakora experience: ketchup. My dad would plead with my mum to make mint chutney, a plea she never failed to bend to. But those were in the days before my dad developed an allergy to vinegar and tamarind. He's never felt the same about pakoras since.

We would have diced potato, pea and onion pakoras. Fish pakora was a favourite with my dad. Paneer pakora is particularly delicious. Or *patra* pakora, *patra* being a spinachy type of leaf that comes tinned and ready to use. Chicken pakora is served to this day in Indian restaurants across Scotland. There have been haggis pakoras, pizza pakoras, and it being Glasgow, Mars Bar pakoras. My favourite however was when my mum had fried all the vegetables and there was a soupcon of the gram flour batter left, coating the bottom of the bowl. Never one to waste, my mum would take a slice of bread, halve it and clean the bowl out with it, removing every last drop of the spicy gram flour mix. This piece of bread would be fried and invariably eaten by my mum since we boys would have consumed most of the pakoras by the time she sat down to eat. By its very definition there was never more than one or two pieces of the bread pakora to enjoy; maybe that's why I loved it so much. Absence made my culinary heart grow fonder. Or maybe it was because I loved to eat with my mum.

I manage to get hold of gram flour easily enough at the roadside market and also pick up a couple of bottles of soda water. There isn't going to be space to prepare everything at Khalil's place, and given it is only a five-minute *shikara* ride from *Merry Dawn* I decide to go back and prep everything there. The pomfret turns out to be easy enough to fillet, each fillet offering three pieces. I reckoned I would only need four fish in total. I mix the gram flour and the seasoning and add the soda water. Obviously the Indian way would be to use plain water but I want to see how the gram flour reacts with the soda water. It seems fine. I peel some potatoes and rush out to my *shikara*. It's getting late into the afternoon and I know I am up against it.

We arrive at Khalil's. He is wearing that look of 'I'm not sure that I want to go ahead with this'. I counter with my look of 'Here's a thousand rupees, we had an agreement'. He begrudgingly lets me onboard. His oil pan is not massive so I will have to cook a couple of fillets at a time, and gauging the heat of the oil will be challenging since Khalil only ever fries the same mashed potato ball snack. I ask him if he will consider changing the oil. This really annoys him. He starts muttering in Kashmiri and throws his hands about the place. I decide to lubricate the situation with money. Again. I have learned much about diplomacy thanks to my western upbringing. It seems however that the more money I offer him, the surlier he becomes. He hands me a tin of oil. It appears that I will have to change the oil myself. Fine, I think.

First things first I need to dispense with the old oil, oil that looks like it is ready to celebrate an anniversary, so long has it been used to fry with. I pick up the *karahi*, the steel-handled frying pan, and look around the tiny space for somewhere to discard it. I feel like Harold Lloyd, shuffling about on the spot, turning one way then the other looking for something that clearly doesn't exist, being watched by a man and his friend who clearly think I am one pakora short of a mid-afternoon snack. Obviously Khalil isn't getting it. I ask him what to do with the oil. He motions to tip it out into the lake. I am obviously not going to pollute an already over-polluted lake. I am seriously flummoxed. I can't just tip it into the lake; that would be wrong. But then how am I going to change the oil? I feel like I have been caught in one of those riddles; the farmer has a chicken, a fox and a sack of grain type riddles. I have to work out how I am going to change the oil. The potatoes are the answer. They are in what looks like a watertight plastic bag. All I need to do is remove the potatoes, pour the old oil into the bag, the new oil into the *karahi* and then pour the old oil into the empty oil drum. Easy. Yeah right.

It is actually relatively straightforward to remove the potatoes from the plastic bag, but I somehow have to hold the bag and tip the oil in. Khalil is clearly not up for helping although he can't help but demonstrate a begrudging interest in my machinations. Eventually I manage to hold the bag and tip the oil and I allow it to pour slowly, leaving a residue of burnt shards behind. I carefully put the *karahi* down and very delicately tie the handles of the bag together. So far so good. Next I need to wipe the *karahi* of its detritus. Instinctively I hand the bag of old oil to Khalil. Instinctively he takes it. Instinctively I smile at him. Instinctively he throws the bag and the oil into the lake. Not only have I polluted Dal Lake with oil, I had also managed to add a plastic bag to the numerous contents that line its floor. But I don't have time to discuss it with him. I clean the *karahi*, turn the flame on underneath to dry it and pour in fresh oil. Meanwhile I slice the potatoes and then chip them. Once the oil hits the required temperature I slip in the first two battered fillets of pomfret. Never overcrowd a deep fat fryer: the addition of anything to hot oil reduces the temperature of the oil; the more you add the lower the temperature becomes and that is how you end up with greasy or undercooked food. Cook less and cook more often. God I'm boring, aren't I?

My first two fillets turn out perfectly. I decide to fry my chips. Now, I am a firm believer in the twice-fried method of chip-making. Fry the chips at a lower heat first, ensuring the inside is cooked. Then return them to a higher heat to crisp the outside and impart that lovely golden-brown texture. I even know some who will bake their chips first, feeling that this gives them a fluffier inner consistency. I have no such luxury. I simply hope and pray that I have judged the thickness of my chips correctly to harmonise with the uncontrollable temperature of the oil. I haven't. The chips cook far too quickly, the outside browning while the inside remains hard and uncooked. (It has to be said that Indian potatoes seem to take much longer to cook than your regular Maris Piper.)

I make an executive decision to dispense with the chips. I am now serving fried fish with Khalil's ketchup. And do you know what? It isn't bad at all, even if I say so myself. Khalil even eats a piece, although I can tell he can't quite work out why I have gone to all that bother.

It's difficult to describe how I feel at this point in my journey. I have travelled almost the entire length of the country yet it has taken me until this point to feel truly proud of the food I've cooked. Admittedly the chips are an unmitigated disaster, but the fish is good. More than that, the fish is the perfect fusion of an Indian and a British recipe, combining my first meal in Glasgow, a meal I have eaten regularly ever since, with my mum's Punjabi food, food I grew up eating every week at home: these are the two halves of my life that make the whole.

I think it is the first meal I've cooked for myself rather than others. To be honest I don't really care what the boatmen think of my deep-fried fish. (I know it would go down a storm on Byres Road.) I think I also very much feel a sense of disconnection with the boatmen of Dal Lake. I don't consider them to be Indian because they don't consider *themselves* to be particularly Indian. They are Kashmiris. I can relate to their plight as a people exercising their right of self-determination. And I have to confess that by this point I am clear that whatever I am, I am most certainly not Indian. Yet I am more than just British. I realise, at this moment in time, that I am a complex blend of both, a blend that changes depending on who I am with, where I am and how I feel on any given day.

For the bulk of my life, ever since that day as a five year old in Bishopbriggs, when I was singled out and not allowed to play with the rest of the kids, my life has been defined by how I am perceived by others, by my appearance. I have been, I am and I will always be a brown-skinned man, with a turban and a rather pronounced belly. I cannot change that, although perhaps a few weekly sessions at the gym might help with the belly. I am who I am, as far as people perceive me. What I feel inside however is another matter altogether. Inside I feel

British. British and proud. Yet I am completely at one with my Indianness. It's not about trying to define myself exactly. I am not 70 per cent Indian and 30 per cent British. Those percentages change constantly. They ebb and flow, like the Dal Lake around the *shikara*s. But at this very moment, watching the darkening sky, my nostrils full of the smell of deep-fried fish, whatever that balance of Indian and Britishness is within me, it feels right. And it is this feeling I carry with me onward to my final destination: Ferozepure and my grandfather's house.

10

ALMOST HOME

I should tell you about my grandfather's house. In its day it was quite palatial, but its day has long since past. The house sits in the middle of a bazaar, a straight row of shops on street level with residential accommodation on the floors above. We have three storeys. Our ground-floor room is accessed by a large sky-blue, double-arched doorway; in the old days we had a water pump in that room and we would have the most excellent baths imaginable. The room has now been rented out to some shopkeeper or other. By the left-hand side of the arched doorway is a small sky-blue doorway, leading up some narrow high stairs. These unremarkable steps lead you to the first floor of 22 Moti Bazaar. This is the main living level. Two public rooms, three bedrooms, a small kitchen and a couple of bathrooms are peripheral to a central uncovered courtyard. This courtyard used to be the focal point of the house. The men would drink their whisky and eat their kebabs here, the washing would be put out to dry here, kids would play here, ladies would gossip here. It all happened here, under the canopy of an ever-changing sky. It was where we would sit and gather in the summer evenings to eat, drink and be merry. The next level up is what we call the *cotee*, the terrace. Back in the day, before the introduction of the western-style 'flush' toilet, it was on this level the *tattia*, the latrines, could be found. No matter how Indian we might feel in our hearts, no matter how much love we felt for the country and how much we enjoyed being here, the single factor that separated us British-born Indians from our Indian-born family was our inability to utilise their different and challenging toilet system. I have never been able to enjoy a squat toilet. My leg joints have never achieved that extreme position of stretching; I have never been clear as to how best gather my garments lest they become involved in my ablutions; and my balance has never been honed to accommodate a passive body position whilst simultaneously evacuating my bowels. Even if I had mastered these complex ways of the east I am most definitely a toilet paper kind of a guy. No matter how compelling an argument is made for the added cleanliness and advanced hygiene of a manually washed arse I still prefer some sort of paper-based barrier between my hand and my faeces. I'm sorry, I just do.

To say the *tattia* were medieval would be doing a disservice to medieval plumbing. There was only one thing worse than having to take a dump in these communal latrines and that was to watch the girl who came in to clean them out every morning. The heaven and hell paradox of the terrace upstairs was that alongside the latrines was this fantastic open area with views over the entire city. We would fly kites, we would play football, we would generally lark around; but whatever we were doing, we were having fun only very irregularly interrupted by someone or other needing to take a dump.

I remember with vivid clarity as if it were yesterday, sprinting up to the terrace one morning, only to be confronted by a goat tied to the balustrade. It seemed a little strange to me that the day before there had been no goat, but I thought it best not to question its sudden appearance. To me, this wasn't a goat, this was a friend. My imagination being what it was, I decided to name my new friend Goaty after some hours of deliberation, and for the next few days, still chewing the last mouthful of breakfast, I would race upstairs to play with Goaty. Perhaps I was at an impressionable age or perhaps Goaty and I had known each other in a past life but I felt some deep almost cosmic connection with Goaty; I think it's the closest I've ever come to loving an animal.

Again, it's with vivid clarity I remember that morning, tucking into a delicious breakfast of pickled meats and parathas. I forced the last mouthful in as I turned the corner onto the terrace looking for my soulmate but Goaty was nowhere to be seen. My emotions were mixed, part of me upset that my companion was gone, another part of me thinking that perhaps in escaping during the night Goaty had at last achieved his freedom. I felt it only right and proper to inform the grown-ups of Goaty's disappearance. Strangely they didn't seem shocked. Their lack of shock soon became apparent when they told me that far from not being present that morning, Goaty had very much been there. On the breakfast plate. The pickled meat I'd so enjoyed for breakfast that morning had in fact been Goaty, my dear, dear friend. Given that I was only ten years old it seems a terrible irony that whilst enjoying Goaty for breakfast, I had been looking forward to enjoying Goaty after breakfast. And so it is clear what I am going to cook when I get to my grandfather's house. It has to be goat. Curried goat. What else? It was what Goaty would have wanted . . .

To say my father has wanderlust would perhaps not fully convey his love for travel, his need to explore. He was born in 1934 and brought up in the city of Ferozepure. If I am anything with regard to India then I am a Punjabi. Regardless of religion and caste my family were Punjabis and I have always felt that that means more than anything else. Then they created Pakistan.

My father was twelve years old when India was torn asunder. The Punjab was slashed into two and Pakistan was ripped away from the wider subcontinent. Borders were hurriedly drawn and redrawn and then drawn again. A man-made line cut through the Punjab and separated people that had lived together, identified with each other for hundreds of years.

The creation of this new nation, the separation of Pakistan from India, defined my very existence. Ferozepure sits but a few kilometres from the border. Given its strategic importance, it was the centre of horse-trading when it came to deciding which side was to be given the city. It is incredible that people, places, histories and families can become the subject of third-party intervention. That third party was of course the British, the Raj, working in concert with self-interested Indian politicians and their apparatchiks. Someone had to draw a line somewhere. That's how man-made borders are created: by men. It's not about rivers and mountains; it's all about politics. Sir Cyril Radcliffe was that someone. A young lawyer with little knowledge or interest in India, he was brought over by Mountbatten in order to effect the impossible: to create a clean line of demarcation that would keep all parties happy and disappoint none. Impossible. The theory was simple: Muslim majority towns and villages were to be given to Pakistan, the land of the Pure, and the rest would remain Indian. Impossibly simple.

At first Ferozepure, with its marginal majority Muslim population, was to be in Pakistan. Then, a few days before the 14 August 1947, the Radcliffe Line was re-sketched, Sir Cyril's pencil heading to the north of Ferozepure, enclosing my father's birthplace and returning it to India. Therein lay my grandfather's fate, my father's fate and mine. Ferozepure became a city defined by its proximity to the border with the newly created Pakistan of 1947, a microcosm for all the chaos of Partition. More than half the city left, their lives on their backs and headed across the still wet ink that marked this new, artificial border. Muslims headed north, and Sikhs leaving the new Pakistan headed south.

Although my family did not physically move, there was a journey to be undertaken for the city around them and for the nation of India. It feels as though my father's whole life was defined by this philosophical journey, albeit one politically motivated; a journey for which the travellers themselves had absolutely no choice. In Ferozepure families were broken; generations of friendships were dissolved. Lives were utterly, completely and irreconcilably changed. The street where my grandfather lived, Moti Bazaar, was predominantly Muslim prior to Partition. One can only imagine the scenes as they left India, left their lives behind.

So picture if you will, Cyril Radcliffe, a green young barrister, fresh from the Home Counties; in front of him a table laid for lunch, a map of India and one freshly sharpened pencil. In amongst all that rests my fate; in amongst that defines my meaning of home. I'm here today, an overweight Glaswegian Sikh because a young English barrister redrew a line on a map. Life's funny, isn't it?

I learned all about this in the late 1990s. It took a few years for me to appreciate this information, and the extent of its impact on my life. At first it was just a good story; then it became my story. There is a part of me that feels that I should never have been born, I should not exist. Millions were brutally murdered during Partition; no one knows for sure how many.

What would have happened to my grandparents, my thirteen-year-old father and his siblings had Ferozepure remained in Pakistan? Would they have made it into Indian Punjab? Would they have avoided the slaughtering hordes? Would they have become those slaughtering hordes? Men became devils, as one old uncle of mine puts it. He looks off into the distance and one wonders what sights scarred and marked his young mind in 1947.

Even if they had survived where so many had perished, surely my father's life would have taken a different path. Momentous events change us momentously. Part of the reason he left Ferozepure twelve years later was because as a border town half its horizon had been slashed. It could no longer look north and thrive as a commercial centre. It had become militarily important rather than culturally or civically important. Ferozepure had stagnated as the army moved in, the city becoming the front line of the newly hewn India. For a man with aspirations as vibrant as my dad, Ferozepure was never going to contain him. And I can't help feeling that his destiny, and consequently mine, rest in the events of Partition. I can't help feeling that on some level I am not meant to be here.

Maybe he would have settled in a small town outside Jalandhar, the then capital of the Punjab. Maybe he would have had his marriage arranged to a woman who was five foot eight instead of five foot two. Maybe that other woman wouldn't have been such an amazing cook and such a loving mother. Maybe he would never have dreamt of leaving India and seeing the world. Maybe he would have become a civil servant and filed paperwork about companies he had never heard of, involved in deals he didn't care about. Maybe I would have never been born. Maybe.

It's a bright morning and early enough still to be described as tranquil. I am leaving *Merry Dawn* for ever. And the Kashmiri dawn seems merry enough. The *shikara* takes me the fifteen or so minutes across the lake, followed by a half-hour cab ride to the airport. The stillness, the calmness of the lake and the valley couldn't be more antithetical to the overbearing security at the airport. As a boy I travelled through a trouble-torn Belfast, but even that experience pales into insignificance when compared to the heightened security at Srinagar airport. I am body checked four times between entering the terminal building and boarding the flight. The entire cab is checked, engine and all. My paperwork is stamped and checked seven times and no hand baggage is allowed on the flight.

As I wait in the departure lounge I witness a microcosm of the Kashmir issue in the context of Indian nationalism. It just so happens that the third one-day cricket international is taking place between India and Pakistan. Cricket is a religion here. All the gentlemen in the lounge are facing the plasma screen, watching intently. The numerous members of the Indian Armed Forces are similarly glued to the screen, their sub-machine guns nonchalantly slung over their all too narrow shoulders. The entire room is transfixed. Although we are on Indian soil the majority of the Kashmiri travellers are supporting Pakistan, the soldiers obviously supporting the flag of the country they had sworn to give their lives for: an uneasy stand-off I think you'll agree. India loses an early wicket. Rather than celebrate euphorically, there is a discernible lack of any sort of reaction from the Kashmiri onlookers. Never before has silence spoken such volumes. I board the plane, feeling as though I am leaving an occupied country.

The thirty-minute flight from Srinagar to Jammu makes an utter mockery of my Hannibal-like ascent in the Sumo Jeep. The seat belt signs are extinguished and then illuminated again within minutes; we barely make it to 30,000 feet. We land without song and dance. I hail an auto rickshaw and cross town through traffic to the railway station, the same railway station I alighted at a few days before. I pass by the army of Sumos waiting to take luckless travellers on an eight-hour adventure. I pass the water supply where my yellow-robed, white-bearded, Adidas-clad holy man had prayed and shouted. I find myself with a couple of hours to kill before the train to Amritsar.

The first thing I notice is the warmth. The temperature is considerably higher than in Srinagar. Srinagar was cold in a way people generally do not associate with India. November sees temperature fluctuate between two or three Celsius and the low teens; it's never warm. At night, temperatures stray below freezing. In Jammu the sun is out and mid-twenties warmth allows my bones to gradually thaw out. I wander up the hill from the Sumos, up towards the station itself, up past the coaches and the urinating men.

No matter where I go in the world, there will be few more scintillating sights, few more vibrant, few more mesmeric than a platform in an Indian railway station. There is always something to watch, always something to do, regardless of the time of day. As I drink a lovely sweet five rupee cup of tea I see hordes of men eating delicious-looking food. Inevitably I feel hungry. It is lunchtime. But eating at a train station would be reckless, almost as reckless as eating rajmah chawal in Peeda.

I sit down at the station canteen, a surprisingly light and airy room with a handful of tables lost in the vast space. A motley crew of insolent men of varying ages mans the servery: no table service. I read the menu on a very retro seventies-style information board where each white plastic letter of each word of each dish is painstakingly pushed into the perforated plastic board. No doubt this is the task that has caused the men behind the counter to become so insolent. They needn't have bothered with the information board since the first three dishes I ask for are not available. No muttar paneer; no aloo muttar and no aubergine. I then inherit their collective insolence and ask what they do have. There is a single answer: aloo channa. Chick pea and potato curry. Sounds good.

Eighteen rupees later I am handed a steel tray with six chapattis, a bowl of potatoes and chick peas, and dollops of the ubiquitous mango and chilli pickles. This was the comfort food of my childhood. But this dish before me is not quite the one I am used to. Not by some way. When I say it is a bowl of potato and chick pea curry, let me be clear. There is a lovely watery brown gravy with soft white potatoes and perhaps half a dozen chick peas secreting themselves within the dish. Food is all about balance. There needs to be the right amount of each component to make a dish work. The mash to mince ratio in shepherd's pie; the pasta to sauce ratio in spaghetti bolognaise; the chick pea to potato ratio in aloo channa. Here there are simply not enough chick peas to justify their existence. It feels wrong, unbalanced. It reminds me of watching the fisherman in Bombay eating. So poor are they, they fill their plates with rice, a cheap and filling ingredient. Beside the rice they place the tiniest amount of flame-red prawn pickle. The bland rice and the fiery pickle combine to create a mouthful of flavour, but the pickle is not cheap, so they ration it tightly and have learnt to make the tiniest amount of pickle spread to the most amount of rice. I have often watched them eat and wondered how they would react to being given more pickle. Would they enjoy the meal more? Or are the proportions they have grown up with, the tiniest dollop of pickle upon the plateful of rice, exactly right for them? All I can tell you is that my handful of chickpeas are by no means the right proportion for me. I feel cheated. Cheated and still hungry.

I return to the platform for my second cup of hot sweet tea. This is the beauty of Indian railway tea. It's intense, like so much of India. There is nothing across this vast country that could ever be described as bland. Every experience, every sensory moment is intense, either in a good way or a bad way. From the beauty of the landscapes, to the sadness of the poverty, everything is heightened. Much like the tea. The tea at Indian railway stations comes in small cups. It is dark brown, very sweet and highly spiced. Any more than a small cup would be too much. But delicious though the tea is, it is still only tea, and there is a definite gap in my stomach, a gap that ought to have been filled by chick peas. I search the platform for sustenance and settle on the ubiquitous banana.

No sooner have I consumed the banana than the train arrives, the Muri Express; train number B102. I am in coach B looking for berth 20. I find myself thanking Rovi, again. He took it upon himself to personally sort out all my train bookings. Where would I be without him? Probably riding on the roof of the train ...

In Britain a four-hour train journey is about as long a journey as I would be comfortable to undertake: the National Express train from Kings Cross to Edinburgh is four and half hours, and a lovely trip it is too when not hampered by rail works or 'the wrong type of snow'. In India a four-hour train ride is a short journey. It is astonishing how quickly my mindset changes and I too view the four-hour journey from Jammu to Amritsar as a brief encounter. The train will head from Amritsar to Delhi and onward to Tata Nagar.

Tata Nagar is one of those places you hear about often and you see it printed lots but never actually go to. It is dropped into conversation and alluded to; someone always has a distant relative in Tata Nagar, or knows someone who has been to Tata Nagar. But no one has actually been there themselves; it's like Carnwadric. When I was boy Bishopbriggs was affectionately known as Spam Valley because all the 1960s Barratt Houses looked a bit like spam tins, lined up neatly in rows.

Bishopbriggs was just another place to grow up, if a little soulless. The only problem was that my school was on the Southside of town in Langside. A fee-paying Jesuit school: only the best for the children of immigrants. The two worlds of Bishopbriggs and Langside couldn't have been more different. The sandstone supremacy of the Southside contrasted sharply with the matter-of-fact modernity of Bishopbriggs. And not only was there such a sharp conceptual distance between the places, there was also a very clear geographical distance. It was two bus rides from school to home, a journey I occasionally had to make solo when my elder brother was off sick. An eight-year-old boy travelling twelve miles across a city on his own: it would never happen today.

In the mornings Mum drove us to school. It was on the way home that buses became part of our lives. The first bus I took from my school in Langside into town was the 45; the legendary 45. The bus took me all the way through town and as far as Colston. Colston was remarkable insofar as it was the point where the city ended and the suburbs started: it was where the fares increased on buses and taxis. The buses that took us into town came from Carnwadric, a suburb in south Glasgow. If I took the bus the other way, towards Langside, I took the 45 to Carnwadric. I lived in Glasgow up until the age of twenty-two. I still have very strong links with the city. My parents live there, my brother and his family live there, I work there and I still call it home. I have travelled the city, but have never in all these years ever been to Carnwadric or met anyone who comes from Carnwadric, or can conclusively prove that Carnwadric exists. Much like Tata Nagar.

The train from Jammu soon fills up. A family decamp in the berth next door, their luggage spilling around the corner. Their daughter, a sweet little girl sporting the Frenchest of bobs, fills her face with masala dosa, a lentil pancake filled with a delicious spiced potato mix. She uses the wide-topped Tupperware dish as a plate and scoops mouthfuls of the potato accompaniment with her already messy fingers. Full-mouthed, she talks incessantly, pausing only to refill herself. She can barely contain her excitement at the journey ahead. We have yet to set off and she has dispensed with her first course and is moving onto her next: samosa. Her legs swing involuntarily, inches above the carriage floor. She is happy. Food does that to you. As the train pulls away from Jammu the little girl tears into pudding.

I doze, I sleep, I sleep, I doze. The train rocks forward and back, backward and forward, in and out of progressively smaller stations, stopping, starting and stopping again. I have no idea how far we are from my destination but get the distinct feeling that we are late. We duly arrive at Amritsar, a massive station, sprawling in every direction.

I would like to be able to tell you how beautiful Amritsar is, how clean and well constructed is the spiritual home of the Sikhs. I would like to tell you that; but I can't. Amritsar, forgive me, is a shit hole. It's horrible. The Golden Temple (Darbar Sahib) is utterly beautiful, possibly the most peaceful

Notice on the train from Jammu to Amritsar

> TRAVELLING ON ROOFTOP AND FOOTBOARD
> ARE PUNISHABLE WITH IMPRISONMENT FOR
> THREE MONTHS OR FINE UP TO 500 RUPEES
> OR BOTH.
> IT CAN ALSO BE DANGEROUS TO HEALTH.

and tranquil of places I have ever had the good fortune to visit. But the rest of the city is terrible. It has all been geared up to serve the pilgrims and tourists that come to visit Darbar Sahib. Streets, alleys and gullies full of the debris of humanity. It's just not a pleasant place to be.

Ferozepure is about 120km from Amritsar. I would like to tell you that Ferozepure is a beautiful city, clean, well constructed, full of stylish architecture and cultural delights. But that would be an unequivocal lie. Ferozepure is also a shit hole. I have chosen to withhold this critical piece of information from you so far, reader, for fear that it may impact on my romantic journey home. But, as I near the place I call home in India, there's no dressing it up or putting a town-planning spin on it. There is a medieval quality to the place: tall buildings, narrow alleyways, the dirt and detritus of life everywhere. As I say, it is a shit hole. But I love this shit hole. It was where my father and grandfather were born. It has given me my most vibrant memories of childhood, those few snatched weeks during summer and Christmas holidays.

I feel I ought to qualify my rather damning description of Ferozepure. Ferozepure used to be a great city, almost princely. Hundreds of years ago the great River Sutlej ran through its heart, bringing with it all the prosperity and trade rivers bring.

Moti Bazaar translates as 'Pearl Market' and twenty yards from our front door on the left, under the arch just past the sweet shop is Heera Mundi, 'Diamond Market'. Ferozepure was clearly the place to be in the fifteen and sixteen hundreds. In the times of the Raj Ferozepure was similarly of great prominence and significance, lying as it did in the heart of the river supply of the state. It had the largest canal headworks in the north of India. This proved invaluable in the irrigation of crops and the Punjab is still to this day the most agricultural of all Indian states, providing the majority of fruit, vegetables and wheat to the rest of the nation, not to mention hydro-electricity from its many powerful rivers.* Can you tell I'm proud?

It is into Ferozepure that I am now heading. Despite the numerous bus and coach services, my uncle has insisted on driving the two and a half hours to pick me up. But that's Billu for you; all six foot five inches of him. Barinder Singh Kohli, known to all and sundry as Billu, or in my case Billu Chachaji.

In the Punjabi family system, which is patriarchal, each relative on your father's side is given a distinct name to describe where they fit in the family hierarchy. The extended family system is driven by hierarchy and status; there's a certain feudal quality to it which is perhaps why the concept is struggling to survive in these more 'egalitarian' times. (It's worth noting that since women are deemed to have left their family to join their husband's family upon marriage, all your father's sisters are *Pooas*, regardless of age and status.)

*Chacha*s are the younger brothers of your father; *thaia*s are older brothers of your father. Since my dad is the eldest I am *thaia*-poor but *chacha*-rich. I have the farmer Billu in

---

*The word Punjab itself means 'five rivers'.

Ferozepure and the renegade Channi in Los Angeles, the ex-army officer who bought the American dream but forgot to keep the receipt. They are my *chacha*s and I, for my sins, am their *pathija*. The *chacha/pathija* axis is regarded as an historically close relationship in Punjabi culture. This may be explained by the fact that in olden times when families were much larger, perhaps ten or twelve siblings, children of the older brothers found themselves much closer in age to their parents' younger brothers. Whatever the social reasoning my Billu Chacha and I are very close.

The Sikhs have long been regarded as a martial race, having been borne out of the need to protect the peace-loving, cow-worshipping, karma-accepting Hindu majority from the all-conquering, architecture-loving, Islam-promoting Moghul armies that spread through Persia into the north of India. In their wake they converted a plethora of new Muslims, often with the use of their quirkily curved swords. There is one crucial difference between Hindus and Muslims: you can become a Muslim in your own lifetime; one simple act of conversion, a belief and love of the Koran and a long moustache-less beard and you are well on your way to Islamic salvation. This is a benefit not enjoyed by the Hindus. They believe in the whole circle of life thing, *dharma*. You are in a cycle of existence that cannot be broken, your behaviour in your last life affects your status in the next and so on. Therefore you cannot become a Hindu: hence the lack of evangelical Hindus with tambourines and guitars.

Billu is a fine example of a warrior Sikh. Not only is he almost six foot five, he is long-limbed, broad-shouldered and charismatically handsome. Add to that his lugubrious voice, his intensely brown eyes and his love of stirring rhetoric and you have a potential military leader on your hands; he's almost

Shakespearian. He has lived his life entirely in Ferozepure, running our land and maintaining the family house. While his sisters married and left for Canada, Malaysia and the UK and his brothers got educated or joined the army, Billu was a constant in an ever-changing world. And while he may not be formally educated, there is little he doesn't know. His knowledge of world affairs, politics and life are self-taught, and consequently his opinions are refreshing in their candour.

A hug and a handshake and then we are off on our way. It's a two and a half hour drive across one of India's most famous highways. The GT Road is not simply a road, it is an institution, a symbol of the Punjab itself. Songs have been sung about it, stories told about it. The Grand Trunk Road stretches across the state delivering and receiving produce and people all through the day and night.

Billu asks me where I want to stop on the way for tea. As if I would know. He tells me about a favourite place of my parents, Hari ka Pathan. There's a little shack by the roadside that makes fresh fish pakoras; as you know, my mum loves fish pakoras. It seems no time at all since my mum-inspired Srinagar fish-cooking adventure. We are halfway home and Billu suggests we stop there for a snack before heading home for dinner. My Billu Chacha can speak English but does so rarely. He prefers the precision, the poetry of his native tongue and talks to me in mellifluous Punjabi tones. The time passes quickly and we find ourselves in Hari ki Pathan. There is a clutch of shops, a few lights and lots of barking dogs.

The shack is nondescript, which, in my experience of Indian street food, augurs well for the quality of the fare. The recently painted hoarding informs us that the shop belongs to Nimmu and Sonu. I assume either Nimmu or Sonu is the white-turbaned man who welcomes us in. My *chacha* asks what fish are available and Nimmu/Sonu takes us over to a large polystyrene box full of freshly caught fish on ice. There's a large fish I don't recognise and a couple of glistening silver catfish. My uncle looks at me; I look blankly back. Billu asks for the catfish.

Nimmu/Sonu instructs one of the gang of young kids hanging around to grab the catfish. The kids burst into life. A boy of about twelve sets the light under the *karahi*, heating the oil for the eventual frying. Another younger boy guts and heads the fish with no little expertise. A third boy opens our beers and another, a study in pre-teenage surliness, brings us glasses and napkins.

Inside the shack the walls are white and plain but are absolutely dominated by Pepsi branding which emblazons three of the four walls. In the great battle of the multinational colas in the late 1990s Coca-Cola lost; India is a Pepsi territory. The only wall clear of the drinks company's red, white and blue logo is given over to a shrine (another sort of marketing, I suppose). A couple of Hindu gods sit by an image of the Sikh gurus; I have a deep admiration for that sort of religious bet-hedging.

Nimmu/Sonu grabs a couple of large scary-looking knives; these are like regulation cleavers except on the top side of the blade, at the furthest most point, the steel twists up and back round, hook-like. Perhaps this is for ease of hanging, or perhaps it is to enable the swift and successful gouging of an adversary's eye in the final throes of bloody hand-to-hand combat . . .

Nimmu/Sonu starts sharpening the knives against each other, making the knives seem even scarier and creating a scary sound. I catch his eye. I'm even more scared. He smiles. I'm not sure that I want to smile back. Deftly he fillets the fish and divides the fillets up into bite-size pieces. A dip in gram flour, salt and pepper followed by a few minutes in the hot oil. Served up on the ubiquitous steel plate with a half lemon slice and some chutney, a blend of mint, coriander and tamarind. It is absolutely divine. The fish has steamed beautifully within the thin batter and the spicy chutney compliments the succulent fish.

We sit and eat our second plate of deep-fried fish and drink our Thunderbolt Super Strong lager beer. It could be Friday night in Glasgow instead of Sunday night in Punjab. All we need is a fist fight and a glassing . . . .

The last hour or so back to Ferozepure is testing. Darkness hasn't so much fallen as crashed, and the empty road presents unexpected hazards; an odd, lone pedestrian, a drunken motorcyclist and an abandoned cart. Thankfully none of these offer any more than a passing difficulty and we are soon in Greater Ferozepure. I have been travelling for weeks and feel ready for the welcome of home. Home: that word again. I can feel the end of my journey almost upon me. Almost.

WHERE THE HEART IS

My name is Hardeep Singh Kohli and I am the grandson of the late Harbans Singh Kohli. And I am home.

I am aware that when I refer to India as home it may seem a little contradictory, given my cast-iron British credentials and the well-documented love of my Scottishness. But within me somewhere still stirs the son of Punjabi soil. As we draw up to my grandfather's house at 22 Moti Bazaar I belong nowhere but in this moment, in this place.

I find it difficult to be objective about Ferozepure. I have never properly lived here, spending a few summers as a child, followed by a handful of trips as an adult, yet this place means so much to me. I get excited if, on those rarest of occasions, I meet someone who comes from Ferozepure. I feel we are kith and kin, instantly bonded. I feel the same way when in the big smoke of London I meet someone from Glasgow. I even smile when I overhear the accent on the tube in London. But my history with Glasgow is *my* history with Glasgow. My history with Ferozepure stretches back for generations; it is a shared history. But when I talk about Ferozepure it still feels like home.

My Billu *Chacha* loves Ferozepure. For him it is a paradise of sorts. Every street has a myriad of shops and kiosks; almost every third shop is food related, be it snacks and starters, *dhaba-*

type cafés or, beloved of Indians, the sweet shops. Food is a very large part of the retail experience in Ferozepure and wherever you look someone is about to eat, is in the throes of eating or has just finished eating. It's certainly a vibrant city. And I suppose that's why Billu loves it.

Our farmlands, an hour or so away from the city, border Pakistan. During the conflict of the 1990s, when India and Pakistan were effectively at war over the Line of Control in Kashmir, the Indian government requisitioned our farmlands and filled the ground full of mines in the hope that it would prevent any Pakistani advance into India. In best keeping with the incompetence of Indian bureaucracy the plans that specified where the mines were placed were 'mislaid'. For years the land was untillable and unusable, remaining dormant while officialdom scratched around for the plans they couldn't locate. Admittedly compensation was offered, but nothing happens quickly in India, nothing except incompetence. For a year my uncle and his family had to survive without income. This he was able to do thanks to the trust and support of local businessmen who were only too happy to defer payment to a later date. Maybe that's why he loves this city.

'Don't you want to know why I'm here?' I ask Billu, his handsome face a picture of peace.

'No. You're here. You're home. That's enough for me.' He doesn't mean what he says in any romantic way. He is the most matter-of-fact man I know. When he says that I am home, that is exactly where I am.

'What do you need to do?' he asks.

'Buy some turbans,' I reply. 'And I need to cook.'

'Fine.'

When Billu says things are fine they invariably are just that. Fine.

As we walk the bazaar and alleys Billu tells me that everything he wants is no more than 500 yards from his front door. This is easily verifiable since he has taken me 300 yards around the corner, past Heera Mundi, to buy some turbans. I love coming to Ferozepure to buy turbans. I love wearing turbans in Ferozepure. It is one of the few instances in life when I am not the only man wandering about with eight yards of pink fabric wrapped skilfully around his head. In Britain the younger Sikh population, what there is of it, tries hard not to draw attention to itself. They wear small sleek black turbans that almost belie the very nature of the turban itself. There is no pride in their turban-wearing. And who can blame them? It wasn't easy growing up in Glasgow in the 1980s wearing a turban; and, for many, even contemporary Britain can be a little unforgiving of the turban. But here in the Sikh heartlands I am joined by tens, maybe hundreds of thousands of other turban-wearing Sikhs who embrace whole-heartedly and whole-headedly the panoply of possibility when it comes to turban colour.

There are four turban shops, each side by side. They have narrow fronts but stretch cavernously away from the dusty squalor of the road. They sell nothing but turbans, which for me is ideal. The shop I favour is no more than a metre and a half wide, more than half of which space is given over to the shelving and the counter which runs the entire length of the shop, perhaps five maybe even six metres in total. Behind the counter, floor to ceiling, are lengths of turban material. Every colour imaginable, and a few that have yet to be given names, grace the shelves behind the industrious workers. The narrow counter itself is six deep in a spectrum of fabrics, all of which have been unfurled and inspected, in the hope of a prospective purchase.

My style of turban is commonly known as the Jat style. There are myriad turban types and variations, but I like to think the Jat style is the precursor to all others, given that the Jats are the farming class, the very roots of the Sikh religion: it all started with us. The Jat style is characterised by its size. It is not a turban for the faint-hearted. Yard wide fabric is purchased to the desired length, a precise art that can make or break the turban size itself. In my case it is eight and half yards exactly. Not eight and a quarter and certainly not eighteen inches short of nine yards. Exactly eight and a half yards. The fabric is then 'doubled', which involves cutting it in half to give two lengths of four and a quarter yards each. Still with me? These are then sewn together along their length giving a final turban material of two yards in width and four and a quarter yards in length. It's a truly beautiful thing.

I have many, many turbans. I am often asked how many, a question to which I don't have a definitive answer; I normally reply that I have at least eight pink turbans. One can surmise the extent of the remainder of my collection based on that statistic alone. Today I am after another subtly different pink turban, as well as a dramatic black, an interesting blue, an autumnal cream and one other colour yet to be decided. I ask for a particular shade of turban and an old bespectacled man with two-day-old stubble, and body odour to match, climbs an unsafe-looking ladder (one that vies with him in the age stakes). He unfurls, flag-like, each roll of material. In the past I have found the choice a little overwhelming, and I have found myself leaving with turbans that would look great on the head of a Punjabi farm hand 50km south of Amritsar but work significantly less well on Sauchiehall Street on a wet Wednesday afternoon when you're looking for change to pay for parking.

My grandfather and my father bought their turbans from this shop, and to this day my *chacha* has his turban needs satisfied by the selfsame vendor. There's something very comforting about being part of history, no matter how small or significant that history may be. But for me, this modest little turban shop, this palace of life, this kiosk of colour, is a direct and tangible link between my Sikh past and my Scottish future. My turban is very much part of who I am. Growing up in Glasgow in the eighties and nineties, to be a fat kid with glasses and a turban was to invite ridicule and abuse. I suffered the slings and arrows of that outrageous warfare as I sought to find a place for myself in society. I had all sorts of identity crises. At one point I wanted to convert to Catholicism. Absurd I know, to move from a groovy, young guilt-free religion like Sikhism into the teeth of an ancient, guilt-laden religion full of self flagellation and self-doubt.

It was a struggle to work out who I was in Glasgow. A real struggle. I was so very desperate to be accepted as Glaswegian, as Scottish. I was fed up of being asked where I came from and the questioner not being happy with my response of 'Bishopbriggs'. I was a brown-skinned child: I couldn't possibly come from Glasgow. Justifying yourself gets tiring.

Moving to London helped, since no one seems to come from London and therefore everyone is an outsider. This must be annoying for those increasingly few native Londoners who feel so marginalised within their city of birth. I may have been born in London but it means nothing to me; I never really lived there as a child. Neither have I ever lived in Ferozepure, but it feels very different.

◈

Back at 22 Moti Bazaar I survey the colour choices of my turbans. I wonder how many turbans have similarly been surveyed by my father and my grandfather. I wish my father were here. I have wished for him at various points on this quest. I would have loved to be with him in Kovalam as I looked out over the Arabian Sea. He would have enjoyed the sun setting over the beach at Mamallapuram. He would have marvelled at Bangalore. I could have done with his presence on the train from Bombay to Delhi. Delhi is always much more exciting with my dad around. And I have always wanted to go to the Kashmir Valley with him as an adult. But more than ever I wish he was in Ferozepure with me now, to see how this journey has changed me. I think he might be a little bit proud. He would never admit as much, but his eyes would give him away.

And I would like him to be here tonight when I cook my final meal. Of all the meals in my life I've looked forward to cooking and eating, I don't think I've ever looked forward to cooking and eating a meal more than this. To say I've waited a lifetime would seem appropriate. But perhaps it is more than one lifetime that I've waited. I think about the life of my father, I think about the life of my grandfather. Perhaps I've waited three lifetimes to eat this meal.

No one tells you how to feel about your ancestry. There's no manual, no almanac that guides you through the complexity of belonging. Who decides where I belong? My parents? Well, if you ask my mum, she would probably regret that her sons have grown up without enough Indian and Punjabi culture. The fact that I am her only son who speaks anything like fluent Punjabi I know disappoints her. My father is a little more circumspect in his opinion. I am sure he feels a tad disappointed that we have not adopted more of our Punjabi roots, but he is a citizen of the world and he seems to have embraced the fact that his kids have rooted so firmly in the land of their birth: Britain.

All these thoughts, and all the thoughts I have had on this quest are bouncing around inside my head. What could be more Punjabi than a Sikh man buying turbans in the Punjab? But this Sikh man has realised through his travels from south to north India that he is more British than he ever knew. If only the natives of Ferozepure could share the great irony of my situation: I grew up looking Indian in Glasgow, attempting to convince others that I was British, whilst working out who I really was; and here I am in my grandfather's town, with turbans purchased from my grandfather's turban maker, feeling very British on the inside and trying to come to terms with looking Indian on the outside, having worked out exactly what I am. From the initial, uncertain steps in Kovalam, through the tranquil self-realisation of Mamallapuram, the confusion of Mysore, the debacle of Bangalore, the clarity of Goa, the misadventure of Bombay, the triumph of Delhi and the conclusion of Srinagar. What a journey . . .

It is evening in my grandfather's house. It would be an understatement to say that I am aware of a certain pressure as I prepare to cook goat curry, knowing that it is a tradition that has spanned decades in this house, in this family. In terms of my lineage, my father, my grandfather and I share a distinct trait: we all love to cook meat. My grandfather would only ever cook meat or chicken, and I have had to tutor myself in the ways of the vegetarian world, slightly against my better judgement. The residual notion that a meal without meat isn't really a meal will stay with me until the day I die, probably a premature death brought on by the consumption of too much meat.

It's quieter than usual in Ferozepure this evening. I stand in the tiny kitchen chopping onions and heating oil, waiting to taste my own goat curry. It seems right that having ventured to bring a little taste of Britain to all of India, I should finish with a flourish and enjoy a little bit of India in that place I call home. The aroma of Indian onions frying in Indian oil combined with Indian spices is the smell of India yet also the smell of growing up in Glasgow. For the first time in my life these are not two different places but the same unified space; and that space is within me. The only sound I can hear now is the sound of frying and the sound of my own heart beating within my chest. I can barely imagine my father standing in this kitchen, cooking the same dish, but I know he did; and I know that my grandfather did. Dinner is ready. All I have left to do is garnish with freshly chopped coriander and eat.

I have worked out where home is. Home is where I want it to be. Glasgow, London or within these four walls at 22 Moti Bazaar, Ferozepure. My journey has seen me travel a subcontinent as a stranger, exploring lives I didn't even know existed. Arzooman; Nagamuthu; Suresh; new people and new experiences. My attempt to bring with me the food of the land of my birth soon became secondary to the search for who I am and how I feel about myself. It is a quest that is just beginning rather than ending.

We sit in the courtyard, my uncle, my cousin and I. The stars twinkle above as we silently eat curried goat with chapattis. There are no words to explain how this feels; there are no words to convey the continuity of history that I have become part of. I only wish my father and my grandfather were here to join me; British me; Indian me; British Indian me; Indian British me. Just me. My name is Hardeep Singh Kohli and I have finally arrived home.

HOKKAIDO HIGHWAY BLUES

WILL FERGUSON

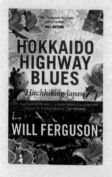

With the same fervour they have for outlandish game shows and tiny gadgets the Japanese go nuts each spring when the cherry blossom sweeps from island to island towards the country's northern tip – Hokkaido. Will Ferguson was celebrating the event in the standard fashion, and after way too much saké announced he would be the first person in recorded history to follow the blossom's progress. And to make it a challenge worth doing he'd hitchhike all the way, relying on the kindness of some very weird and wonderful strangers. The resulting travelogue is one of the funniest and most illuminating books to be written on Japan.

'Mr. Ferguson is a very gifted writer.' Bill Bryson

'A mild stroke of genius . . . savagely hilarious.' *Sunday Herald*

'The road book of the year . . . a warm-hearted account with a generous helping of satire.' *Daily Telegraph*

£7.99

ISBN 978 1 84195 288 8

www.meetatthegate.com

BATTING ON THE BOSPHORUS

ANGUS BELL

Following a chance encounter with a psychic, Angus Bell sets off on an 8,000-mile, Skoda-powered road trip across Eastern Europe in search of a cricket match. It's a gloriously batty adventure involving fingerless fielders in the Czech Republic, Serbian MI6 agents and the realization that England's most eccentric game is being played with passion in the strangest corners of the continent.

'Very funny. Dave Gorman meets Andrew Flintoff in clothes borrowed from Billy Connolly.' Hugo Rifkind, *The Times*

'Weird and wonderful . . . one of the maddest, most enterprising cricket tours of all time.' *Guardian*

'It deserves to be as big a hit as the blow Bell dealt a cricket ball on the bridge over the Bosphorus, propelling it from Europe to Asia.' *Daily Telegraph*

£8.99

ISBN 978 1 84767 290 2

www.meetatthegate.com

LANARK

ALASDAIR GRAY

Lanark, a modern vision of hell set in the disintegrating cities of Unthank and Glasgow, tells the interwoven stories of Lanark and Duncan Thaw. A work of extraordinary, playful imagination, it conveys a profound message, both personal and political, about humankind's inability to love, and yet our compulsion to go on trying.

First published in 1981, *Lanark* immediately established Gray as one of Britain's leading writers, compared with – among others – Dante, Blake, Joyce, Orwell, Kafka, Huxley and Lewis Carroll. This new edition includes an introduction by William Boyd as well as the author's fascinating addendum, the 'Tailpiece' (2001).

'I was absolutely knocked out by Lanark. I think it's the best in Scottish literature in the twentieth century.' Iain Banks

'Remarkable . . . Lanark is a work of loving and vivid imagination, yielding copious riches.' William Boyd, *Times Literary Supplement*

'When dawn comes up and retires in dismay, we find ourselves in the presence of an overpowering surreal imagination. A sage of a city where reality is about as reliable as a Salvador Dali watch.' Brian Aldiss

£8.99

ISBN 978 1 84195 907 8

www.meetatthegate.com

THE ASSASSIN'S SONG

M. G. VASSANJI

In the aftermath of the violence that gripped western India in 2002, Karsan Dargawalla, heir to the shrine of a mysterious medieval sufi, begins to tell the story of his family and the now destroyed shrine. After a bitter quarrel with his father that led him to abdicate his birthright, Karsan made a new life for himself in suburban British Columbia. But when tragedy strikes in Canada and India, he is drawn back after thirty years to see if anything is left for him . . .

A story of grand historical sweep and intricate personal drama, *The Assassin's Song* is a heartbreaking ballad of a life irrevocably changed.

'A poetic lament which grips your heart . . . An unforgettable novel.' Yasmin Alibhai-Brown, *Independent*

'It treads that line between the intimate and the epic, and builds to a powerful, heartbreaking, redemptive ending.' Tahmima Anam, *Guardian*

'*The Assassin's Song* is both particular and universal, which is one of the marks of great literature. Historical novel, bildungsroman and terrorist thriller all rolled into one.' Giles Foden

£8.99

ISBN 978 1 84767 283 4

www.meetatthegate.com